The Jewish Hour

THE JEWISH HOUR

THE GOLDEN AGE OF A TORONTO YIDDISH RADIO SHOW AND NEWSPAPER

MICHAEL MANDEL

Now and Then Books
Toronto 2016

THE JEWISH HOUR: THE GOLDEN AGE OF A TORONTO YIDDISH RADIO SHOW AND NEWSPAPER, by Michael Mandel. Copyright © 2016 by the Estate of Michael Mandel and Now and Then Books. All rights reserved. No part of this publication may be reproduced in any form or by any means, electronic, mechanical or otherwise, except for brief passages quoted in the context of a critical review, without prior permission from Now and Then Books.

Cover design: Jon Stancer/Parade and Now and Then Books.

Order online from www.nowandthenbookstoronto.com

Library and Archives Canada Cataloguing in Publication
Mandel, Michael, 1948- , author
    The Jewish Hour : the golden age of a Toronto Yiddish radio show and newspaper / Michael Mandel.

Includes bibliographical references.
ISBN 978-0-9919009-7-8 (paperback)

    1. Radio broadcasting, Yiddish—Ontario—Toronto—History. 2. Radio broadcasting—Ontario—Toronto—History. 3. Radio programs—Ontario—Toronto—History. 4. Yiddish newspapers—Ontario—Toronto—History. 5. Jewish newspapers—Ontario—Toronto—History. 6. Jews—Ontario—Toronto—Intellectual life. 7. Jews—Ontario—Toronto—Social life and customs—20th century. I. Title.

HE8699.C2M364 2016   384.54097 13'54   C2016-904819-5

Note: Musical selections from the various Jewish Hours have been made available online free of charge. To access these tracks, please visit the website www.soundcloud.com and enter the search phrase "Jewish Hour - Mandel." (Subject to changing conditions.)

CONTENTS

Acknowledgments 7
Foreword 8
Introduction 12

Chapter 1
"First Jewish Radio Hour Calls Forth Joy"
16

Chapter 2
Max Mandel — From Apt to Toronto
49

Chapter 3
The First Year of the *Kanader Nayes*
65

Chapter 4
Pre-War Years
85

Chapter 5
War Years
151

Chapter 6
Post War Years
211

Appendix
Music from The Jewish Hour
289

About the Author 325

For my children
Max, Giulia, Lucy, Tevi and Orly
and their children and their children's children,
and for my wife Karen,
and my sisters Marilyn ע״ה *and Sharon*
and their families and children's children,
and in loving memory of my parents,
Max and Hilda Mandel ע״ה

ACKNOWLEDGEMENTS

For their invaluable help with this project, the author would like to thank Harry Arthurs, Mike Burstein, Donna Bernardo-Ceriz, Cantor Louis Danto ע״ה, Evelyn Dorfman, Sharon Fuller, Harry Glasbeek, Karen Golden, Chris Halonen, Rabbi David E. Herman, Sarah Kerzner ע״ה, Giulia Mandel, Lucy Mandel, Max Mandel, Ernie Marmurek, Irma Penn, Henia Reinhartz, Nochem Reinhartz ע״ה, I. Reisman, Harvey Rudnick ע״ה, Stella Rudolph, Roberta Saltzman, Ellen Scheinberg, Alex Serota, Dara Solomon, Leo Spellman ע״ה, Nathan Tinanoff, Gerry Trefler ע״ה, the Dorot Jewish Division of the New York Public Library, the Jewish Heritage Centre of Western Canada, the Jewish Public Library of Montreal, the Judaica Sound Archives, the Ontario Jewish Archives, Osgoode Hall Law School of York University, the YIVO Institute for Jewish Research, and the York University Libraries.

Grateful acknowledgements are made to the family of the late artist Mayer Kirshenblatt for permission to reprint his painting of the interior of the Apt synagogue (page 48); and to the Ontario Jewish Archives for permission to reprint the photos of the Dworkin shop (page 24) and the Israel parade on College Street, Toronto, in 1948 (page 210).

FOREWORD

MY FATHER HAD A YIDDISH RADIO SHOW on a variety of radio stations from 1936 to 1953. They called it "The Jewish Hour." All over North America there were these shows and his was the Toronto one. The centrepiece of these shows was Yiddish song, and my father left lots of beautiful recordings made for the show. But the shows also had drama, poetry, culture, politics and news. In the early days of radio, shows were often linked to newspapers and this one was linked to an extraordinary Yiddish newspaper called the *Kanader Nayes* (the *Canadian News*), that came to your door or your news stand inside the great New York Yiddish newspapers, primarily *Forverts* (*Forward*). The people who produced the *Kanader Nayes* newspaper were activist intellectuals in what could fairly be said to be the main current of Jewish opinion: socialist (but anti-communist), Zionist and Yiddishist. In Canada, the mass of the Jewish population was of recent immigration, Yiddish speaking and working class.

Through the music and adventures of "The Jewish Hour" and the pages of the newspaper that sponsored it, this book takes us on a journey back to a rich and pivotal time in recent Jewish history, when the Yiddish-speaking immigrant, newly arrived in the North American Diaspora from the *shtetls* of Eastern Europe struggled to make sense of the new world through Jewish eyes, and even to try and transform it.

The story starts with my modest quest to learn more about my late father's radio show, armed only with a group photograph of "Greenfild's Jewish Radio Hour скос" and some scratchy old 78 rpm records, one of which was a singing commercial. This leads me to the discovery, not only of the radio show, but of the whole world of this generation of immigrant Jews, through the fragile, almost crumbling pages of the Yiddish newspaper, the *Kanader Nayes* (1935–1954) that sponsored the show and lovingly chronicled its many ups and downs. The newspaper, put out by a remarkable group of journalist activists, turns out to be a window that opens onto this world, its everyday life and also its great events and controversies, from the politics of Communism and Socialism, the rise of Nazism, the war, the Holocaust, the struggle for the State of Israel and the ultimately vain effort to save the Yiddish language. The accounts in the paper, translated from the original Yiddish, allow us to feel what it was like to live these events and provide us with fresh and immediate insights into them, insights that seem to have been forgotten over the years. They allow us to savour Jewish passion, wisdom and humour from a unique time in history, a real "Jewish Hour."

The story is illuminated by the pages of the newspaper itself, presented in facsimile, and a series of re-mastered recordings of great Yiddish songs (translated and transliterated) recorded specially for "The Jewish Hour," many well-known and some never heard before, including Second Avenue show-tunes, cantorial masterpieces, war songs, folk songs, poems set to music and, of course, the singing commercial.

Toronto was a medium-sized Jewish centre of the time, not unlike many throughout the world. In the case of the protagonists of the *Kanader Nayes*, it was linked by the publishers' personal, business and ideological connections to the centre of the Jewish world, New York City, and the leading Jewish/Yiddish newspaper, the *Forward*, of which the publishers were the sole importers in Canada.

But there was, in fact, one Jewish world during this period, as there may well be said to be today, and this is a universal story lived by Ashkenazi Jews throughout their Diaspora during this last great outburst of Yiddish culture. Beyond that, it is the story of any newly arrived immigrant who desperately tries to live in two worlds at the same time, preserving the old culture while trying to adapt to, and even shape, the new one.

The story loosely follows the life of the musically and dramatically talented Max Mandel, a young Jewish immigrant from the venerable *shtetl* of Apt in Southern Poland, who arrives virtually penniless in Toronto, gravitates to the local music scene and lands on the first (permanent) Jewish radio hour in Canada, where he rises to be a star and a "darling." It charts his career in the studio and on the stage to his premature and much mourned death in 1953 while preparing for a new show. It tells of the bitter competition between rival radio shows and the no-holds-barred debates between their partisans that vividly reveal the aspirations and anxieties of the Jewish community.

All this we learn from the pages of the Yiddish newspaper that sponsored the show, showcased it and published many articles and letters to the editor debating its quality. But, besides radio, all the streams of Jewish culture and politics pour from these pages. There is the fascinating local talent, including itinerant cantors who moonlighted as opera singers or jewellers, synagogue choir boys who moonlighted as Irish tenors, local musicians with communist sympathies singing the praises of the Soviet Union, "wunderkind" acrobatic sisters, a right-wing choir, a left-wing choir, singing groups with names like the "Harmony Girls," a blind accordionist, a "Yiddishe shikse," future classical music stars, and so on. Because Toronto was one of the important stops on the itinerary of the big international

Jewish stars, we get to meet in their prime such huge personalities as Jacob Ben Ami, Moyshe Oysher, Molly Picon, Herman Yablokov, Morris Schwartz and his Art Theatre, Menashe Skulnick, Sholom Secunda, Joseph Rumshinsky, Aaron Lebedeff (both in his prime and past it, according to a later reviewer), Pesach'ke Burstein, Lillian Lux, Miriam Kressin, Maurice Rauch, Sally Josephson, Chaim Tauber, Ludwig Satz, Jennie Goldstein, Leo Fuchs, and Cantors Moshe Koussevitsky and Liebele Waldman. As well, we meet the literary and political stars who came and enthralled the community, including Golda Myerson (before she was Golda Meir), Chaim Weizmann, "Red" Emma Goldman, Sholom Asch, H. Leivick and many more. Through the debates and reporting in the pages of the newspaper, we get an unobstructed view of the dramatic and traumatic issues of these times, and through the ordinary stories and advertisements in the paper, many of which now make us laugh, we experience the everyday life of the immigrant Jew in good times and bad.

INTRODUCTION

> I knew only two boys in our neighbourhood whose families were fatherless, and thought of them as no less blighted than the blind girl who attended our school for a while and had to be shepherded everywhere. The fatherless boys seemed almost equally marked and set apart; in the aftermath of their fathers' deaths, they too struck me as scary and a little taboo. Though one was a model of obedience and the other a troublemaker, everything either of them did or said seemed determined by his being a boy with a dead father and, however innocently I arrived at this notion, I was probably right.[1]

WHEN I FIRST READ THAT PASSAGE from Philip Roth's quasi-autobiographical novel, *The Facts*, I took it very personally. Roth was remembering when he almost lost his father at the age of eleven. My own father died when I was not yet five and I was both very bad and very good, bringing my mother great *tsures* and great *nakhes* in turn.

What Roth did not know, because his own father survived, was that sons who lose their fathers when they are young spend the rest of their lives looking for them. My mother made sure that my father was always around in one way or another, because she never stopped holding a torch for him, and she had learned loyal widowhood from her own old-world mother. But I didn't really find my father until the day I flipped open a dusty volume of an old Yiddish newspaper from 1936, the *Kanader Nayes* (pronounced Ka-*NA*-der *NAY*-es according to the strange way Jews pronounced *Ka-NA-da*) and his picture appeared with the caption "Max Mandel, artist on the

---

[1] Philip Roth, *The Facts: A Novelist's Autobiography*, New York: Farrar, Straus & Giroux, 1988 pp. 13–14.

Jewish Radio Hour." Not only did I find my father, I found his whole world. I found the radio show that was one of his great loves, but, on top of that, the wonderful newspaper that sponsored the show, the magnificent people who put out the paper, and through the paper and them, the entire world of the first-generation Yiddish-speaking immigrants from Eastern Europe, their struggles and ideals, their music and culture, their catastrophes and triumphs, from the six-year nightmare of the Holocaust to the realization of their wildest Zionist dream, to the decline and fall of their adored Yiddish language. This is the world I have been privileged to revisit and that I want to describe to you.

In English, we always called the radio show "The Jewish Hour." I set out to find the radio show, but on the way discovered "The Jewish Hour" in a much bigger sense: a unique time in Jewish history, as seen through the very eyes of the Yiddish-speaking immigrant struggling to find a way in a new and unfamiliar place.

A Brief Note on Translation

Astronomers say that stars burn brightest just before they die. In many ways this is a story about the last glorious outburst of Yiddish, the common tongue of the Eastern European Jew for about a thousand years. It's worth remembering the significance of the Eastern European Jew to the whole Jewish people: before the Holocaust, the vast majority of the Jews of the world were Eastern European, either living there or recently transplanted to America. On the other hand, it was only in the hundred years before the Holocaust that Yiddish became a literary language, and the newspapers, songs and theatre that figure so heavily in our story came to be written. But the Germans murdered most of the speakers of Yiddish and those who remained alive in the Diaspora gradually stopped speaking it, and adopted the language of their host countries. In the case of Israel, home to about half the world's Jews, that language was Hebrew, which replaced Yiddish as the distinctively Jewish language, hard as the Yiddishists fought against it. Until Zionism, Hebrew was employed by Jews only in the synagogue.

So for a long period, of which our story might be considered the finale, for most Jews, Yiddish and Jewish were a single entity. In fact, in the Yiddish language, "Yiddish" *means* "Jewish." The word is very similar, of course, to the German "Jüdische." Yiddish, in fact, is a mostly Germanic language written in Hebrew characters, albeit with a strong admixture of ancient Hebrew. There is a bitter irony in this, of course, and many Yiddishists resist the German connection, but it is impossible to avoid. I once gave a concert of Yiddish songs in Florence in which I included the tear-jerker *"A Yidishe Mamme"* (A Jewish Mother). All the Florentine Italians (Ladino[2] speakers) were smiling back at me as if I were singing "Happy Birthday," but the few German (gentile) friends I had invited from the European University Institute were bawling their eyes out because they understood almost every word.

My mother always referred to the radio show as "The Jewish Hour." It would never have occurred to her generation to translate *"Di yidishe shtunde"* as "the Yiddish Hour." When speaking English, these people only used "Yiddish" if they were referring specifically to the language. That is the only course to take for a book like this. *"Yidish"* will be translated as "Jewish" (and *"Yid"* as "Jew") with only one exception, when we are referring specifically to the language.

---

[2] Ladino is the specifically Jewish language spoken by Jews originating in Spain. Instead of old German, the main non-Hebrew component is old Spanish. It is spoken by Sephardi Jews, such as those who comprise most of the Florentine Jews.

A Brief Note on Transliteration

In this book I have largely adhered to the canonical system of Yiddish transliteration used by the YIVO Institute. But I make exceptions where the YIVO system results in a word which reads too differently in English, like "mame" instead of "mamme" for "mother," or "rebe" instead of "rebbe" for rabbi.

Another problem of transliteration specific to this book is the rendering of names that only appear in the original material in Yiddish. I struggled a lot with this and I know I've made mistakes. So I ask the forgiveness of anyone who knows better how the person in question wrote their name in English. On the other hand, when I *do* know the way a person spelled their Jewish name in English—Chaim Weizmann, for example—I feel compelled to break with the YIVO in transliteration.

CHAPTER 1

"First Jewish Radio Hour Calls Forth Joy"

TEACH LAW FOR A LIVING, BUT MUSIC is my first love. I'm a singer and I even studied opera in Italy, but I never made it further in the professional opera world than a few productions in the chorus of the Canadian Opera Company, one step above a spear-carrier.

Yiddish music was a different story, due to the fact, I suppose, that my father was a gifted singer of Yiddish song. When he died, he left a stack of sheet music and 78 rpm records, his own and others. As a child, everybody always wanted me to sing Yiddish, but I wasn't all that enthusiastic about it, naturally. Little did I know that they were all pining after my father. To them I was his kid; to me, I was me. My oldest sister Marilyn remembered us being "royalty" in the old days, but I knew nothing of it. I was the baby of the family, only four when my father died. I performed some Yiddish numbers at my own bar mitzvah with Sam Silver's orchestra, he, a pianist from my father's old radio days. After that, I left it behind. When my mother got sick with the illness that would ultimately take her life, I took time off from my opera studies (and my law teaching) and worked up my father's old repertoire for a concert for her birthday. After she died, my sisters and I put together a cassette tape—remember those?—of my father's old songs to give the proceeds to a memorial fund at Toronto's Baycrest Geriatric Hospital. Around the same time, I got a (very modestly) paying job as a tenor soloist with the Toronto Jewish Folk Choir. Little did I know then my connection to *them*. That brought me back to my father's records and I started to gravitate to the Yiddish music scene, giving concerts, mostly in

Toronto, but also in Italy where I spent a lot of time (teaching law). At one point, I was, I dare say, the reigning tenor at the "Yiddishland Café" in Toronto produced and directed by the marvelous Henia and Nochem Reinhartz and alongside a bevy of sopranos. I worked as a choir director at the Toronto Winchevsky School and we even produced a mock-up concert version of my father's radio show there. This is perhaps rather too long a way of saying how I came to be flipping through those newspapers at the Ontario Jewish Archives.

I was actually on assignment from the Ashkenaz Festival to look into the origins of Yiddish radio in Canada. The festival director had the idea of doing a local version of what Henry Sapoznik had created in New York, "The Yiddish Radio Project." They called me because of my authentic link to Jewish radio through my father, by now pretty well known in the small circle of Toronto Yiddish music by way of my concertizing. But all I really had to go on were the assurances of everybody that my father was a big star and that stack of 78s, one of which was him performing a singing commercial sung to a popular Yiddish tune. I also had an old photo of a group of Jewish guys in suits, my father smack in the middle, under the caption "Greenfild's Jewish Radio Hour. скос." The picture had hung on my wall since my mother had passed away. That was eighteen years earlier, so I couldn't call on her for help. She had talked to me only in vague terms about my father's past radio career. In fact (sadly typical, I guess) I had only got really interested in these things after she was gone.

So I'm sitting in the Archives on or about June 7, 2004, flipping through really dusty volumes of old Jewish newspapers from the 1940s—so old they literally crumbled in your fingers if you were not really careful. I had asked the archivist, Chris Halonen, for old

Jewish newspapers and he brought me volumes of several different ones from the 1940s: the *Yidishe Zhurnal* ("The Jewish Journal" —"The Daily Hebrew Journal" was its refined English title), the *Vokhenblatt* ("The Weekly Broadsheet"), the *Jewish Standard* and the *Kanader Nayes*. It was in the latter volume that, sure enough, I found a little ad for the radio show (Sunday, October 24, 1943):

Jewish Radio Hour
Every Sunday from 4:30 to 5:30 in the
daytime over station CKTB
1550 kilocycles, managed by
Max Mandel and Sam Yuchtman.
For information telephone Randolph 7453[3]

As I flipped through the volume, sure enough, I found the ad in every issue of the paper. I was delighted, of course, but, as I remember it, a little underwhelmed, at least compared to what happened next. What happened next was that I asked Chris Halonen for a volume from the 1930s. He brought me more *Kanader Nayes* and I opened

---

3 This, it turns out, was my parents' home telephone number.

up the 1936 volume at random and started gingerly flipping through the pages, back to front (in other words, gentile style), when what do I see, but my father's dashing wedding picture, which, like every father's son, I had seen on walls and mantle pieces all of my life, but which had been taken two years before the date at the top of the newspaper. The caption read in Yiddish: "Max Mandel, Artist on the Jewish Radio Hour."

Above it was a picture of "Greenfild," the guy from the photograph, with the caption "S.M. Greenfield (this, I later learned, was the way he actually spelled his name in English), general director and announcer of the Jewish Radio Hour." And beside that was a story starting "Jewish Radio Hour (conclusion from page 1)." So I flipped to page 1 and this is what I saw:

In the middle of the front page on the right-hand side:

**ערשטע אידישע ראדיא
שטונדע רופט ארויס פרייד**

"Ershte yidishe radio shtunde ruft aroys freyd"
("First Jewish Radio Hour Calls Forth Joy")

And here, in translation, is what the article said:

> Last Sunday, Ontario Jews had a pleasant surprise: suddenly the radio began to speak a familiar language, our own mother tongue, Yiddish. It was reported to us that some Jews of the older generation interrupted what

they were doing to make a *shehekheyonu*.⁴ This was the first time that they had heard Yiddish on the airwaves.

The program was excellent regarding both the choice of material and the artistic execution. The artists who participated were as follows: the musical-literary director of the above radio hour was the trained Cantor Stolnitz, his capable son—one of the province's best singers and a scholarship winner at the Toronto Conservatory, the sweet singer of folksongs Max Mandel, the Toronto Symphony Orchestra violinist, Mr. Agronoff, and in a successful recitation, the stage darling and movie actor Benny Adler.

There were also speeches by Mr. J. Glass, K.C., M.P.P, President of the Toronto Zionist Council, and Mr. K. Hurwitz, Secretary of the Labour Committee. Mr. Greenfield, the director of the Hour, was the announcer. He gave an appropriate speech and conducted the program as if he were a radio announcer from a long way back.⁵ His voice was clear and strong.

Mr. Henry S. Rosenberg, President of the Ontario Zionist Region had sent a message that was read. The world also heard a *mazel-tov*⁶ for the new Jewish institution—the Jewish Hour—from the *Kanader Nayes*.

From now on, the Jewish Hour will be heard each Sunday morning from 9.30 to 10.30 on station CKOC. Do not forget to turn on your radio next Sunday for new surprises.

Talk about "calling forth joy!" My Yiddish was weak and I could only make out a few of the words ("First Jewish Radio Hour" and "the sweet singer of folksongs Max Mandel") but it was enough to send me hopping around the room barely able to control myself, whispering excitedly, showing the piece to every one of the studious senior volunteers working away on their clippings and photographs.

---

4 A traditional blessing in gratitude for living long enough to experience a happy, long-awaited occasion.
5 This was expressed metaphorically in Yiddish: "as if he had been a radio announcer from the six days of creation"—"*Azoy vi er volt geven fun di sheyshes yimey bereshis on a radyo anonsirer.*"
6 A congratulatory good luck greeting.

My journey back to the world of my father had begun. My Yiddish gradually got stronger as, dictionary in hand, I translated article by article. And there were lots of articles on the show because, as I soon found out, the newspaper was the show's sponsor! Hence the prominence given to a show that hardly figured at all in any other press of the time, English or Yiddish (not a word in the rival *Yidishe Zhurnal*, for example). But the *Kanader Nayes* lovingly chronicled each show and the careers of the artists. It had letters to the editor about the show and it debated its value and reported on its ups and downs. The *Kanader Nayes*, owned and operated by the prodigious Dorothy Dworkin, soon came to consume my attention as much as the radio show. In fact, the stories of the *Kanader Nayes* (1935–1954) and Max Mandel's various Jewish Hours (1936–1953) were almost entirely co-extensive.

The show at Ashkenaz came off but without my participation. I was supposed to star as my father, but I soon developed "artistic differences" with director Theresa Tova, the details of which are better not gone into here. After a few weeks of rehearsal I quit, with the excuse of a misunderstanding over rehearsal schedules.

Freed of that burden I decided to do a real and proper history of the show. After a period, Chris Halonen wanted to rid the Archives of the disintegrating newspapers in favour of microfilm and I eagerly accepted them. I donned surgical mask (the vapours emanating from these papers was truly awful), put dictionary to hand and started to translate. The characters and their dreams and nightmares came pouring out of the yellowed pages. Some of them I knew as a child, some were relatives of friends, others I actually met up with later, or their surviving children.

But my biggest discovery was the newspaper itself.

The *Kanader Nayes* was a bi-weekly newspaper published by the remarkable Dorothy Dworkin and her activist brother Maurice Goldstick. Actually, it wasn't an independent newspaper but rather a local *insert* that Mrs. Dworkin had stuffed—sometimes by her young grandson Harry Arthurs, a future Dean of Osgoode Hall Law School, who gave me my first job—into the New York Yiddish papers Dworkin imported to Toronto by virtue of her shipping business, "*D. Dworkin's shifs kontor,*" "D. Dworkin's Shipping Office," run out of premises, since demolished, at 525 Dundas Street West.

She had worked in the business since 1917 alongside her husband Harry Dworkin, a huge figure in Toronto Jewry, whose funeral in 1928 at age forty, after being struck by a car, brought thousands into the streets and made headlines even in the English papers. By the 1920s he had built an empire around the shipping office run by him and his brother Edward: "E. and H. Dworkin, wholesale tobacconists, importers and exporters, steamship and banking." For the largely immigrant Jewish Toronto, this was a focal point for the whole community, first of all, because it was Dworkin's business to arrange passage for Jews from Eastern Europe and that enterprise didn't end after their arrival. Families came gradually, and when the pioneer arrived, they would save to buy passage for their relatives. My mother came as a sixteen year old, worked in an uncle's clothing factory, and then brought her sister, brother, and mother over in instalments.

But it wasn't only a ticket that Dworkin arranged, it was also the all important "papers." According to Canadian filmmaker Harry Rasky, who was named after Dworkin, these papers were sometimes questionable" papers.[7] For instance, my aunt Dvoreleh and her

---

[7] Harry Rasky, *The three Harrys*. Oakville, Ont.: Mosaic Press, 1999.

daughter came as *sisters*. But the job didn't stop there. The travel agent in those days was a combination lawyer, politician, immigrant aid society and vocational agency.[8] Harry Dworkin, and later his widow Dorothy, were serious philanthropists, also on the retail level, and there are many stories about them paying for passage when a relative in Toronto could not afford it. Now, the shipping office dealt in imports and exports of things as well as people. Packages were sent and money wired to relatives in the old country. One important line of imports were the hugely popular New York Yiddish daily newspapers, which were then distributed to the various outlets in the city, and later even home delivered, and into which the *Kanader Nayes* was inserted twice weekly as a local supplement.

Harry Dworkin was not only a businessman, but also a socialist and community activist.[9] He was slated to run as an alderman for the Socialist Party in 1916, but gave up his candidacy in favour of friend Jimmy Simpson, who later became Toronto's only authentic left-wing mayor for a brief period in the 1930s. Dworkin himself later ran for alderman but lost. Harry Dworkin was also one of the founders and funders of the Labour Lyceum,  built in 1929, a large building at 346 Spadina Avenue, just around the corner and up the street from the *shifs kontor*, which housed Jewish unions uncomfortable with the anti-Semitism they found in Toronto's Labour Temple on Shuter Street; later the building was refurbished into a series of Chinese restaurants. Dworkin, at the time of his death, was chairman of the Labour Lyceum's board

---

8 Ben Kayfetz, "Recollections and Experiences with the Jewish Press in Toronto," Polyphony, Summer 1984, pp. 228-231.
9 *Dictionary of Canadian Biography Online*, Vol. 15.

of directors. Its huge hall would be the scene of many banquets, lectures, concerts and, ironically, High Holiday services, because Dworkin was militantly anti-religious. His Dawes Road Cemetery tombstone, entirely in English and Yiddish, lacks all the traditional religious references (such as the usual: תניצב״ה standing for the words "May his soul be bound up in the bond of eternal life", or naming him as "son of"). But it notes in the Yiddish (not English) that he was an איד איבערגעבענער ("devoted Jew"). Dworkin's personal anti-religiousness did not at all prevent him from immersing himself in Jewish affairs—another manifestation, one supposes, of the old conflict between Judaism as a religion and Judaism as a nationality. Besides his work for Jewish Labour, he was also a delegate to the first conference of the Canadian Jewish Congress in 1919. It's not known whether Dworkin's personal antipathy to religion was shared by his widow or by her socialist brother, but, if it was, it never prevented the *Kanader Nayes* from giving *khazans*, rabbis, shuls and religious holidays their usual place of respectful prominence in the news and commentary, even if the content and orientation were mostly secular; you could even find the occasional poking of fun at religion in the satiric column "*Off der yidisher gas*" ("On the Jewish Street").

The Labour Lyceum was across the road from the main Jewish theatre landmark of the city, the Strand Theatre, 287 Spadina, "corner Dundas" as they used to say, of which, more later.

Dorothy Dworkin

As large a figure as Harry Dworkin cut in Toronto Jewry, his widow eclipsed him in lasting accomplishments. Dorothy Goldstick Dworkin came from Latvia, then part of the Russian Empire, as a girl of fourteen in 1904. Both Dorothy and Harry came from the Courland region of Latvia; she was born in the town of Windau. Very soon after arriving, she started to work at Toronto's first Jewish free medical dispensary on Elizabeth Street, run by the Hebrew Ladies' Maternity Aid and Child Welfare Society. While still a teenager, she went to study in Cleveland, obtaining a diploma in Ohio in nursing and midwifery and then becoming one of the first Jewish nurses in Ontario. There was no Jewish hospital at the time, but a great many felt a need for one among the highly religious immigrant community, so that they could eat kosher food while in hospital and speak in their mother tongue to the staff. Jewish doctors also found it virtually

MISS DOROTHY GOLDSTICK
President of the B"noth Zion Kadimah
Nurse of the Jewish Free Dispensary

impossible to gain access to the anti-Semitic regular hospitals. In 1920, when the Toronto General Hospital refused to provide a wing with a kosher kitchen and Yiddish-speaking staff, Dorothy took a leading role in a drive that led to the purchase of a building at 100 Yorkville[10] and the establishment in 1922 of the Toronto Jewish Convalescent and Maternity Hospital, renamed the Mount Sinai Hospital in 1923, where most Toronto Jewish babies, including me, would subsequently be born. All forty Jewish doctors in the city joined the staff in 1923. Dworkin was the first president of the Ladies Auxiliary and secretary of the board until it moved to its present site in the hospital district at University Avenue in 1953. In 1943, a building at 101 Yorkville, then across from the hospital was purchased by the doctors for the hospital and it was named "Dorothy Dworkin House" in recognition of her work.[11] The *Kanader Nayes* worked tirelessly for the hospital, giving prominence to its every development and every fund-raising benefit event.

Dworkin was also active in socialist politics, being elected one of three Toronto delegates to the first "All-Canada Conference of the Jewish Worker Committee." Dorothy married Harry in 1911. When he died in 1928, she was thirty-eight and came into his part of the *shifs kontor* business.

The Kanader Nayes

In 1935, Dorothy Dworkin started to publish the *Kanader Nayes* as an insert into the Yiddish newspapers that she imported from New York. There were three dailies and one weekly: *Forverts*

---

10 The façade of the building has been preserved, now owned by Teatro Verde, a design store.
11 *Kanader Nayes*, December 5, 1943, on the front page, naturally.

("*The Forward*"), *Der Tog* ("*The Day*"), *Der Morgen Zhurnal* ("*The Jewish Morning Journal*") and *Der Amerikaner* ("*The American*"). Subsequently added was the *Di Tsukunft* ("*The Future*"). They arrived in Toronto by overnight train and were distributed on the morning of the day they were published. The great advantage for the *Kanader Nayes* was that the New York Yiddish papers were far more widely read, in Toronto at least, than the local Canadian Yiddish papers, namely the *Yidishe Zhurnal* of Toronto, the *Keneder Adler* ("*Canadian Eagle*") of Montreal, and the *Yidishe Vort* ("*Jewish Word*") of Winnipeg. The New York papers pre-dated the local press by at least a decade and, with their big budgets, they carried lots of old-country news and attracted high quality literary talent. New York was the largest Jewish city in the world, with 1.6 million Jews in 1920, almost a third of its population, having a valid claim to being the centre of the modern Jewish universe. The local Toronto Jewish press, on the other hand, was always on the verge of bankruptcy.[12]

During the 1930s, there were about 45,000 to 50,000 Jews living in Toronto, one-third of all those in Canada (Montreal was slightly larger). Toronto was a middle-sized Jewish population centre by world standards. The Jews of Toronto were mostly of recent immigration, mostly from Poland—according to one authority, mostly from the south-central Kielce area[13]—and virtually all of them claiming Yiddish as their mother tongue. Though they made up less than ten percent of Toronto's population, Jews were the largest non-British ethnic group by far. They were concentrated in the downtown "Wards." Spadina Avenue, a few steps from where Dworkin's was

---

12 Shmuel Mayer Shapiro, *The Rise of the Toronto Jewish Community* (Toronto: Now & Then Books, 2010), p. 57.
13 Gerald Tulchinsky, *Canada's Jews: a people's journey*. (Toronto: University of Toronto Press, 2008), p. 210.

located, was essentially a Jewish street, as Jewish then as it is Chinese now—in both respects different only in size from New York City's Lower East Side.

The *Kanader Nayes* editors, writing on the paper's thirteenth anniversary—its "bar mitzvah"—on April 23, 1948, described the origin of the paper this way:

> **Our Bar Mitzvah**
> About fifteen years ago a few of Toronto's Jewish business leaders of the time came to us with the request that we should put out a Jewish newspaper. They complained that the Toronto Jewish organizations were all at the mercy and the caprices of the publicity agents, who made them pay heavy sums of money for their publicity, which was of doubtful value. Moreover, these businessmen pointed to the happy situation that one of the current publishers of the *Kanader Nayes* was the Toronto distributor of the great daily and weekly New York Yiddish newspapers. "This fact," they underlined, "gives you the means, immediately, with the very first issue, to be the Canadian Jewish newspaper with more readers than any other Canadian Jewish newspaper." We confess that we were not persuaded right on the spot. The matter of a paper was at that time completely strange for us. It seems certain that if one of the current publishers of the *Kanader Nayes* had not herself been a victim of the publicity agents, the *Kanader Nayes* might never have been born. Today's Jewish Mount Sinai Hospital had at that time undertaken a modest campaign to raise some tens of thousands of dollars to enlarge the hospital. We had turned, as usual, to the publicity agents to do their job, for the immediate reward of honour on this sinful earth. But these important publicity businessmen demanded a price for their wares that amounted to a significant percent of the relatively small campaign goal. The result was that the campaign committee, of which one of the current publishers of the *Kanader Nayes* was a member, decided instead to carry out the campaign with circulars inserted into the New York Jewish newspapers, which were sold in Toronto. The public read the many thousand circulars and gave

money for the hospital. From this was born the idea of circulating a Jewish newspaper in the New York Jewish newspapers.

In other words, a Yiddish insert into the New York papers was good business for local advertisers, including, it must be said, Mrs. Dworkin, whose advertisements for her various enterprises along with those of her brothers, profitable as well as charitable, could always be found in the paper.

According to Harry Rasky, one additional motivating factor for Dworkin herself was that Jewish emigration to Canada, the mainstay of the family business, had been cut drastically after 1929. Mrs. Dworkin certainly didn't hide the fact that one of the goals of the *Kanader Nayes* was to expand the circulation of the New York papers she imported by making them more attractive to Canadian readers. As she wrote in the first issue of the *Kanader Nayes*: "The only thing that has impeded us in the constant enlargement of the number of readers of the New York newspapers has been the fact that the New York papers have lacked a little local Toronto colour." However, she claimed a community, rather than a business purpose for this: "For us, this is more than a matter of business." In fact, the paper had an unabashed ideological outlook that was also an important ingredient in its birth.

One of the key figures at the new paper, H.M. Kirschenbaum, had been managing partner and editor of the *Yidisher Zhurnal*, the main Toronto Jewish daily (located right across the street from the *Kanader Nayes* at 542 Dundas Street West—the building still exists) from 1915 until a bankruptcy sale in 1931, when he left in search of other journalistic enterprises, several of which failed, before he joined the *Kanader Nayes*.[14] An article by Kirshenbaum in the first issue of

---

14 Shapiro, *op. cit.*, p.51-52.

the paper, strongly hints at political reasons for his departure, as well as offering a glimpse at the open personal bitterness of these Jewish newspaper rivalries:

> It is precisely four years ago today that I was torn away from the Jewish reader. To be exact, Friday night, *Shabbes hagadol*[15] of 1931, they came into my office and notified me that the new management didn't need me anymore. And that my sixteen years connected to Toronto Jews, living with them, knowing all their suffering and cries, were put aside and others were to take my place. It was four years ago today that they published my article "The hunt for leaven" with my name removed. . . . A significant fact of my life, which has deeply engraved itself in my memory.

In the same article, Kirschenbaum wrote that, in the meantime, he had stayed working with the "Zionist Socialist movement," which about sums up the distinct ideological bent of the *Kanader Nayes*.[16]

Although known by detractors as "Mrs. Dworkin's "*bletl*" (little sheet)[17] and even her "*shmateh*" (rag), it was in fact her brother, Maurice Goldstick, who was the editor in chief and driving intellectual force behind the paper. Maurice Goldstick was a socialist like Harry Dworkin, and a Zionist as well. By the time he assumed leadership of the paper, Goldstick had a long career of activism at his back. He had been a local leader of the *Poale Tzion* (literally "Workers of Zion" or Labour Zionists) and its associated fraternal organizations, the *Farband*, the Jewish National Workers

---

15 The Shabbat before Passover.
16 "The paper appealed to both major ideological elements in the Jewish community-pro-Bundist, because Mrs. Dworkin continued the tradition of her late husband Henry Dworkin who was active in the socialist movement, and pro-Zionist, because Maurice Goldstick was a devoted Zionist." Kayfetz, *op. cit.*
17 "They [the Jewish communists] also laugh at us for being 'Mrs. Dworkin's little sheet' [מרס. דווארקין'ס בלעטעלא] instead of Stalin's gigantic newspaper. M.G." [Maurice Goldstick], "A chat with an old friend," *KN*, Oct. 27, 1937.

Alliance (*Yidish Natsionaler Arbeter Farband*) and the *Arbeter Ring*, the Workmen's Circle. The influence of these movements in the Canadian Jewish community of the early twentieth century, as in the rest of the Jewish world, can be gauged by the fact that Goldstick was elected the first vice-president of the Canadian Jewish Congress at the inaugural congress in March 1919 as the Toronto delegate with the most votes. In his history of the Socialist Zionist movement in Canada, Simon Belkin described Goldstick as a "dynamic" leader who had "had great influence in the Arbeter Ring circle." [18]

On Goldstick's retirement in 1954, which was quickly followed by the closing of the *Kanader Nayes*, he revealed that he had written *every lead editorial* over the nineteen years of existence of the paper. It was no coincidence that the paper's ideological outlook was not only like Goldstick's own, but also that of its star New York import, the *Forverts*, with whose functionaries Goldstick and Mrs. Dworkin had strong personal ties. One of these was Baruch Vladek, manager of the *Forverts* and a much revered labour leader and civic politician, who had been elected to the New York City Council. He was given dignitary status by the paper whenever he came to Toronto.[19] In practical terms, this meant the paper supported the establishment of a Jewish state in Palestine, supported labour over capital, supported Yiddish as the language of the Jewish people, was socialist, even, at least in the beginning, Marxist—you can still see the faces of Marx and Engels in relief on the gloriously restored *Forverts* Building (1912) at 175 East Broadway in New York City. But from the start and

---

18 Simon Belkin, *The Labor Zionist Movement in Canada 1904 to 1920* (Actions Committee of the Labor Zionist Movement in Canada, Montreal: 1956), pp. 135, 169).
19 "B. Vladek, manager of *Forverts* speaking at a mass meeting at the Strand Theatre," *KN*, January 10, 1937, p 8.

increasingly so, the paper was anti-Communist Party and anti-Soviet. The major splits in the world socialist movement had occurred in the 1920s and the Zionist parties, including the *Poale Tzion* itself, had been completely suppressed in the Soviet Union by 1929.

The paper's socialism and anti-communism found local expression as electoral support for the newly formed Canadian Commonwealth Federation (CCF), the forerunner of today's New Democratic Party (NDP), which has never come close to forming a national government, though it has had some sporadic success in this regard at the provincial level. The ideology of the party was originally socialist, but it has become very moderate in modern times and has dropped this designation. The paper also waged a campaign against what was known as "dual unionism," the practice of the Communist International of forming its own unions and competing for workers' allegiances on the shop floor.[20] Anti-communism was not the mainstream position in the 1930s that it was to become in the 1950s, especially among Jews, but it came natural to Zionists. This was because the Communist Party, run from the Soviet Union, was anti-Zionist in the whole interwar period, backing the indigenous Arab opposition to Jewish aspirations in Palestine, an opposition that was often violent. Nevertheless, the Jews of the Wards gave huge popular and electoral support to the Communist Party and Mrs. Dworkin, either differing from her brother on this, or simply catering to the market, had no problem selling elaborate guided tours (described below) to the Soviet Union until 1937.

But, by 1937, the great terror was underway in the Soviet Union and, though it was not specifically anti-Semitic, it did not spare

---

20 Ruth Frager, *Sweatshop Strife: class, ethnicity, and gender in the Jewish labour movement of Toronto, 1900-1939*. Toronto: University of Toronto Press, 1992, pp.182ff.

Jews, even some prominent Jewish Bolshevik political and military leaders, who were put on trial and executed. The terror led to open Jewish editorial war in Toronto between the Socialists and the Communists. The *Kanader Nayes* carried on an anti-communist crusade, though with only middling success among the Jews. In the local elections of 1937, Jewish communists won election as aldermen in the Wards, and J. B. Salsberg was launched on his long political career. In further local elections of 1938, the communists had less success and the paper even took a little credit for it. Salsberg remained the paper's arch-enemy until the mid-war years when the Russians became our allies against Hitler. Then he was transformed into a respected statesman.

Clearly the *Kanader Nayes* was a matter of much more than dollars and cents to the people who ran it. Nor was it by any means a purely political organ. It had the highest cultural and intellectual aspirations. It aimed to be a local paper for the thinking Jewish community. In the editor's words in the first edition, "This means that we undertake to inform the reader of everything that occurs in our country and our city that a modern intelligent Jewish citizen needs to know."

The Yiddish Radio Show

In early 1936, the *Kanader Nayes* decided to sponsor a Yiddish radio show. Sponsoring a radio show was not an unusual thing for a newspaper to do in the mid-1930s, though there was a strong love-hate aspect to the relationship. Newspapers were the unchallenged mass media for literally hundreds of years before the arrival of radio on the scene. By the 1930s, radio was everywhere and newspapers, fearing the competition, bought their own stations, which they would use as promotional devices. As would happen a generation later with television, most Canadians listened to the American shows. The stars were often Jewish (Jack Benny and Eddie Cantor, alongside Amos 'n' Andy and Fibber McGee and Molly), but there was also a distinctly Jewish radio in the United States, centred in Brooklyn with its huge Yiddish-speaking audience.

Yiddish radio started to establish itself in New York around 1927 when the newspaper *Der Tog* launched a program on WABC in Manhattan, broadcasting at 11 AM on Sundays. It lasted until 1932, when its time slot was taken over by the *Forverts*, Mrs. Dworkin's star import, which had also taken over station WEVD and created "The Forward Hour." The station itself had been created in 1927 by the Socialist Party in honour of its deceased leader Eugene V. Debs—hence the "EVD" in the name. So, here were precedents for Mrs. Dworkin. You could even hear Jewish radio hours in Toronto broadcast over WGR from Buffalo, New York in the early 1930s.[21]

There was actually a Canadian precedent for newspaper-sponsored Yiddish radio, though it was in far away Winnipeg, more remote than New York from the ken of Toronto Jews. The newspaper in question was *Dos Yidishe Vort*, which like the *Yidisher Zhurnal* had a more genteel English name, the *Israelite Press*. On November 30, 1931, the paper announced that it had arranged a "local high-class Jewish radio program," the "*Yidishe Shoh*," [22] to be heard each Sunday on CKY starting the following December 6.

However, on February 22, 1932, the paper announced the twelfth

---

21 *Toronto Daily Star*, April 1, 1931, p. 26: "10:45 [PM]—WGR—Jewish Hour."
22 "Jewish Hour" – "*Shoh*" means "hour," not "show", in Hebrew and Yiddish, though it is pronounced "sha'a" in Israeli Hebrew. "*Shtunde*" also means hour in Yiddish, being derived from the identical word in German.

and last show of what was now described as a "series of shows." Nothing more would be heard until November 9, 1934, when a second series was announced and the three-year hiatus was explained as due to a "useless wait" for the "radio commission to give radio programs to the Jewish citizen, as they do for other nationalities." The problem seems to have been that radio station CKY, one of the oldest in Canada, was a *public* station and not a private station like the one "The Jewish Hour" would operate on in Ontario. It was operated as a monopoly by the provincial government through the Manitoba Telephone System. So there were political obstacles to overcome, which were hinted at in an article two years later when another "first of a series" was announced.

Political obstacles might also be said to have prevented any Jewish Hour from being heard in Quebec until the 1960s, notwithstanding Montreal's pre-eminence among Jewish communities. There was privately-owned radio, but it was overwhelmingly French, clerical and xenophobic, as was the province.[23] Nachum Wilchesky[24] started his Jewish broadcasts on CFMB when it opened in 1962, billed as "Canada's First Multilingual Broadcaster," which may have been true for Quebec, but was wrong by a generation for the rest of Canada.

There appears briefly to have been a show in Vancouver as well. A letter to the editor of *Di Yidishe Vort* on June 3, 1932, page 6, bitterly complained of its low quality: "It's been stressed enough that the radio hour, which should demonstrate folk character, musical

---

23 Tulchinsky, *op. cit.*, pp. 301ff.
24 In a sweet coincidence that neither Nachum Wilchesky nor Max Mandel lived to see—the two men never even met—two of their grandchildren fell in love in Toronto and were married in 2010.

37

education and aesthetic taste, was transformed into a radio-shame."²⁵

So was the *Kanader Nayes* right to claim the "first" Jewish hour for itself? The editors later hedged a bit with "the only *permanent* Jewish radio hour in Canada."²⁶ And that's how Cantor Stolnitz described it in his book of many years hence.²⁷ From the radio pages of the various newspapers, it appears that there were even local Toronto Jewish hours on CFRB dating from as early as 1931. However these were sporadic and had long ceased to broadcast before 1936. An article about "The Jewish Hour" in the *Kanader Nayes* of August 19 put it this way:

"All other such undertakings . . . have ended just as quickly as they began. . . . Why has the Jewish Radio Hour had more luck than other Jewish radio hours and half-hours which we have had in Toronto before the hour?" For the record, it might be said that the *Kanader Nayes* show, which was intended to be permanent and did, indeed, in one form or another stay continuously on the air for many years, had some claim to pre-eminence over all these other examples. But why not give Winnipeg and CFRB their due, and simply say that the *Kanader Nayes* show was one of the first Jewish radio hours in Canada?

The People of The Jewish Hour

Let's return to the account of the first episode of the Toronto show quoted above. Who were these people? A lot can be said about a few of them, others not so much.

---

25 There is a play on words here in Yiddish: the Yiddish word for shame is *shandeh*. So *"radio-shandeh"* is a play on *"radio shtunde"* – "radio hour."
26 *KN*, June 7, 1936, p. 2, emphasis added.
27 N. Stolnitz, *Music in Jewish life/Negine in yidishn lebn* (Toronto, 1957), p. 253.

Nathan Stolnitz
"the musical-literary director, the trained Cantor Stolnitz"

Nathan Stolnitz was born in Goworowo, Poland in 1893, then settled in storied Vilna, and came to Canada in 1926. He was not only a *khazan* but also an authority on *khazans* and their art. The author of many journal articles and three books, he was active in cantors' organizations across the continent. He was to play a big, if short-lived, role in the radio hour.

Samuel Stolnitz
"his capable son—one of the province's best singers and a scholarship winner at the Toronto Conservatory"

Samuel Stolnitz followed in his father's footsteps. He was already concertizing as a *khazendl* (child cantor) with his brother in Vilna before coming to Canada at age twelve. In his early years, he flirted with classical music and performed opera locally, but he eventually settled on a long career as a *khazan*, culminating in twenty years at the Holy Blossom Temple in Toronto, from which he retired in 1966.

Mr. Agronoff
"the Toronto Symphony Orchestra violinist, Mr. Agronoff"

The Toronto Symphony archives have no record of Mr. Agronoff's ever having played with the orchestra, which doesn't mean that he did not, only that he was probably never a permanent member of the orchestra.

Benny Adler
"the stage darling and movie actor Benny Adler"

Although he had the famous Adler name, Benny Adler was not

a member of the luminous New York family. Benny Adler, born in Rumania in 1886, was by 1936 a well-established American Yiddish theatre actor who had recently had a big part in the first Yiddish talkie, the critically acclaimed anti-Nazi and anti-war *The Wandering Jew* (1933). Adler very effectively plays the bad guy role of a German Nazi sympathizer who is the false friend and rival of a persecuted Jewish artist played by Jacob Ben-Ami. Adler had come to Toronto for a March 1, 1936 concert at the Strand Theatre, but stayed on for a second on March 22, with performances in smaller centres in between.

Although a big farewell evening had been held for Adler on March 25 in the Labour Lyceum, in fact, he stuck around for the first few episodes of the radio show. His connection to Toronto and the *Kanader Nayes* was very strong. He would return and spend the entire 1937–38 season doing numerous performances in repertory at the Spadina Theatre. He came back frequently and was appearing in Toronto as late as 1954.

John J. Glass
"There were also speeches by Mr. J. Glass, K.C., M.P.P., president of the Toronto Zionist Council"

John J. Glass was a Jewish Liberal Member of the Ontario Provincial Parliament from 1934 to 1943, very active in Jewish causes. His presence in the studio shows that the inauguration of "The Jewish Hour" was indeed a big community event.

K. Hurwitz
"Mr. K. Hurwitz, secretary of the Labour Committee"

Not much is known about Mr. Hurwitz, but his organization was a branch of the famous New York-based Jewish Labour Committee founded in 1934 as a trade union response to the rise of Nazism in Europe. The Committee gave material and moral support to Jewish labour in European countries and the anti-Hitler underground, both before and during the war, and organized boycotts and mass protests against Fascism abroad and at home. Its leading personality and first president was Baruch Vladek, which indicates its Labour Zionist orientation and underlines once again the strong ties between the *Forverts* and its Canadian cousin, the *Kanader Nayes* and the *Kanader Nayes*'s radio show.

S. M. Greenfield

Finally we have the godfather of the whole enterprise. According to the *Kanader Nayes* report:

> Mr. Greenfield, the director of the Hour, was the announcer. He gave an appropriate speech and conducted the program as if he were a radio announcer from a long way back. His voice was clear and strong.

Sam Greenfield was definitely *not* "a radio announcer from a long way back." He was, up until that moment, a debt collector and, as such, one of the *Kanader Nayes* most devoted advertisers. His first ads appeared in June, 1935:

S.M Greenfield & Co.
Licensed Bailiffs & Collectors
1 ADELAIDE ST. E.
WAverley 2878

Do you want quick and efficient service, collecting rent or other debts that are owed to you, then you should turn to Greenfield and Company, 1 Adelaide Street East, telephone Waverley 2878; in the evening Melrose 3181. It costs you nothing if we collect nothing. We speak Yiddish.

Greenfield was soon a kind of poster boy for *Kanader Nayes* advertising. One front page reprint of a letter from him had him singing the praises of the *Kanader Nayes*: "I have got better success through your newspaper than through any other Jewish newspaper in which I have advertised before." Greenfield subsequently expanded a bit to debt *creation* as well as collection: "We collect rents and other debts; we lend money on mortgages and automobiles, we manage properties."[28] Greenfield continued advertising in almost every edition of the *Kanader Nayes* up until just a few weeks before the radio show first broadcast. Perhaps he advertised on the show itself, though we have no record of it. Perhaps Greenfield's zeal to start a radio show derived from his faith in the power of advertising. Greenfield would continue to be a major player in Jewish radio, so there will be more to say about him. And of course, we'll have a lot to say about:

"the sweet singer of folksongs Max Mandel"

One picture is worth a thousand words, though, and if we don't have a snapshot of the inaugural program of the Jewish Radio Hour itself we have something very close to it. On the front page of the *Kanader Nayes* of April 1, 1936, alongside the account of the first

---
28 *KN*, January 19, 1936, p. 4.

Jewish Hour and stories of alleged police interference in the recent municipal election and of the plenary meeting of the Canadian Jewish Congress in Montreal, there was also a loving account of a *"zay gezunt ovnt"* (farewell evening) for Benny Adler, who was supposed to have been ending his Toronto engagement, but who, in fact, stayed around for quite a while after. The event had taken place on the eve of the first Jewish Hour broadcast. Here's the account:

> **Adler evening a colossal artistic success**
> The farewell Adler concert which took place Saturday night in the Labour Lyceum was beyond doubt an artistic achievement of the first rank. From Benny Adler's presence alone this would already be obvious. Everyone who has had the good fortune to see Mr. Adler on the stage, whether live or in the movies, was allowed to expect that, at a concert prepared for him by his intimate Toronto admirers, even he himself would triumph.
>
> This expectation was completely fulfilled to such an extent that Benny Adler surprised even his friends with his expressive recitations. The great wonder of the evening, however, was that every single one of his local artist-friends who had come to honour Benny Adler, was infected with Adler's artistic spirit. And they themselves began to "speak like prophets."
>
> It will be enough to list the names of the Toronto artists and to say that the artistic contributions from each one of them was worthy of the greatest and most beautiful theatres of America. And here are their names: the talented comedian and "master of ceremonies" Max Mandel, the gifted musical cantor Nathan Stolnitz, his scholarship son with the golden tenor-baritone voice, Sam Stolnitz, the sweet folksong singer Yacubovitch with his succulent tenor, the recitalist, a professional actor, Mr. Fogel, the pianist accompanist Shifra Goldstick.
>
> However, perhaps more than everyone, because this is a supernatural phenomenon, the two Pasen sisters, children, but children who could together both walk around on their hands, these *wunderkinds* won the hearts of the audience. It will not be any exaggeration to argue that Hollywood has never seen such a thing. Two little

children presenting themselves and performing with a talent such as Benny Adler, will give you an idea of what those in attendance saw.

The audience was roused more than anything else when Moyshe Shapiro announced that we were not yet letting Benny Adler leave Toronto and that he would perform theatre in Toronto the week of *Pesakh* (Passover).

The event was clearly delightful, even if it appears to have been presented under somewhat false pretenses. But that's not the reason we're lingering over it, which is rather the even more delightful coincidence that a gorgeous photograph exists of many of the evening's participants, fresh with the excitement of the performance that had just taken place. We can guess that it had just taken place because neither of the "supernatural phenomenon," the Pasen sisters, are in the picture, though a closely contemporary picture of them at a Mount Sinai Hospital musical evening appeared in *Kanader Nayes* of January 19, 1936.

Evelyn went on to a very distinguished singing career in Canada and the United States as a mezzo-soprano. She and her sister live in Toronto, but Evelyn has no recollection of the evening, saying they were probably kept back stage until their performance and then taken home. Hence the deduction that the group photograph was taken after the event and not before. Here it is:

The photograph includes not only the characters of the show, but of the *Kanader Nayes* itself, and can serve as a kind of *dramatis personae* for our story. The picture did not come out of my family album, though it could have. I had never seen it until 2005 when I spotted it in Cantor Stolnitz's book, *On Wings of Song* (1957). Then the original popped out of the Dworkin papers at the Ontario Jewish Archives.

Some of the people in the photograph still remain to be identified, but most are known.[29] Seated in the middle, rather whimsically, is the guest of honour, Benny Adler. Beside him, the very young and gifted Sam Stolnitz, looking supremely confident for his twenty-

---

29 When Harry Arthurs and I compared notes on the picture, he knew about half the people and I knew most of the other half.

two years. His father, Nathan Stolnitz is standing in the second row, second from the left. Seated beside the younger Stolnitz is the pianist Shifra Goldstick. Behind her, standing, extreme right in the second row, is her father, the activist editor of the *Kanader Nayes*, Maurice Goldstick. Seated on the extreme left in the front row is my mother, Hilda Mandel, all of twenty-four years old, looking very happy. Second from the left in the back row is Morris (Moyshe) Shapiro, the one who announced at the end of the evening that Adler would be staying on. Shapiro was a man of diverse talents, for many years a theatrical prompter and, latterly, a Yiddish theatre impresario. He was also a court translator, who wrote of his experiences in the *Kanader Nayes*. He appears, though, like so many of these people, to have earned his daily bread in a more prosaic way, in his case as a star insurance salesman. The distinguished-looking man beside him is unknown to me. Standing in the second row, third from the right, is "the learned Professor Golecki," a lecturer and "specialist commentator" for the *Kanader Nayes* on "political and social events."[30] Beside him, in the very centre of the picture, looking appropriately regal, is Dorothy Dworkin.

Beside her, with Moyshe Shapiro's hands on his shoulders, is the twenty-seven-year-old Max Mandel.

---

30 "Moscow trial a "frame-up" says Prof. Golecki in lecture," *KN*, March 7, 1937, p. 5; "Grigori Gershuni, The Greatest Jewish Revolutionary," *KN*, September 5, 1937, II-1; "F.M. Dostoevsky,"*KN*, Sept. 25, 1946, Section 2 p. 1; "Problems of Socialism," *KN*, September 23, 1949, RH section 3, p. 1.

CHAPTER 2

Max Mandel — from Apt to Toronto

MAX MANDEL WAS ONE of tens of thousands of poor Jewish immigrants from Eastern Europe who poured into Canada in the first three decades of the twentieth century. He came to Canada on May 6, 1927 as an eighteen-year-old—born December 14, 1908—from the little *shtetl* of Apt on the Vistula River in South-Central Poland near Kielce and Krakow.[31] The name on his passage was "Majer Mandel" which was pronounced MANdl. This ultimately became Max ManDEL. He followed his father, Leybish, who had come the previous year, who in turn had followed his parents-in-law Yakov and Miriam Cohen, who lived at 60 Henry Street, Toronto, just one street over from the future Apter synagogue. Max was soon joined by his mother, brother and four sisters, and even a niece (masquerading, as mentioned earlier, as a sister for immigration purposes).

"My little town, Apt," never left the heart of this Apter. He davened at the Apter synagogue, where he ultimately became president, he put on many benefit concerts for the Apter survivors of the Holocaust, and he was buried, along with many of his relatives, in the Apter section of the old Dawes Road Jewish cemetery in Toronto.

Apt was small—no more than 8,000 people, about two-thirds Jewish—but not tiny by shtetl standards, no "*mizmoyr l'soydeh in a kleyner siderl*" that one senior davener at a morning minyan once

---

[31] The town's Polish name is Opatow and its Yiddish spelling is אפטא.

dismissed a colleague's town to me as.[32] Apt also had a noble history. It was the sight of an imposing church dating from the twelfth century, still standing, not to mention a beautiful synagogue dating from the 1600s, destroyed *after* World War Two, but depicted in detail by Mayer Kirshenblatt.

In fact, the Mandels had actually immigrated to Apt during my father's lifetime from the even smaller town of Ozharov (Ozarow), which is listed on Max's passport as his birthplace.

Max remained a very devoted and active Apter *landsman* all his life. The *Apt Yiskor (Remembrance) Book* has this to say about him:

> He was the successor to Avram-David Freiberg. He was President of the Apter Friendly Society and directed the campaign to finish the construction of the building, which is called the Apter Centre.[33] Max was a gifted singer. He also had other artistic abilities. He was the top leader in the Apter Aid Society. He organized concerts, the profits from which were devoted to help townsfolk (*landslayt*), survivors and also other townsfolk throughout the world. He also composed the little song *"Mayn Shtetele Apt"*— re-worked from Moyshe Oysher's song. It was sung at all Apter concerts. Being all of a few years over forty he was torn away from his Apter work, which was so dear to him.[34]

The Oysher song referred to is *Belz, Mayn Shtetele Belz* (*Belz, My Little Town, Belz*) sung by Oysher in the 1937 film *The Cantor's Son*, composed by Alexander Olshanetsky with lyrics by Jacob Jacobs. Belz was a shtetl about half the size of Apt, about 100 kilometers to the east. You would think Max's Apt song would have been

---

32 *"Mizmoyr l'soydeh"*—Psalm of Thanksgiving [מזמור לתודה] is a very short prayer in the morning service for which one rises briefly—a *"mizmoyr l'soydeh* in a small prayer book" is a davener's metaphor for "tiny."
33 I had my bar mitzvah there eight years after he died.
34 *Apt: A town which does not exist anymore.* (Apt Organizations in Israel, USA, Canada and Brazil: Tel Aviv, 1966), p. 396.

considerably different to merit such a comment, but, according to several reliable witnesses, the only difference was the substitution of the word "Apt" for "Belz"!

Apt was a minor timber trade centre in the Middle Ages. Toronto Apter S. Waverman wrote that the "surrounding landscape was completely enchanting, with sheets of black fields, gigantic forests and little peaceful lakes, which every visitor marvelled at,"[35] whence all those "*beymelen*"—little trees—of the songs. After the expulsions from Germany in the fourteenth century following upon the Black Death, and later from Spain following the Inquisition and the final defeat of the Muslims in 1492, Jews poured into Poland where they were welcomed for their famous commercial talents and trading connections and, hence, where the atmosphere was much more tolerant. Apt's importance increased towards the end of the sixteenth century, which, by no coincidence, was when Jews began to settle there. The Jews were city dwellers in a world of peasants; they were skilled in crafts and trade and finance. By the mid-seventeenth century, Poland had eighty percent of the world's Jews.

But after a "golden age" of Polish Jewry in the fifteenth and sixteenth centuries, the war-ravaged seventeenth century was very insecure for Polish Jewry. They were victimized by invading soldiers and also by Polish soldiers and civilians, with a sharp increase in blood libels.[36] Matters improved especially from the end of the eighteenth century, when Apt began to change international hands. Poland was partitioned three times between Austria, Prussia and Russia during the period 1772 to 1795. Under the second partition in 1793, the Jews

---

35 S. Waverman, "My City Apt," *KN*, January 6, 1946, p.2.
36 The blood libel was a claim that Jews kidnapped and murdered Christian boys to make matzah. When a Christian boy died inexplicably this would be the cue for a lynching or a pogrom.

of Apt came under Austrian rule, a situation which lasted until 1807 and under which the Jews prospered, relatively speaking. This was also the period in which they were made by the authorities to adopt the names we often now associate with East European Jews, Mandel being one of them. It means "almond" in German and Yiddish, probably shortened from Mandelbaum, "almond tree." After the Austrians were defeated by the French in 1807, Apt came under French rule in the Duchy of Warsaw and, upon Napoleon's defeat in 1815, it was annexed to Congress Poland, effectively under the thumb of the Czar of Russia until the end of the First World War. However, Apt remained outside of the Pale of Settlement and hence conditions were somewhat less oppressive than in backward Russia. The Jews of Apt, as with most of Congress Poland, escaped the pogroms following the assassination of Tsar Alexander II and again during the revolutionary period around 1905. The Bialystok pogrom of 1906 was the worst of these, with a hundred Jews murdered. Max's wife Hilda (my mother) was from Bialystok, a large industrial city far to the north-east of Apt, but she was born after these events.

Apt and its Jews seem to have done quite well during the nineteenth century, as the city developed small factory and cottage industries. The Austrian army occupied Apt during the First World War; the Austrians and their German allies had a more tolerant view of Jews, indeed saw them as natural allies against the Russians. The occupation was a period of greatly increased freedom for the Jews, who were even allowed to form political parties forbidden under Russian domination. The end of the war saw a kind of retribution by returning Polish armies, and a short wave of anti-Semitism; Jews continued to leave in droves; about 75,000 emigrated to the United States in 1921 alone. Open immigration to the United States quickly ended and the destination of choice became Canada. That didn't last terribly long either, as the doors virtually closed to Canada in 1929 with the Depression. In "My City Apt," his post-Holocaust reflections for the *Kanader Nayes*,[37] Toronto Apter S. Waverman writes that the reasons for the mass departure were compound:

> With Poland's independence there began the exodus from Apt, the way it began for all Polish Jewry. From that day on, young and old were going around worrying: what will be tomorrow? The youth sought to flee into the far away and the idealists went to the land of Israel. Then there was no White Paper. Many travelled to America. The Polish chauvinists also forced out Polish Jewry. They opened cooperatives all over with the slogan "*Svoi do svega*" ("Poles buy from Poles"). The merchants stopped stocking goods and the stores became empty. The famous Apter carriage-drivers worried about their haggard horses. The times became bitter. Grabski and his followers scourged Polish Jewry, not just with taxes, but also with pogroms.[38] Fascism was raging even before Hitler arrived.... Whoever had the chance to emigrate, emigrated, and those who stayed hoped for better times, until 1939, that dark year for Polish Jewry.

For those remaining in Poland, the 1930s were a period of increasing repression and economic collapse, political instability and anti-Semitism. There were boycotts of Jewish shops, quotas on Jewish students in universities, and pogroms. The end came with the Nazi occupation of 1939–45, during which, in the words of the Apt *Yiskor* book: "The German murderers uprooted every trace of Jewish life in Apt."[39]

The town was built around a rectangular marketplace which,

---

37 *KN*, January 6, 1946, p.2.
38 Wladyslaw Grabski, leader of the anti-Semitic National Democratic Party, introduced an anti-Jewish taxation policy that was said to contribute to the exodus of Jews from Poland.
39 *Ibid.*, p. 20.

in my father's day had a market twice a week. There were all the trades and crafts necessary to sustain a population, right down to the "oldest profession" itself. Jews were the large majority, over sixty percent of the population, concentrated, for the most part in one section of the town. The Poles were the vast majority of the peasantry in the surrounding countryside. They would bring their unfinished wares to market where the Jews sold them finished goods. There was cottage industry, notably in brushes, and a few factories, the most famous of which was Mandelbaum's soap, candle and oil factory with the sign of the elephant. All this is vividly depicted in the beautiful folk paintings of Meyer Kirshenblatt, who left Apt just in time and, late in life, painted his memories of the town and described its workings in intimate detail. To know Apt or any *shtetl*, you just have to read his book, *They Called Me Mayer July*. [40]

Apt was a centre of Jewish learning renowned in the Khasidic world for some of its figures. Apt was the birthplace of the *magid* (preacher) Reb Yisrael of Koznitz, one of the four founders of Khasidism in Poland. In the beginning of the nineteenth century, Reb Abraham Joshua Heschel, "the Apter Rebbe," served as *admor* (Khasidic dynasty head) and rabbi of the town. The Apter Rebbe was a disciple of the even more famous Rabbi Elimelekh of Lyzhinsk, one of whose descendants was the American civil rights activist Rabbi Abraham Joshua Heschel. Apt also had the distinction of being a centre of enlightenment and this was no mere boast, as one of the most esteemed of modern Yiddish writers, I.L. Peretz, actually came to marry a girl from Apt for the sole purpose (according to him) of being with her mathematician-philosopher father. It is usual for Apt

---

40 Mayer Kirshenblatt and Barbara Kirshenblatt-Gimblett, *They Called Me Mayer July: Painted Memories of a Jewish Childhood in Poland before the Holocaust*, University of California Press, 2007.

to claim Peretz as a *"landsman"* because of this. However, to call Peretz an Apter is stretching things considerably, considering the fact that the marriage ended in divorce after five years.

In the period between the two wars, Apt was mostly orthodox and boasted, besides the beautiful synagogue, four *batei midrash* (houses of study) and five Khasidic *shtiblekh* (small prayer halls) as well as other places of worship. Despite its small size, every conceivable political grouping could be found there: the Zionist Organization with its youth groups *Hashomer Hatzair* and *Hekhalutz*, the *Mizrakhi* (religious Zionists), Revisionists, *Poale Tzion*, *Bund* and Communists. The cultural life was rich. All the tendencies had their schools, in Hebrew, Yiddish and Polish, and there were organized drama and sports clubs. S. Waverman writes of a spirit of tolerance:

> In general, however, the residents of Apt had respect for the "other-believer." On Sabbath nights, after *cholnt* [Sabbath stew], the elders and the Khasidic section of the people used to go and hear a Lithuanian *magid* [itinerant preacher] in the city *beys hamidrash* [study-house]. The radicals used to go strolling around on Tsozmirer Way to the famous "Kanye" swimming hole, singing their socialist songs and carrying on romances with the good Apter daughters.[41]

When the Mandels left in 1927, there was still no electricity or running water in the homes, and there were no cars or buses, just horses and carriages. There were only a handful of private telephones. A hopeless poverty had settled on Apt as elsewhere in Poland. Like many Poles and Jews from the *shtetls*, the Jews of Apt were also leaving the economic backwardness of the small town for the big cities, with their factory jobs. As the 1930s wore on, the town saw more and more overt anti-Semitic agitation. In 1936 the organized

---

41 S. Waverman.

violence started. On one of the market days, a group of hoodlums, along with area farmers, attacked Jewish stores and stalls. They stole goods, beat the owners and their families, and tried to break into houses. Even though thirty Jewish Apters were injured, the rioters were treated with leniency by the police and courts.[42]

The great calamity struck on September 6, 1939, when the German army, having attacked Poland five days earlier, arrived in Apt and started their incomprehensible reign of terror, extortion, enslavement and, ultimately, mass murder. The Jews of Apt were separated from the Poles, expelled from their homes and made to live in a ghetto in unsanitary and crowded conditions, forced to wear the Star of David, made to pay extortionate fines, deprived of their businesses, subjected to forced labour and random and punitive killings of the most sadistic sort. If you want to cry long and hard, see Kirshenblatt's painting of a grandmother made to watch her whole family being shot before being shot herself. In 1941, a ghetto was established with Jews from outside of Apt herded in. During October 20 to 22, 1942, a mass "liquidation" was carried out. The 500 fittest Jews were sent to forced labour, 6,000 were sent to the death camp Treblinka, and a few dozen were made to gather and inventory the abandoned possessions of those who were deported, forced to clean the deserted area, and, on the completion of these tasks, taken to the cemetery and murdered by the German beasts.

On the eve of World War Two, Apt had a Jewish population of 5,200. At the end of the war, only 300 remained alive, mostly forced labourers. A few returned to Apt at war's end, but they found a hostile and menacing local population and quickly left.

---

42 "Opatow," Encyclopedia of Jewish Communities in Poland, Volume VII (Poland). Translated from *Pinkas Hakehillot Polin*, published by Yad Vashem.

The Mandels were among the tiny, fortunate minority to leave Apt before the Holocaust. It must strike every Jew whose parents were born in Europe how lucky we really are just to be alive.

A New Life in Toronto

With immigration to the United States almost entirely cut off after 1924, Toronto was the preferred destination for Eastern European Jews in the 1920s, slightly ahead of Montreal (34.5% to 26.6%) and way ahead of Winnipeg (19%).[43] Max Mandel sailed from Liverpool on the *SS Minnedosa* on April 29, 1927, third class of course. The passage took eight days. The passenger manifest lists his occupation as "farm labourer," which was a new one on me, but was no doubt what he had been advised to say, given the preference of Canadian immigration authorities at this time.[44]

According to the manifest, Max arrived with the princely sum of eighty cents. What did he do in Toronto? The family had a millinery shop in Apt. In Toronto, Max's father Leybish started out as a peddler of firewood by horse and carriage, then went into second hand clothing, a venerable Jewish trade. Max started out working in a factory on College Street making pants, but ultimately went into the family business with his father and his brother Harry. They would fall out badly, leaving much pain and bitterness. According to his brother's family, Max neglected the business for the radio show. According to our side, his evil brother used this as a pretext to push him out of the business. Who knows where the truth lies?

At some point after his arrival in 1927, Max started to gravitate

---

43 Gerald Tulchinsky, *Canada's Jews: A People's Journey,* Toronto U of T Press, 2008, p. 199.
44 *Ibid.*, pp. 220 ff. Almost everybody on the *Minnedosa* seems to have listed the same occupation.

to the Toronto Yiddish theatre scene. He joined an amateur theatre club (where he met his future wife, Hilda), helped out backstage with professional productions and sang and performed comedy in restaurants for free with other aspiring thespians. Max is described in a *Kanader Nayes* news story as "local talent" in the categories of song, drama and comedy. It appears from a caption in the *Jewish Standard* that he directed at least one legitimate theatre production, Clifford Odets' *Waiting for Lefty* in 1936, in Yiddish. Of course, Max wouldn't have discovered music and theatre in Canada. His obituary no doubt had it right when it said "the art of the stage was in his blood," especially if we expand "stage" to include pulpit. In Hebrew, there is no difference; both are expressed by the word "*bimah*." Like many of the singers of his generation in Poland, Max came to singing on the stage via *khazunes*, the sacred synagogue chanting of the Jewish cantor. According to an aunt, he trained as a *khazan* in Apt and was known as *der yunginke khazndl*, the young cantor. How *widely* he was known is impossible to say. There were many such *wunderkinds* in the old country and the new. But I do not want to doubt anything about my father any more after finding that he was indeed the radio star he was said to be!

His old country training is clear from the two examples of *khazunes* on the recordings he left behind. But when he came to Toronto he seems to have wandered far enough into secular musical pursuits so that his father, an important Apter *landsman*, declared him not *frum* (pious) enough to lead services at the Apter shul. This was somewhat the reverse of *The Jazz Singer*, but aped such famous cases as Moyshe Oysher, the singer turned cantor, whose congregants were said to have walked him to shul on *Shabbes* because they questioned his piety, that is whether he would otherwise drive a car. In fact, many,

Down-town Toronto as seen from the water-front. In the left foreground is shown part of the New Union Station. Above it rises the tower of the City Hall. At the extreme right, the spire of St. James Cathedral 1927

many cantors crossed over to the secular arts. According to the late Toronto entertainment entrepreneur Johnny Lombardi, who shared space on CHUM radio with Max in the 1940s, my father was an opera lover. My mother once told me she sewed a clown's costume for my father to sing in. I assumed it was Leoncavallo's *Pagliacci* (*Clowns*) but it was more likely to have been Herman Yablokov's *Der Poyatz* (*The Clown*) of 1933.

By the time Max arrived, Toronto was a major manufacturing and banking centre with a thriving cultural life of museums, sports arenas, theatres, concert halls, a university, a symphony orchestra, and the rest. It was not Paris, London, New York, Rome, or even Warsaw, which had about twice Toronto's population. At 600,000 souls, it was about the size of Lodz. And, indeed, the 45,000 Jews of Toronto far outnumbered the Jews of Apt. Whereas the Jewish populations were roughly a third to a majority in shtetls like Apt and in big European cities like Warsaw, Lodz and Bialystok, Jews in most North American cities like Toronto were only a small minority.[45]

45 "Bialystok," Jewish Virtual Library; Rebecca Weiner, "Lodz," Jewish Virtual Library; "Warsaw," Jewish Virtual Library.

However, the feeling of minority status was greatly mitigated because the Jews clustered in the downtown Wards Three, Four and Five, bordered by Dovercourt, University, St. Clair and the lake, and in these areas they actually dominated. As a population, they were incredibly diverse in a way the shtetl dweller would not have thought possible. My father's marriage to a blue-eyed Jew from the big town of Bialystok on the Polish-Russian border is an example. Jews from England? Germany? Reform Jews? The Holy Blossom Congregation, the oldest in Toronto, was entirely Reform by 1920. Max's experience of Toronto Jewry must have been something like one's first visit to Israel: "You mean all these people are *Jewish*?" As elsewhere in the North American Diaspora, the Jews from the various shtetls formed *landsmanshaftn*, "friendly" or "sick benefit" or "benevolent" societies, consisting of fellow former residents of their hometowns: Apter, Ivansker, Lugover, Stashever, etcetera.

Work was also different than in the old country. Now the Jews worked in factories larger than anything they'd seen in the shtetl. Toronto Jews completely dominated the thriving mass clothing industry (the so-called "needle trades"—dress makers, cloak makers, hat makers, pant makers, furriers). They were the workers and they were also the owners. In this there was not much difference from the Polish shtetl Jew experience of migration to the larger towns like Lodz, also dominated by the textile industry. Shocking as this must have been in the old and new countries alike, they were at least prepared for the union and political tendencies that reproduced themselves even in small towns like Apt.

When the Great Depression hit, Jewish immigration was cut to a trickle, with only 5,000 Jews allowed into the country between 1933 and 1945. Nazism also found its Canadian sympathizers. In 1933, the year Hitler became chancellor of Germany and started his reign of persecution of Germany's Jews, a number of very public anti-Semitic incidents occurred in Toronto. In one case, an insurance company cancelled Jewish contracts; in another a GENTILES ONLY sign appeared at a dance hall.[46] The first mass anti-Nazi demonstrations took place in Toronto in July, 1933, with 25,000 participating, following the one organized by the American Jewish Congress earlier in the year in New York City. That same summer a Balmy Beach Swastika Club was formed and started harassing Jews in the Beaches area. In August 1933, they erected swastikas at a dance. Fifty Jewish youths marched on the club, but a clash was averted by the police. Jews were attacked on Kew Beach by swastika wearers. The climax was the Christie Pits riots. First, Nazis in the stands taunted a Jewish baseball team with slogans and swastikas. A few days later, Jewish players and fans were assaulted. Jewish self-defence clubs were trucked out to the park and fighting continued for six hours. Jewish shops were vandalized and passersby harassed. The violence petered out, but a Nazi sympathizer party (the Union Party) was formed, and vandalism and discrimination continued.

The Depression hit its depths in 1933 and 1934 and this, too, was a radicalizing and unifying experience for Toronto's Jews. Jewish philanthropies were severely weakened by it, making life very difficult for all the immigrants who were dependent on them, especially the many ineligible for government relief because of length of residency or family unification requirements. Dorothy Dworkin's Mount Sinai Hospital teetered on the edge of bankruptcy and the Brunswick Avenue Talmud Torah actually went bankrupt and closed for nine

---

46   Stephen A. Speisman, *The Jews of Toronto: A History to 1937*. Toronto: McClelland and Stewart, 1979, p. 332.

weeks, unable to pay teachers' salaries. The community rallied to save these organizations through independent collections and benefit concerts and the establishment of the United Jewish Welfare Fund of Toronto. The long-dormant Canadian Jewish Congress was re-established in 1933 in response to the rise of Nazism in Germany. Future *Kanader Nayes* editor Maurice Goldstick got involved again as the chair of the committee to reorganize the Ontario Division and immediately the large contingent of Jewish communists was ousted from the CJC. This wasn't just Goldstick's personal bias, but reflected a long-standing mutual animosity. In 1923, the communists left the Workmen's Circle, mirroring world-wide developments in international socialism. They established their own association, the Labour League, subsequently the United Jewish Peoples' Order, their own newspapers *Der Kampf* ("*The Struggle*"), subsequently the *Vokhenblatt* ("*Weekly Broadsheet*"), with leadership coming through the *Frayhayt* ("*Freedom*") from New York. They even had their own choir, the Frayhayt Gezangs Farayn ("Freedom Singing Association"). The socialists' cultural organization was the Arbeter Ring and their political movement Poale Tsion, given expression in the influential *Forverts* newspaper of New York. Unions were also divided along party lines, even in the same plant, a phenomenon called "dual unionism."

The socialists and communists, while hugely influential in the Wards and in the Jewish organizations were marginal influences on the bigger political scene, but Jews themselves were far from marginalized. In 1934, David Croll, who had been mayor of Windsor, was elected as a Liberal to the Ontario provincial legislature and became the first Jewish cabinet minister (Labour and Welfare) in the Hepburn government. He was joined as an MPP by J. J. Glass and E. F. Singer. The revived Canadian Jewish Congress also sought mainstream influence in its fight against anti-Semitism at home and abroad. It tried to keep immigration open by taking responsibility for all German-Jewish refugees and it joined the American Jewish Congress boycott of German goods; it opposed discrimination in recreational facilities and employment. All the while, it maintained as low a profile as possible for Jews.

So this was the political cauldron into which the *Kanader Nayes* and its Jewish Radio Hour were launched.

קאנאדער נײעס
Canadian News
Printed in Toronto

SUNDAY, APRIL 14th   TORONTO, ONT.   VOL. 1, NO. 1

באגריסונג פון מעיאר דזשימי סימפסאן

מעיאר
דזשימי סימפסאן

באגריסונג פון הא
דוד קראל

אונזער צײטונג

די פארשפרײטער פון נעדרוקטעז װארט

באגריסונג פון א
ציוניסטישען פירער

ה. ש. קאושדאו אין שטאט

סטרענד טעאטער װערט צוריק די היים פון אידישען װארט

מילנערי ארבעטער צוריס בײ דער אביב

CHAPTER 3

The First Year of the Kanader Nayes

THE FIRST EDITION of the *Kanader Nayes* was issued on Sunday, April 14, 1935. It announced that it would be issued Sundays and Wednesdays, a promise it kept until October 1939, when it trimmed itself down to a Sunday-only supplement.

The Sunday edition was actually issued on Saturday night and often announced events of that very evening. After the war it moved to Friday. Its masthead motto was the sage: "If you wish to understand the world, you must know your own land." It declared its partisanship with the somewhat coded: "Encourages and supports all progressive movements." It had a union label. It proudly (if unnecessarily) pointed out: "When you buy a New York newspaper, look inside and you'll find the *Kanader Nayes*."

The front page was framed by an article from each of publisher Dorothy Dworkin and editor Maurice Goldstick.

Dorothy Dworkin's article, "The Distributor of the Printed Word" (*Di Farshpreyter fun gedruken vort*) was a fairly frank explanation of the new paper as an attempt to increase the readership of the New York Yiddish papers by adding local colour, though not just as a matter of pure business. It shows just how much these Jews saw themselves as part of one Jewish world:

> It's already a number of years that I and my family have occupied ourselves with the technical side of the distribution of the Jewish word in Toronto. For us, this is more than a matter of business. Keeping the old reader and winning over the new reader of Yiddish newspapers from New York has for us always stood above the material income that we have gained from them.
>
> Our New York newspapers represent all the

[ideological] tendencies present in Jewry. It doesn't matter if a reader is always in agreement with everything that his newspaper writes. The fact that the language of his paper is Yiddish is enough guarantee that the reader is someone who will remain attached to the ideals that our paper stands for. . . .

The only thing that has impeded us in the constant enlargement of the number of readers of the New York newspapers has been the fact that the New York papers have lacked a little local Toronto colour. That will now be the aim of the *Kanader Nayes*, which will occupy itself exclusively with Canadian and Toronto matters. The appearance of the *Kanader Nayes* will thus be a victory for us and for the reader of the New York newspapers.

Maurice Goldstick's article, "Our Newspaper" (*Undzer tsaytung*), set his sights somewhat higher, but still saw Toronto as only a "province" of New York:

> Our great sister newspapers, through which we make our "debut" and together with which we will be distributed in Toronto, save us a lot of effort. They, the giants of the Yiddish journalistic field, with their powerful financial resources, their hundred thousand readers, they alone are able to attract and maintain the cooperation of the best writers of our time. No provincial newspaper can undertake this.
>
> We don't even measure ourselves with these grown-up, well-developed and culturally beautiful sisters of ours. We're just happy to be delivered together with them.
>
> The journalistic world theatre, we leave entirely to them. We are going to make our appearances on the relatively smaller stage called Canada, mainly with the part of the stage called Toronto.
>
> This means that we undertake to inform the reader of everything that occurs in our country and our city, that a modern intelligent Jewish citizen needs to know. . . .
>
> The publisher and the manager of the *Kanader Nayes* are old idealists. They have deeply interested themselves in the hardships and aspirations of the working masses and in the destiny of the Jewish people. Nothing which will improve and make more beautiful the life of our people will escape their attention.

The *Kanader Nayes* will always encourage and support all constructive efforts and all progressive movements. It will struggle for the Jews as citizens and for the Jews as a people.

מעיאר
דושיעי סימפסאן

The front page of the *Kanader Nayes*'s first issue had the usual "greetings" with photos that such an enterprise always kicks off, with the biggest one being from Mayor Jimmy Simpson, a friend and political comrade of Dworkin and Goldstick. Simpson was a trade unionist and socialist politician who had fought in the 1920s against Communists in the Ontario Labour Party. He successfully ran for mayor as a CCF candidate in 1935, but was defeated the following year. On page 2, there was an editorial note that would seem ultra-leftist today:

Simpson's Victory
We congratulate our worker mayor Jimmy Simpson on the victory which he recorded against the united and well-organized capitalist forces concerning the question of the salary cuts of the city employees.

The front page also had greetings from Henry S. Rosenberg, a Zionist leader, and the Hon. David Croll, then Minister of Public Welfare for the government of Ontario. Other stories on the front page included the announcement of visiting Jewish dignitary Khayim Shloyme Kazdan, one of the founders and leaders of the Central Yiddish School Organization in Poland: "He'll be in Louis's restaurant on Spadina Avenue on Saturday night. Come and meet him." A story about the "complete victory" of the millinery workers union noted, "The new gains are: a forty hour work week, a raise in salary and fuller control by the union."

And then a story about Jewish Theatre, something dear to Mrs. Dworkin's heart as it was to the entire Jewish community: "Strand Theatre will once again be the home of the Yiddish word." This story announced a Yiddish operetta *Oy America* for the second day of *Pesakh*. And it also referred to trouble between the management and the public the season before: "Last season saw a *broyges* [angry conflict] between the theatre managers and the theatre-going public. Mr. Axler longed for his public and the public longed for a Yiddish word. Mr. Axler assures us that, as long as Toronto Jews want it, there will be Yiddish theatre—Toronto Jews, what's your answer?"

Axler had managed the Standard Theatre from its opening in 1922. It was a unique institution, built with community subscription, designed at least in part by Toronto's first Jewish architect, Benjamin Brown, specifically to house live Yiddish theatre. Increasing competition with smaller theatre venues up the street, and especially

with the movies had forced it to close in 1934 for re-modelling as a movie theatre. When it re-opened as the Strand in 1935, Axler was committed to continuing to provide Yiddish theatre and live entertainment alongside the movies, and it continued in this way until the war years, when it became the Victory Theatre, a modern movie house. Then it became a burlesque house, which is how I remember it, a Chinese cinema called the Golden Harvest Theatre and, ultimately, a bank with shops.

The Strand, as mentioned, was also used as a movie house and on page 3 of its first edition, the *Kanader Nayes* announced a double bill of Hollywood movies: *Going Hollywood*, with Bing Crosby and Marion Davies, and *Baby Take a Bow*, starring Shirley Temple ("the wonder child") along with "a coloured comedy." A "coloured comedy" referred to a genre of black-face vaudeville of the sort seen

in Al Jolson movies; this was probably a "live" act presented alongside the movies. The Jewish connection was that it was to benefit the Young Men's Hebrew Benevolent Association. There was also a big ad for a Jewish movie, *Live and Laugh*, a "*Yidishe talkie*" playing this time at the Labour Lyceum, involving a bevy of New York Yiddish stars including Menashe Skulnick, Max Wilner, Seymour Rechzeit, Chaim Tauber, Miriam Kressin and Khazan Mordechai Hershman and his choir—a vaudeville-type review, held together by the thinnest of comic plots. This, too, was a benefit performance arranged by the Minsker Relief Association.

Support for the Jewish benevolent associations and charities was a major function of the paper. The groups all advertised in the paper and, in addition, there was a feature entitled "Around the Benefit

Societies" which would later become "Around the Organizations," announcing membership campaigns, fund-raising dinners and other activities of the Minsker, Kelzer, Ivansker, B'ney Yakov, Pride of Israel, Mozirer and Radomer Sick Benefit or Friendly Society.

Not all of the cultural events reported in the first edition of the *Kanader Nayes* were of the popular variety. High-brow events were warmly supported, such as a Rambam commemoration in the local Brunswick Avenue Talmud Torah auditorium put on by the education committee of the Canadian Jewish Congress, for the 800th jubilee of Moses Maimonides (nicknamed Rambam), the revered twelfth-century Jewish philosopher.

The paper was steeped in politics, above all Jewish politics. The lead editorial combined what would become two defining features of the better part of its existence, the fight for Israel and against Nazism, by calling for donations to *Keren Hayesod*. Otherwise known as United Israel Appeal, the fund was set up in 1920 as the central fundraising organization for Israel throughout the world, raising money for immigration from Europe to Israel:

> The Jews of Toronto, who are themselves immigrants, understand the situation of our own brothers imprisoned by destiny. They know the terrible economic hardship which oppresses the Jews in the Eastern European countries. Everybody knows what it means for a German Jew to make the exodus from today's bloody Hitlerish Germany. Until now, the *Keren Hayesod* has been supported by the Zionists or those who stood close to the Zionists. Now it must be supported by all Jews. Once Israel was a future Jewish homeland. Now it is already a Jewish homeland for hundreds of thousands of Jews . . . Jews of all classes do your duty!

The paper also touched on non-Jewish political and non-political stories, such as the scandal over questionable electricity contracts made by the prior Conservative provincial government to the benefit of certain Quebec magnates, a robbery at a union office in Montreal, and upcoming federal elections. There was also a novelty story "Married in February, divorced in March," about a Jewish couple in Montreal, though the headline was a real exaggeration: the marriage actually lasted thirteen months, and not just one as the headline implied.

A lot of the paper was promotional, even if not nearly as covered in advertisements as the newspapers of today. A lot of it was for the various Jewish "progressive" activities thought worthy of support by Dworkin and Goldstick: an announcement for a "linen shower" for the Mount Sinai hospital, Mrs. Dworkin's favourite charity, the adoption of a union charter for the kosher butchers, a Pesakh concert at the Workmen's Circle School, a parents' meeting at the

Brunswick Talmud Torah, the Daughters of Israel charity campaign kick-off for the end of April, and the United Palestine Appeal, which had already raised $15,000.

There was also individual promotional material, basically professional notices with pictures, disguised as news stories: "Dr. W. B. Horwitz, back in Toronto after being away for two years" ... "Dr. M. V. Selznick 329 Bloor St. W. who is recently back from Europe and doing post-graduate studies in women's childbearing and sexual illnesses." Then there were the classified ads (stores, apartments and houses for rent) and the commercial ads, such as "Kosher for *Pesakh* Macaroni and Cheese fresh everyday" at Aaron Ladovsky's United Bakers at 338 Spadina.[47] If all else failed it was at least an advertising sheet for the Dworkin's many enterprises. There were ads for the newspaper itself:

> Toronto business people—Now you have an opportunity to advertise—Every advertisement will be read in every Jewish house that has a New York newspaper.
>
> To the readers of the New York Jewish Newspapers—The New York newspapers now arrive in Toronto the same day they are printed—Peddlers sell the newspapers around 5 o'clock in the morning—At the newspaper stands ask for them in the morning right when you go to work.

The Dworkin–Goldstick relatives and associates were well-represented. Edward Dworkin, wholesale tobacconist at 525 Dundas West; Maurice's brother David's "diverse law practice," and the *Kanader Nayes*'s news editor's printing business: "Order your printing from the Progress Printing Co. where everything will be beautiful—good—cheap . . . H. M. Kirshenbaum, A. Vinick Owners." Mrs.

---

47 A restaurant still operating to this day, but at a more northern locale appropriate to Jewish migration patterns.

Dworkin certainly did not neglect her own shipping business, nor did her ads hold back from tugging at the heartstrings of the new immigrant. Throughout the first year of the paper, every holiday was occasion for Mrs. Dworkin to remind her readers of their poor relatives in Europe. From August 9, 1936:

> *Yontif and your relatives*
> Remember that Yontif is again at the door
> Your poor and downhearted relatives in Europe look forward a whole year for the few dollars that you send them at Yontif. If destiny has decreed that they should suffer a whole year, see that, at least during the Yontif days, they will live somewhat better—send them a couple of dollars.
> MONEY SHIPPED TO ALL LANDS
> Dworkin's shifs-kontor—D. Dworkin & Co.—525 Dundas St. W.

Mrs. Dworkin had a knack for mixing business with politics as in this ad in the lead-up to the Berlin Olympic Games of 1936:

> **VISIT THE LAND OF ISRAEL**
> The Jewish protest has not helped
> Tens of thousands of sportsmen, anti-Semites and just uninformed persons will soon travel to Hitlerland to see the Olympic Games.
> Make known your contempt for all this open and hidden Jew-hatred. Let them make friendly with bloody Hitler in Berlin.
>   You, however, should go and see the world-
>   **RENOWNED PURIM CARNIVAL**
>   in
>   **OUR TEL AVIV**
>   Tens of thousands of Jews visit the land of Israel
>   **PURIM AND PESAKH**
> Join this multitude.
> And it will also cost you a lot less.
> Come to us and we will give you all the information
>   **D. DWORKIN & CO. . . .**

One Dworkin enterprise that revealed persistent ideological tensions in the Jewish community not only of Toronto but the entire world, was the one advertised in the paper of April 24, 1935, a "wonderful vacation trip" to Russia. The Russian tour was something that Mrs. Dworkin took a personal interest in and would carry on annually for the next three years. She tried to make the first tour into a high-class cultural affair by enlisting two esteemed musicians, advertising them as "the two official escorts on the cultural tour." The first was a young Boris Berlin, her compatriot and a young professor of piano at the beginning of a long and illustrious career at Toronto's Royal Conservatory of Music. The other was Alberto Guerrero, who would become the celebrated teacher of Glenn Gould, one of Canada's few true cult figures in the classical music world.

The ad re-appeared frequently in the paper up until departure. It soon became a trip to "*Soviet* Russia" and was paired with a celebratory ad from Intourist itself:

U.S.S.R.
See it with your own eyes.
Soviet Russia
The most enchanted country in the world.

When Boris Berlin returned from the tour he gave an interview to the *Kanader Nayes* in which he couldn't praise the new Russia enough:

> He remained three weeks longer than he had planned. He was surprised at the strides that Russia had made.... Mr Berlin says that in art, music, drama and painting Russia has now taken a place of honour ... To the question we asked him about the life of the masses in Moscow, he answered that in no other country in Europe had he seen so much people's happiness and joy as in Russia.

The following year saw a repeat of the tour which was now billed as the "yearly tour." It was led once again by Boris Berlin, this time joined by the baritone Irving Levine: "Get to know the greatest historical experiment which is now being carried out in the Soviet Union." Dworkin herself planned to conduct the 1937 tour:

> Journey to the Soviet Union
> See the celebration of its 20th year jubilee ...
> 3rd annual Soviet tour personally led by Mrs. Dorothy Dworkin on the Empress of India

This barely concealed pro-Sovietism must have lived very uncomfortably with the anti-Sovietism of Maurice Goldstick. Dorothy Dworkin was by no means unique in her enthusiasm for the Soviet Union, as this quote from the Yiddish movie *The Wandering Jew* of 1933 demonstrates: "In Russia, a Jew, imagine, has hammered out a new social system, perhaps the future of the social systems of the world." But anti-Sovietism would win out among Jews in general and at the *Kanader Nayes*. The Arab revolt in Palestine against mass Jewish immigration and against the British rule that promoted it had begun in the spring of 1936, becoming very intense during the summer, with a great loss of Jewish life, limb and property. The communists (including local Jewish communists in Palestine) supported the Arabs. In the local Toronto elections of 1936 the *Kanader Nayes* went after the communists. When the communists had a surprising electoral success with the election of alderman J. B. Salsberg and a school trustee, the paper reported: "He would have had more votes if his party hadn't last summer so sadly boasted about the Arab pogroms against the Jews in the Land of Israel." In March, 1937 the paper was denouncing the Moscow show trials of August 1936 and January 1937, which involved a greatly disproportionate number of Jewish defendants. By the end of the year, the paper was equating communism with fascism and claiming the former was essentially anti-Semitic. Dworkin's third Soviet tour, to be personally conducted by her, and advertised in adoring terms—"If you want to learn about the greatest event in history: the coming of a new human society, or you want to be with relatives, who you have left there years ago"—never came off.

Besides Dworkin and her relatives and friends, other early advertisers included Moyshe Grafstein, whose famous silk store was a constant presence in the paper. On July 7, under his usual ad there appeared (coincidentally, no doubt) a picture and story about his "musical family," the seven Grafstein sisters—Sholom Aleichem's Tevye had nothing on him—two trumpets, two saxophones, an accordion, a violin and drums.

And many gentile institutions took the opportunity to reach

א מוזיקאלישע פאמיליע

אויפ'ן בילד זעגען די
גראפשטיין
שוועסטער
וועלכע האבען געהאט
גרוים ערפאלג. ביים
אויפטריטען צו א קאנ-
צערט אין גראנאט

קלוב אויף סט. קלעיר עוו. די פאמיליע די קינדער פון גוט באקאנטען **משה גראפשטיין** אר-
בייטען איצט ענערגיש זיך צו פארפאלקאמען אין מוזיק, און וועלען מאכען א טור איבער קא-
נאדע און די פאראייניגטע שטאטען. ווי זיי וועלען געבען א רייכע קאנצערטען.

their Yiddish-speaking customers: Toronto's major retail store, the T. Eaton Company (*Ot firt op di Kale*—"There goes the Bride"); the *Toronto Star* advertised its want ads in Yiddish; the Ministry of Highways its road safety advice; and, in the summer months, the Salvation Army advertised its Fresh Air Camp at Jackson's Point on Lake Simcoe.

The project Mrs. Dworkin would always be identified with was the Mount Sinai Hospital, which the paper promoted as much as possible. The big day, what the paper called the *yontif* (religious holiday) of the hospital, was May 19, 1935:

Canadian News
קאַנאַדער נייעס

Sunday, May 19, 1935   10 PAGES   9   10 מיי   זונטאָג, 19־טער מאַי, 1935   VOL. I NO. 1

מאָונט סיני האָספּיטאַל ערעפֿענונג היינט 3 בײַטאָג

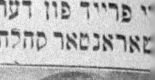

די פֿרייד פֿון דער שאַראַנטאַר קהלה

ראַבײַ ש. שאַקס
וועלכער וועט היינט נעמען אַ טייל בײַ דער ערעפֿענונג

וועלכער ערעפֿנט היינט דעם האָספּיטאַל

ע. ק. סינגער קיו. סי.
פּרעזידענט פֿון מאָונט סיני האָספּיטאַל

פאַרערס קאַנוועגשאַן באַהאַנדעלט וויכטיגע אַרבייטער פֿראַגן

פאַרערען שפּרייזינגערע אָפּהיטונג פֿון זונטאָג געזעצען

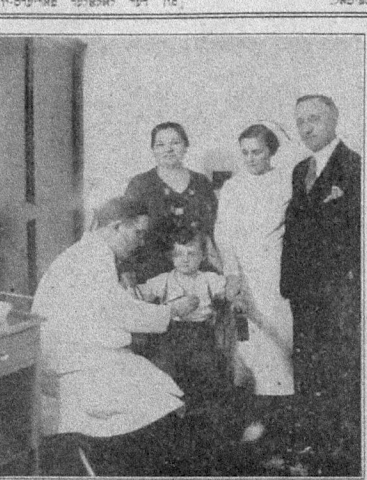

אַ בילד פֿון דער האָספּיטאַל דיספּענזערי

לעזט היינט די נייעס

א. פּלאַן, קאַשיררער

> *The Yontif of the Jewish Toronto*
> Mount Sinai Hospital opening
> Today – 3 o'clock in the day
> Presidents of organizations and societies are invited
> to the opening
> The Jewish public is asked to come to
> the Embassy Club Bloor and Bellaire
> from which they will go to the hospital
> so as not to disturb the sick
> Mayor Simpson will officially open the hospital
> A beautiful program and reception will be prepared

The May 19 edition added six extra pages devoted entirely to the opening of the refurbished and expanded hospital, including an article by Dorothy Dworkin entitled "Our Jewish Hospital," with pictures of the building and all the personalities involved.

Not only Mrs. Dworkin's big projects, but also her little ones had no trouble making it onto the front page. For example, right smack in the middle of the front page of the May 12, 1935 edition there was this:

> Mazel Tov.
> The editors and management wish
> Mrs. Dorothy Dworkin
> and
> Mr. and Mrs. Rackslin,
> Mazel Tov on the birth of their
> son and grandson.
> May the new member of the family have much
> happiness and health.[48]

---

48 Or "Jewish boy wins national contest" (with a photo of my boss as a nine-year old in suspenders). "Harry Arthurs, 9 year old, son of Mr. and Mrs. A. Arthurs, a grandson of Mrs. Dorothy Dworkin, has, in a national contest in which took part children from all Canada's schools, won a prize for his essay on the Battle of Quebec. The essay, which was excellently written, was printed in the children's journal 'Canadian Heroes' which is issued in Montreal for all Canada."

But there were more serious matters, of course, to keep the paper's writers busy. In the mid-1930s, their first priority was to defend Jews against rampant anti-Semitism at home and abroad. Here are some of the headlines: "Hitlerites want to be active—Mayor Simpson snaps shut their hopes"; "Kingston University smeared with swastikas"; "Social workers convention closes with a sharp attack on Hitlerism"; "Bill in Quebec Legislature aimed against Jews"; "Toronto must not discriminate."

Naturally, the paper reported everything to do with the Canadian Jewish Congress and strongly supported its call for a boycott of German products. When the Nazis passed the Nuremberg laws in September, 1935, the *Kanader Nayes* editorial of September 22 sounded a prophetic alarm:

> **Nazi Boycott**
> The decrees against the German Jews are taking on an entirely more determined character. The Nazi spokesmen proclaim from day to day their determination to proceed with and enforce the annihilation of German Jewry. As they are cannibals, one must take them at their word. They will indeed take all measures necessary to starve and get rid of the Jews from Germany. And since no state in the world is going to take up our grievance, there remains for us only one instrument with which to carry on our struggle with Hitler—the relentless boycott of all that comes from or that can bring something of profit to Germany, as long as it is governed by the Nazi criminals.

The paper's support of workers' struggles was also unstinting. In the summer of 1935 British Columbia relief workers organized the "On to Ottawa Trek" to protest Depression conditions, and when they were stopped by the RCMP in Regina, riots ensued. The *Kanader Nayes*'s reporting was sympathetic to the strikers, and when a march of Ontario workers arrived in Toronto, it was enthusiastically covered:

Hunger marchers arrive in the city
Not minding the rain which they encountered, the Ontario hunger marchers were joyous when they entered from various points in the province. The marchers paraded yesterday in Queen's Park and demonstrated before the Parliament buildings.

Naturally the *Kanader Nayes* supported union action, especially Jewish union action. An ad for the locked out Butcher's Union cried:

Don't eat the workers' flesh! Local 68 of the Trade and Labour Congress in Canada appeals to Toronto Jewish workers not to buy any meat except in butcher shops that have the union sign

The paper maintained its partisanship for the moderate Left at all levels of Canadian politics. It fought hard, but in vain, for Jimmy Simpson's re-election as mayor of Toronto with a huge ad covering two-thirds of page 3 in its December 25, 1935 edition and a front page headline endorsement on December 29: "Nature has created Jimmy Simpson for Office. Now the citizens have to re-elect him." The *Kanader Nayes* also wholeheartedly backed the CCF in its first official federal election campaign in 1935, publishing its entire official platform as its lead front page story and appealing for support from "all those who believe that Canada, blessed with our natural riches and possessed of our machinery for the fabrication of wealth, must not suffer indefinitely from poverty, unemployment and insecurity." Front page headlines highlighted the political speeches of CCF leaders ("Banks, Railroads, Radium, Must Be Nationalized—Woodsworth").

The CCF candidate in Spadina, Dr. Jacob Romer, was given a daily column in the paper for two weeks before the October 14 election to promote his campaign. On the eve of the election, an entire page was devoted entirely to "The CCF leaders—a page of their candidates"—although the incumbent Liberal Samuel Factor was able to purchase as much space in the paper for his advertisements. All of this support for the CCF turned out to be in vain, as the Liberals triumphed in Spadina and the country as a whole. Romer finished dead last behind the other four candidates, three of them Jewish.

One of the paper's missions was to promote Jewish culture. So the big holidays of *Rosh Hashana* and *Pesakh* were celebrated with special, extra-long editions that included greetings and long pieces of fiction and non-fiction. The annual Hadassah Bazaar was also given due prominence.

Yiddish musical theatre had a place of honour, especially when big stars came to town, such as the "King of Song" Herman Yablokov, and "the Yiddishe Shirley Temple," Gloria Goldstein. But equal prominence with the pop stars was given to famous Jewish poets and lecturers who treated Toronto as an important stop on their tours of Jewish centres. Among them were the much-beloved New York worker's poet H. Leivik, renowned journalist and author Emil Ludwig, literary critic Shmuel Niger in an evening honouring the "grandfather" of Yiddish literature, Mendele Mokher Sforim. An editorial, "Our Mendele," celebrated his legacy. A Jascha Heifetz performance at Massey Hall was mentioned in all the papers, but only the *Kanader Nayes* announced him as the "famous *Jewish* violin artist."

CHAPTER 4

Pre-War Years

THE PAPER HAD BEEN RUNNING for almost a year when on March 25, 1936, the front page headline announced: "The opening of the Jewish Radio Hour Sunday morning," featuring a big picture of "the noted and cultivated Jewish singer" Sam Stolnitz, as well as "the world famous artist" Benny Adler and Mr. Mandel, the "local dramatic talent." The second biggest story on the front page was of the "Zay gezunt" evening for Benny Adler planned for March 28. Granted, this was not a huge news day ("Talmud Torah children in McCaul synagogue," — "Montreal dogs go on relief" — "Ten Canadians win in the Irish lottery"), but you'd think some of the other stories deserved greater prominence than to be dwarfed by the radio show and the Adler evening. But the Jewish Radio Hour was the *Kanader Nayes*'s baby and the publishers weren't taking any chances with its success.

The opening of the show on Sunday, March 29, 1936 once again got front-page billing: "First program of the Jewish Radio Hour, today Sunday morning . . . has called forth unheard-of joy in all circles of the Jewish community. . . ." The radio show stayed right on the front pages for months afterwards. Every Sunday (i.e. Saturday night) paper would give a more or less detailed line-up above the fold and, at least for the first while, the Wednesday paper would give a review. The second show was, of course, "a colossal success:"

> The program included a special number in honour of the 60th jubilee of Shaul Tchernikowsky, composed by Prof. Zaludkowsky, and sung by Khazan Stolnitz and his two sons: Sam and Simon; a pair of numbers by Max Mandel;

> a dramatic recitation by the beloved Benny Adler; a violin solo from Mr. Agranov; a short address by Mr. S. M. Greenfield; a song from Miss Singer, and news of the week from the *Kanader Nayes* and read by news editor Mr. Alexander Brown. Benny Adler brought forth tears with his art-recitation "The Tramp." Mr. Max Mandel's numbers were of the highest artistic level, and the Stolnitz family placed the Jewish Radio Hour among the most beautiful radio programs on the American continent.

Miss Singer was fourteen-year old Ada Singer, pictured in tallis in a subsequent edition of the *Kanader Nayes* in a "pants role" from *Yankele*. Alexander Brown was at that time Ontario secretary of the Canadian Jewish Congress and a future director of the Jewish Teachers' Seminary. His reading of the news of the week became a steady fixture of the show and was clearly a way of advertising the *Kanader Nayes*. The Stolnitz brothers were reunited here as when they had been child cantors in Russia. Professor Zaludkowsky was Detroit cantor Elias Zaludowsky, a friend of Cantor Stolnitz and the subject of his "number," Shaul Tchernichowsky, was a famous Russian-born poet who wrote in Hebrew and was, in 1936, living in Palestine. Next Sunday's paper announced "a rich holiday [*Pesakh*] program":

> A choir of 60 men will appear in national songs. A part of the program will be dedicated by Cantor Nathan Stolnitz to the 40th jubilee of the Cantors' Association of America and Canada. A succession of gifted artists will take part, including the well-known Benny Adler, who is leaving Toronto at the end of the week. Mr. Alexander Brown will once again present the news of the week, gathered specially for the Jewish Radio Hour from the *Kanader Nayes*. A number of letters are coming in, both to the radio station and to the editorial board of the *Kanader Nayes* in which the writers express their great happiness with the Jewish Radio Hour, and the hope that the hour will remain as a permanent part of Ontario Jewish artistic and cultural life.

A choir of sixty men! That must have been quite a convoy that rode out to Hamilton that Sunday morning. No doubt, for convenience's sake alone, the participants in the show would have preferred Toronto to Hamilton, which was at least an hour away from Toronto by car (still is, with all the traffic). Sunday after Sunday, they would pack up in several cars, often taking the whole family (my sisters remember playing in a Hamilton Park while the show was on). CKOC is one of the oldest radio stations in Canada, established in 1922 and still operating as an "oldies" station at this writing, very near the same place on the AM band as it did in 1936 (1150, to which it moved from 1120 in 1941). Like many early stations, it was owned and operated by a radio supplier, Wentworth Radio and Supply Co. (originally Wentworth Auto Supplies Ltd.) to give purchasers something to listen to. By 1936 it had a very powerful 1,000 watts with which to reach Toronto. Its studios were above the store in the Wentworth Radio building at 32 John Street North, now, alas, a parking lot. One can only assume that it was cheaper to go to Hamilton than to operate in Toronto, and CKOC had plenty of power. There was also a sizeable Jewish community in Hamilton to add to the audience.

In the following week's paper, the surprising identity of the big choir was revealed:

> A good impression was made by the national Betar choir, which last week took part in the program with a number of songs.

Betar was (and is) the right-wing Revisionist Zionist youth movement formed by Zev Jabotinsky in the 1920s. The Revisionists wanted to "revise" the more moderate Zionism of Ben Gurion to push immediately for a Jewish state in all of Mandatory Palestine, using force if necessary. So, it seems that the ideology of the *Kanader Nayes* had little to do with the programming of the Jewish Hour! As the paper would write of the show, "the Jewish Radio Hour is not a party platform which is just uni-directional, but rather an important general instrument for all kinds of shades and directions of Jewish cultural communal life." This was proved by the fact that in June, a couple of months later, the show was featuring the "Freedom Singing Society," a choir of seventy-five which had a large proportion of Jewish Communists. Subsequently, it became the Toronto Jewish Folk Choir of the leftist United Jewish Peoples Order and is still singing as I write. It was this very group that hired me as a soloist in the 1980s. Even at that late date, the wonderful people of this choir blended an authentic tradition of Jewish music, *yidishkayt* and old-fashioned "progressive" politics. Some of the original members were still singing in the 1980s and still going on peace marches and friendship visits to the Soviet Union. No doubt, some of the singers I sang with were there that day, to sing before or after Max Mandel performed the comic sketch of "the hard-luck Jew." One of the choristers, the late Max Kelsen, was an old friend of my father's. He assured me that my father had sung with the choir, "שטילערהייט", *shtilerheyt*, in other words, "on the quiet", because the choir was "political," and Mr. Kelsen assured me my father wasn't.

Let's return to the April 12, 1936 show with the Betar Choir. Besides the choir, the show was also Benny Adler's last appearance and the first by Khazan David Glick. Glick was a part-time cantor whose main source of income was a jewellery store, which he advertised in the *Kanader Nayes*. He was the father of Srul Irving Glick, one of Canada's leading composers of Jewish music, not yet two years old at the time. It must have been about this time, or even on this very day, that the photo of "Greenfild's Jewish Radio Hour. CKOC" was taken, because both Glick (with the unmistakeable eyes of his famous son) and Adler are pictured in it, along with Joe Barsht, Agranov, Max Mandel, Alexander Brown, Nathan Stolnitz, and S.M. Greenfield:

The April 19 show promised "new features (with "features" simply transliterated into Yiddish as "פיטשורס") including a 'Gypsy Girl' and the 'Happy Chasid' in a number of songs and recitations. The page 1 announcement was accompanied by a page 2 editorial bursting with pride over the radio show:

> Without noise and without clamour a Jewish individual has favoured us with a new culture-organ, which possesses colossal possibilities for the Jewish cultural life of our province—the Jewish Radio Hour. Before he came out in public with his plan, Mr. S. M. Greenfield, the initiator, manager and announcer of the radio hour, came to us and put it before us. The idea immediately appealed to us and we promised him that we would help popularize his plan, because we instantly saw what a terrific achievement this could be for the Jewish masses of our city and province....
>
> And now, after only three programs have been performed, one can already make an evaluation of this hour. It is our opinion that Mr. Greenfield's radio hour has a very great significance for the Jews of Ontario. The local talent who have participated in it have nothing at all to be ashamed of in comparison with the talent who perform in other American programs. We believe that, just as the material performed on our radio hour is better than what has come over the air-waves from the United States, so, too, are the performers better than those presented in the States. It has been a complete pleasure to find out that Toronto possesses such capable artists.
>
> The future of this hour is dependent on two things: on the quality of the programs and on the financial revenue that will be made for the management of the hour. Concerning the quality, we can expect that it will always stay at the proper level. This, the programs of three Sundays have demonstrated. But, as far as the material side is concerned, this is completely another matter that has nothing to do with the management, only with the listener. When the Jewish institutions and business community understand that the Jewish Radio Hour is not only an important Jewish cultural institution, but also an extraordinary and effective advertising organ, they will use the radio-hour to advance their own interests, and in such a way, assure the existence of the radio hour.
>
> We congratulate Mr. Greenfield on his success that he has already achieved and wish him luck and blessing in the future.

It's clear that there is no little self interest in this assessment. But it is still important to keep in mind how different radio was at this time than it is now. The main thing, of course, is that there was no television, no video rental, or even record players of any great quality, with records of a duration of more than three minutes in the distant future. So this was *it* as far as home entertainment was concerned. Of course, there was a whole range of radio programming available to the listener, but a couple of things distinguished these programs. First, their high cultural aspirations. They did not only do music, though they did lots of that. They did theatre and comedy and politics and religion. And they were live, not a series of recordings, but authentic local talent performing one-time only. Add to this the rarity for any particular new immigrant community of having a show by and about your own people in your own mother tongue and we can get some sense of the significance of these shows to Toronto Jews.

Alongside the cast of regulars—Mandel, Cantors Stolnitz and Glick and Alexander Brown with the news of the week—the shows featured a constant stream of guest appearances. Some of these were of the height of seriousness, including religious leaders such as "the widely esteemed prominent Rabbi Sh. Sachs" who gave a talk on a "timely and important theme," and Rabbi Axelrod from Hamilton, "with a short talk in Hebrew", and community *makhers* [big shots] Mr. Henry S. Rosenberg, chairman of the United Zion Appeal. For the tenth show, there was "the well-known learned Professor Golecki, who in a learned way brought out the importance and significance of a permanent Jewish radio show for the Jewish community of our land."

But entertainment was the Radio Hour's main objective and pride of place was given to visiting show-people, such as New York comedienne Sally Josephson and Rochelle Rosenfeld, "the esteemed show-woman from New York" who would "sing some numbers." Rosenfeld was appearing in a Maurice Shapiro production at the Labour Lyceum (*Who is She?*), tickets being sold at Dworkin's shipping office. Her local co-star, Felix Fogelnest, also appeared and stayed on as a regular. Lacking the really big names of the New York Yiddish stage (the "boyars" as the paper called them), the show announced an "improviser" would appear to impersonate David Kessler, Jacob Adler and Boris Tomashevsky.

One big name visitor to Toronto who did not appear on the show, but who was featured by the paper, was Golda Meir, the future Prime Minister of Israel. In 1936 she was still Golda Meyerson, but, at thirty-eight years old, already famous as a Zionist leader. Her picture shared the front page with the radio show on May 10, 1936. Born in Russia and brought up in Milwaukee, she moved to Palestine in 1921 as a member of the *Poale Tsion*. By the time of her visit to Toronto, she was on the executive of the *Histadrut*, the national Jewish labour union in Palestine. Hence she was very close in ideology to the editors of the *Kanader Nayes* and spoke not only at the King Edward Hotel but also at Dworkin's Labour Lyceum and at a private function of the Land of Israel Labour League. The *Kanader Nayes* advertised her as "one of the best speakers that the Land of Israel possesses:"

> It is expected that a large audience, especially of young people, will come and hear her tonight because Madame Meyerson is known as an energetic and capable speaker – she is well-versed in Palestinian life and has, in fact, spent the major part of her years in the Land of Israel.

The Jewish Radio Hour was Zionist, too, of course, but it aimed to be more cultural than political. It highlighted Jewish culture by celebrating all manner of "jubilees" and *yortsayts*.[1] On Victoria Day, Canada's national spring holiday "in honour of the birthday of the deceased Queen Victoria which will be celebrated tomorrow over the whole country as a holiday," the program was dedicated, not to Queen Victoria, but to the twentieth anniversary of the death of Sholem Aleichem and to the memory of Nachum Sokoloff, the recently deceased president of the world Zionist Organization. Apropos of Sholem Aleichem's *yortsayt*, a couple of weeks later the *Kanader Nayes* ran an editorial in which it argued that the fact that Sholem Aleichem was a Jewish hero said much about the Jewish people:

> The great Akhad Ha'am[2] says in his essay about Moses that it is not important whether such a man as Moses really lived in the world or is simply a legendary personage. What is important is the idea that the people have created concerning what makes greatness in their leader.
> It is the custom of all peoples to honour the memory of the people who they consider to be folk-heroes. Here, a people shows its true face. Exactly as one can understand an individual by his friends or by the books he reads, so one can evaluate a people's spiritual state from the men it honours. If it honours a Shakespeare or a Goethe, it is a cultural people; if it worships a Hitler or a Goering, it is, if not a murderer people, then a deluded people.
> The same general rule is also applicable to the Jewish people, and according to that principle we certainly belong to the intellectually and spiritually rich peoples. The recent Mendele celebrations confirm this.[3] The

---

1 Literally, "year times," meaning the anniversary of death, the typical Jewish occasion for remembering a deceased loved one.
2 Literally, "one of the people," the pen name of Zionist thinker Asher Ginsberg (1856-1927).
3 Mendele Mocher Sforim, the pen name of Sholem Yakov Abramovich (1836–1917), a Yiddish novelist, considered the "grandfather" of Yiddish literature.

outpouring of honour for him that has been expressed in *yortsayt* celebrations over the whole world testifies that the Jews are, above all, a book-people.

Literary criticism is not our vocation and this is not the place for it. Let's leave that to the specialists. But you don't have to be a literary critic to place Sholem Aleichem in the first rank of our Jewish classics. We believe that, if a poet possesses the power to arouse such interest in his creations as has Sholem Aleichem, this alone is already a certificate of greatness.

Who else among us Jews is so often quoted, both by the intellectuals and by the people, as is Sholem Aleichem? Sholem Aleichem's work is precisely like the legendary *manna*, of which the Jews partook while coming out of Egypt—each was able to extract from it the taste that he alone desired. When a simple man who has an inclination to humour reads Sholem Aleichem, he will laugh heartily and have lifelong pleasure from it. Or, if the reader is a man with good light and penetrating eyes, he will find in Sholem Aleichem's little stories, not only the stuff of laughter and for passing the time, but also pictures of himself, his brothers, sisters, neighbours and acquaintances. In the humorous narratives he will find lessons about morality. He will hear the suppressed groan of a broken heart and he will see how tears (invisible from the surface) pour from the pained victims of fate or of barbaric men.

In such creations can each reader intuitively sense the authenticity that is one of the pre-conditions of classic status. Our Sholem Aleichem has given us this, and so he is exalted by us, and that is the spontaneous stimulus created by Sholem Aleichem's *yortsayt* celebration throughout the whole world, Toronto included.

In July the show celebrated a "double *yortsayt* of our national-folk figures, Dr. Theodore Herzl, the greatest political leader of our time," and Chaim Nachman Bialik, "the very brilliant national poet."

Alongside its regulars and big name guest stars, the Jewish Radio Hour always made room for lesser known talents. A "Miss

Taub" would sing "The Prayer" by Avram Reisen. A "Miss Warren," a member of the Detroit *Halevi-Hazamir* Choir, would sing the *Hamavdil* by Rumshinsky, or the "soprano singer from Hamilton, Sonia Laskin", and an actress "Madame Mira Kritzer," all never to be heard of again. On the other hand, the list of regulars kept expanding. The May 3 show introduced Isaac Swerdlow, who had just returned from New York and a period with the renowned Maurice Schwartz Art Theatre to become a leading figure, along with his actress wife Adele Swerdlow, in Toronto Jewish Theatre. Born in Odessa, Swerdlow came to America in 1923, and from 1933 lived in Canada. He would have a long career on the Yiddish and English stage. His wonderful old-world talents are on full display in the 1954 CBC Radio production of Ted Allen's *Lies My Father Told Me*, in which he stars as Zeyde.[4] Swerdlow introduced a strong theatrical element to the radio show. On the show with the Freedom Singing Society, he read from Kipling's poem "Boots" (one assumes in Yiddish translation), on the plight of the British soldier fighting Britain's imperial wars in Africa. Swerdlow both performed and directed on the show; in 1936, he directed a scene from A. Zeitlin's comedy, *The Wise Men of Chelm*, having played in the piece with Morris Schwartz Art Theatre.

Other early regulars on the Jewish Radio Hour included the pianist Joseph Barsht, who later changed his name to Barsh. He came from a family of old-world *klezmorim*, his father having played in the Szpilman family orchestra of Ostrowiec. That orchestra included

---

[4] Ted Allen, *Lies my father told me* (Toronto, Scenario Productions, 2000).

the father and grandfather of the famous Wladislaw Szpilman, the subject of the Oscar-winning movie *The Pianist*, whose cousin Leo Spellman settled in Toronto after the war and worked on radio with Max Mandel. Spellman is the pianist on some of the remastered recordings on "Music from the Jewish Hour." Barsh subsequently moved to New York and had a long career in the Jewish theatre.

The violinist Maurice Turk lasted much longer on the Toronto Jewish music scene, playing on the radio and at weddings and bar mitzvahs for many years. Two "fiddle solos" of his also appear on "Music from the Jewish Hour;" sometimes he was joined on the Radio Hour by another fiddler named Pearl Grunevetter. After my father died, Turk was supposed to become my violin teacher, and he may indeed have given me a lesson or two, but I soon lost my violin at a Jack Benny "photo-op" at the Toronto airport sometime in the 1950s. A bunch of kids playing violins were supposed to greet Benny for the photographers when he got off the airplane. All of the kids were given old broken violins, so, to be like the others, I discreetly put down my brand new one and took a broken one—the good one was never returned. That pre-empted my studies with the maestro and my career. Who knows, but I may have been sawing away in some orchestra instead of teaching law.

There were also singers galore, including two members of the musical Barkin family, tenor Jacob (Jack) Barkin and sister Sara, a pianist and soprano. Like Sam Stolnitz, Jack Barkin flirted with opera to finally decide on a cantorial career; he was Stolnitz's successor at Holy Blossom Temple. Another tenor later turned cantor was Joseph Yacubovich who changed his name to Harry Jacobs. This greatly confused a letter writer to the *Kanader Nayes* who admired the new Jacobs but wondered what had happened to

Yacubovich! Saul Weinberg, Moyshe Gutkin, and Albert Gamze were other local talents that filled out the roster in the first months of the program.

The dominant figure in the early days of the show was Cantor Nathan Stolnitz, the "musical-literary director" as he was designated. The Polish born and Vilna bred Stolnitz was deeply involved in all aspects of cantorial art. He was the organizer of the Cantors Assembly of North America and wrote many articles and a couple of books on *khazans* and *khazunes*. He promoted the show and the paper—and himself, why not?—to a network that included important old-world personages such as Zalman Reisen, journalist, co-founder and director of the YIVO institute in Vilna (at the time a part of Poland), and author of a lexicon of Jewish literature. The brother of the poet Avram Reisen (the subject of one of the Radio Hour's "jubilee" shows), Zalman was imprisoned and killed by the Soviets during World War Two. On May 27, 1936, the paper proudly printed a letter to Stolnitz from Zalman Reisen as a news story entitled "A letter from Zalman Reisen to Nathan Stolnitz about the Canadian Jewish Radio Hour."

Stolnitz was a regular performer on the Radio Hour, chanting the memorial prayer to organ accompaniment on the many *yortsayt* shows, and even taking over the reading of the news of the week from Alexander Brown. Naturally, Stolnitz's family made frequent appearances on the show. His very talented son Sam appeared often as well as Sam's younger brother. Sam sang the beautiful *"Meyerke Mayn Zun"*[5] on the tenth show and a duet with his sister, Rose. The Rose and Sam duet was part of a "musical "surprise" (simply transliterated as "סורפרייז") that, unfortunately, had to be cut short due to bad timing—this was live radio, after all! They were back on the next show to do a complete version.

Cantor Stolnitz was not the only one to bring family members on the show. Max Mandel brought on "Mrs. Max Mandel," in other words, my mother, who never once mentioned being on the radio show, so it was something of a shock for me to see this. Then I remembered that Max and Hilda were said to have met at a theatre club, and in this particular instalment of the Jewish Hour (June 28, 1936), it was announced that there would be the first episode of "a special feature—a "life picture" which has been specially written for

---

5 A gorgeous rendition exists on CBC Records by Canadian soprano Catherine Robbin. When I asked Ms. Robbin, a colleague at York University, where her impeccable Yiddish came from, she told me she had been coached by *khazan* David Glick's famous son Srul Irving Glick.

the radio show and which will be performed by the Jewish Radio Hour players." A "life picture" ("*lebens bild*") was a genre of theatre that tried to portray "real" life and "real" characters, by mixing tragic, comic, and sentimental elements. It originated in the Viennese theatres of the eighteenth century and became very popular among twentieth century Yiddish writers. The following week, the paper announced the second episode of "Life picture," with Y. Swerdlow, Fogelnest, Max Mandel, N. Stolnitz, S. M. Greenfield, and "two new talents, Miss Rudnick and Shirley Lieberman." Miss Rudnick was my mother, now using her maiden name. I remember Shirley Lieberman, who left no known theatrical legacy, as a friend of my mother's. Shirley's husband Ernie was a midway games entrepreneur who gave me a job as a teenager hawking hats at the Canadian National Exhibition. Ernie dabbled in many diverse enterprises including race horses and even radio shows.

The Jewish hour's first summer saw the worst heat-wave in the modern history of North America, before or since. Five thousand deaths occurred in the United States making it the worst natural disaster in the history of the United States or Canada. You think current summers are hot? Temperatures exceeding 44°c in Manitoba and Ontario claimed the lives of 1,180 Canadians (mostly the elderly and infants), 600 in Ontario and 225 in Toronto alone. Four hundred of the deaths were caused by people who drowned seeking refuge from the heat. The *Kanader Nayes*'s front pages were full of it. It didn't deter the radio show, although summer found its cast members sojourning in some summer resorts under the heading of "outreach." On July 5, the whole cast was enjoying the hospitality of Schechter's Hotel—one of the *Kanader Nayes*'s advertisers—in Hamilton after the show.

The following week Greenfield and Stolnitz visited Buffalo to meet and greet with the Jewish community there, with hopes of expanding the show into upper New York State:

> . . . the established Canadian permanent Jewish Radio Hour has called forth great interest not only in Ontario but also among all the Jews of Buffalo, Rochester, Syracuse and other cities of Western New York State. Both Toronto guests got a very friendly reception there and were invited to address several Jewish organizations. . . . The Jewish Radio Hour will, from now on, stay in constant contact with a pair of representatives from Buffalo—well-known local Jewish cultural community leaders, lawyer Solib and the druggist Mr. Astor. Also Mr. Price, a dedicated community man who is well known among the wider Jewish masses in Buffalo, has become interested heart and soul in helping out for the benefit of our Jewish Radio Hour. From now on, from time to time, selected Jewish talent from Buffalo and other neighbouring towns will also take part in the radio programs. This greatly strengthens the hand of the managers of the Jewish Radio Hour and gives a firm basis to hope that this institution will be able to be presented at a proper level and will truly be one of the most important Jewish radio hours on the American continent.

What Did the Listeners Think? "The Readers Write"

From the point of view of its sponsors and operatives the show was doing fabulously, but do we know what the listeners were thinking? In fact we do. Though the show was studiously ignored by the rival Yiddish papers and the English press, we have a treasure trove of letters written by listeners to "The Readers Write" section of the paper, in inimitable Jewish immigrant style. Now you might think critical letters would have been censored or even suppressed, but you would be wrong. Some contain merciless criticism, and others are decidedly mixed. Furthermore, some of the letters are highly partisan. So they make for great reading at this distance. Take the first letter published (all the emphases are mine):

> Distinguished Editor of the *Kanader Nayes*:
>
> I want to request some space in your distinguished newspaper to express my opinion about the Jewish Radio Hour.
>
> First of all comes a heartfelt thanks to Mr. Greenfield, the director of the undertaking, for the task that he has taken on of spreading the Jewish word through the airwaves, and I hope that Mr. Greenfield will continue his good work so that we will have nothing to be ashamed of about our radio hour compared to others.
>
> *To speak truthfully, the first two radio hours were a lot more beautiful and better than the last two.* I very much do not want to be a critic, but since you announced on the radio that everyone can express his opinion, I want to give an evaluation.
>
> Friend Yacubovitch, certainly, I have completely enjoyed. Mr. Brown, the announcer of the weekly news has been wonderful. *The other numbers have not been bad.* And I want to say now a pair of earnest words. Having a Jewish hour, it is the duty of every Jewish businessman to see that it is able to exist, because that is the best way that the Jewish word can be spread. I know that there are many Jewish businesspeople who advertise themselves through radio, so why not support such a beautiful institution as the Jewish radio? Not having been able to sustain a Jewish theatre, we should at least be able to sustain the Jewish Radio Hour.
>
> In closing, I would like to thank you, friend Greenfield, for the pleasure that you have created for us until now and let us hope that you will continue to. *I hope that the Jewish Hour does not become commonplace and that the resources that come forward do not cheapen the beautiful Jewish Radio Hour.*
>
> With esteem,
> *Yitzhak Limonov*

Similarly with the next one:

> The question which you ask every Sunday of whether we need a Jewish radio show is, without doubt, [to be answered] with, yes, the Jewish Radio Hour is an important bedrock of Jewish culture and is justified not only in Toronto, but more so in all the towns and villages of Ontario where Jews live and the Jewish word cannot reach them otherwise than through the airwaves; and Mr. Greenfield, as the one who made this possible, deserves a great thank-you.
>
> Also, there is nothing to complain about in the program itself. *I would not at all want to criticize and evaluate who is better or worse. Naturally all the talent cannot be of the "nobility,"* but it is very hard to speak about your radio hour and not mention such talents as Swerdlow in recitation and Max Mandel as singer and showman. There was a really a special grace to his sketch of "The Hard-Luck Jew" which he performed more beautifully than beautiful the second Sunday. Also, Turk's fiddle solo and his accompaniment for the singers cannot be forgotten. Let us hope that your Jewish Radio Hour will become widely popular and the above-mentioned talent will remain a permanent feature on your Radio Hour.
>
> An especially good impression is made by the guest speakers you have every Sunday. The week's news, which is taken each week from the *Kanader Nayes*, is a great bedrock of the Jewish hour, *even though the news was much better read during the first programs when Mr. Brown was summarizing it.*
> With esteem,
> L. Berman

The comment about the quality of news reading was, in fact, a huge swipe at Cantor Stolnitz, who had recently taken over the reading of the news. However, one of his supporters responded in the next edition:

> As a constant reader for your worthy newspaper, I want to express a heartfelt thanks to the *Kanader Nayes* and also to Mr. Greenfield for making it possible to hear a Jewish Radio Hour, which makes for extraordinary pleasure.

> I wait with impatience every week for the enjoyment it brings. With this letter, I thank the Jewish forces who take part in the program as, for example, Mr. Mandel, the beautiful Jewish folksinger, Mr. Joseph Yacubovich, the Stolnitz family etc.
>
> *A special thanks to Khazan Stolnitz for reading the news that the Kanader Nayes has provided.*
>
> David Glazer, 342 Bathurst St.

(The letter writer spelled Bathurst "Betoyrst" [בעטויירסט] in Yiddish, somewhat the way the paper spelled Churchill: "Choyrchill" [טשויירטשיל]. The Yiddish spelling of English names seems to have depended on the speller's pronunciation. Another letter writer spelled Bathurst "Baterst" [באטערסט]. I had to laugh when I read the way another letter writer spelled Huron Street in Yiddish: יורען סטריט —"Urine St.," exactly the way my mother used to pronounce it, to her children's delight.)

There were some letters of pure praise:

> I want to congratulate friend Greenfield for his magnificent radio hour last Sunday, the 5th of July. I hope that we will have the privilege every Sunday of hearing Goldfaden's music and also *Khazanish* melodies.
>
> The hour is over so quickly and all the talent has been excellent.
>
> Your friend,
> *Sh. Y. Birnboim*

One that is especially dear to me is this one:

> Permit me to write in the readers' section a few points about the Jewish Radio Hour: it is so important and necessary to have a Jewish Hour in Toronto, I am certain, because the Jewish Radio Hour awakens the Jewish heart. I personally would not get up so early on Sunday, but, because of the Jewish Radio Hour, I get up even earlier so I won't be late for the radio show, because it is worth so much to me. *It is a great pleasure to hear a Yiddish word and especially to hear the young, gifted and talented singer, Max Mandel. His singing is simply a pleasure to hear. Every word*

is so clear and heartfelt. I would never tire of hearing him sing and declaim.

I can say the same about the monologues of Mr. Isaac Swerdlow. This is authentic Jewishness. Thanks are due to all those taking part in the Jewish Radio Hour.

With greetings,
Royze Spring

Not everybody agreed with the choice of favourites:

Reading a letter from an earlier number of the Kanader Nayes *about the Jewish Radio Hour, I was astonished that the letter writer gave such a one-sided review of the various programs.*

As we all know, happily, taking part in the Jewish radio program has been a whole series of excellent artists such as Benny Adler, Fogelnest, Sam Stolnitz, Rochelle Rosenfeld and others who weren't mentioned in the letter at all. These artists have at least contributed exactly as much if not more to the interest in the Jewish Radio Hour as those mentioned by the letter writer.

We wish the Jewish Radio hour and its producer Mr. Greenfield full success, and hope that it will continue the same kind of programs as it has up to now.
Mordechai Schwartz

As is the rule with writers of letters to the editor in all newspapers in all places and all times, the writers often used the subject to talk about themselves and their philosophy of life. Thus Jacob Krakowsky of "Baterst Street:"

Do Jews need to have a Jewish Radio Hour?
My answer is that the Jews in Canada need to have a Jewish Radio Hour every day of the year. Why do other peoples have radio programs day and night without end that cost millions of dollars, to advertise their businesses? In my opinion, for us Jews here in the free land of Canada it is necessary to have a Jewish Radio Hour. It is necessary to the same extent as a hospital, a doctor, food, clothing, or a house. Apart from our body, we also have a soul and our poor soul grieves and weeps in our body; we don't give it anything. For the others, one never hears the

radio not playing, it is joyful in every house, every nation hears its language, its song, its word. They are proud that their children have radios. But with us, just like *"Moyshe Kapoyer,"* ⁶ our children can have no hour "nevermine."⁷ Our Jews in Canada are not such a poor people.

You have and need such a moving, beautiful radio hour. Advertise your businesses, even if it costs a few dollars, you will lose nothing. We want to laugh and laugh loud like all people. We have no energy left after grieving for 2,000 years in which we have been weeping and sighing every minute, and one speaks only about the most recent time, we have heard and read of the troubles, the suffering, the pain of our homeless sisters and brothers and for what?

We must have a Jewish Radio Hour and beautiful one, too. The American Jews can help us. "Nevermine" money, we want to laugh. Laughing is healthy. One hour of laughing gives us the energy for a whole week. Sholem Aleichem, the great Jewish poet and writer, wrote for long years so that we should laugh. It is a *nakhes*⁸ to hear the Jewish Radio Hour. Thanks to the *Kanader Nayes*, Mr. Greenfield, Mr. Mandel, Mr. Swerdlow, Mr. Foglenest and the good, gifted young singer Mr. Stolnitz, and his father, the music and literary director of the radio hour and all who take part in the Jewish Radio Hour.

From my side, I ask all Toronto Jewish businessmen to advertise their companies so that they can continue with their singing and acting. We also ask that Mr. Greenfield continues on with the sketch that has just been heard for the first time. We thank all who already helped with it. I hope that you will also follow me and laugh the way I've been laughing all my life. Laughing is healthy.

With esteem,
Jacob Krakowsky

---

6 *Moyshe Kapoyer*, literally "upside-down Moyshe," who does everything backward, was a character created by the *Forverts* humorist Jacob Adler, who wrote under the pen name of B. Kovner.
7 "Nevermine" is clearly a dig at the way some Jews said "never mind."
8 Naches (נחת) is a fairly untranslatable Hebrew/Yiddish word meaning the pleasure one gets from recognized achievements—almost universally used now as what parents feel when their children do well.

But the criticism kept coming, albeit usually leavened with praise.

> Permit me in your eminent newspaper to express my view concerning the Jewish Radio Hour. Every Sunday I simply have pleasure from it. . . .
>
> As a resident of Toronto, I have believed for a long time already that Jewish Toronto must recognize its failure in that such a sizeable population has not been able to maintain a Jewish theatre. So, I believe (and may no evil eye look upon us), and I underline this, that Mr. Greenfield, above all, is a man worthy of a little recognition. I am very happy that we have such Jews.
>
> *Since I'm already writing, I want to say to you that the programs are not yet so good. If the management wants to make the radio show into what it needs to be, they must not allow it to be too vulgar. There has to be sanctity. If we have reached the stage of being able to spread the Jewish word over the air waves, that opportunity has to be used well. Those songs that are already so old should have been left out of the programs.*
>
> I sincerely thank Mr. Stolnitz for the news which he reports. I thank Mr. Yacubovich, friends Fogelnest, Swerdlow and Mr. Mandel, the young Mr. Stolnitz and the other artists. *When you appear again, see that your songs are a little longer. I like you better as singers than as actors and players.* Also a special thanks to the *Kanader Nayes* for your cooperation.
>
> And let us all together involve ourselves in supporting the Radio Hour.
>
> With thanks, *Yitzhak Lisinov*

With all the debate about Stolnitz's reading of the news and the classiness or lack of it of the show of which he was "musical-literary director," perhaps one should have been prepared for the shake-up that took place two weeks after this letter on July 26, 1936. The front-page roster for the show simply announced Alexander Brown as the news reader, but, buried at the bottom of page 3, two articles beneath an article celebrating Stolnitz's engagement to lead High Holiday services at the Labour Lyceum ("Stolnitz Engaged"), under the title "Withdraws from the Jewish Radio Hour" appeared this stark note:

> Worthy Editor,
> Permit me through your distinguished newspaper to announce that I have withdrawn from the Hamilton Jewish Radio Hour and no more bear any responsibility for subsequent programs.
> Respectfully,
> *Cantor Nathan Stolnitz*

This was never explained, nor did it receive any comment whatsoever from anywhere in the paper, or, indeed, the rival *Yidishe Zhurnal*. And, though the Stolnitzes continued to have an excellent rapport with the paper, with every cantorial success of either father or son reported and with the elder Stolnitz continuing to write articles for the *Kanader Nayes* on musical subjects into the 1950s, the elder Stolnitz never appeared on a radio show connected with the paper again.

Nor does the loss of Stolnitz seem to have been lamented much by the listeners. As if to rub it in, the following week's paper had a letter praising his replacement:

> Permit me through the columns of your important newspaper to put in print my enthusiasm for the Jewish Radio Hour from last week. . . . A special thanks is coming to Mr. Alexander Brown from the *Kanader Nayes* for his summary of the news of the week. It was a pleasure to hear his language, diction and clarity.
> Respectfully,
> *Sh. Glass.*

In honour of the twentieth edition of the show, the editors of the *Kanader Nayes* held a contest for the best letter on the subject of "Why do we need a Jewish Hour?" The winner was published on August 16, 1936 and it put the show in the context of the darkening international horizon—in fact, it had far more to do with the context than with the radio show itself:

> **First Prize Winner, Jewish Radio Hour Letter Contest**
> Why do we need a Jewish Radio Hour?
> A chain of scorn, humiliation and torture has, in recent times, encircled Jewish life throughout the whole world. From one side we are put upon with economic decline, and from the second side everything we hold dear and holy is dishonoured.
> In certain European countries they want not only to destroy us physically, but what is even worse, they want to ruin us spiritually, they want to kill our souls, our culture, a culture which was fashioned under the worst and saddest historical conditions, our culture which has been soaked through with the blood of the best sons of our people, has become a target at which they have lately begun shooting from the otherwise beautiful world.
> There have been brought to life many ghosts of the past which try hard to do their destructive work against Jewish culture, which is in essence the noblest and most humanitarian, and which carries within itself the most beautiful pearl of human ethics.
> In the free lands, we experience a certain coldness and weakness which indeed brings us to the brink of despair. We cover up our culture as if it had become a discarded one, a foreign one, and especially the youth are daily becoming more and more torn, alienated and estranged, and they enter ever more in the assimilationist stream, which has brought us the saddest consequences in our historical journey.
> The youth who have already almost forgotten our folk-language are in need of a means of rescue, a means which will at the same time renew and plant the values of Jewish culture.
> This, in such a time, is the service that can be done so fully by a Jewish Radio Hour.
> The radio, in general, has recently become the most powerful cultural force throughout the whole world. Hitler has thus, through the radio, poisoned a whole people. Mussolini has thrown the Italian youth into the flames of death using this most beautiful invention, and has poisoned the minds of people against us through

the radio. Why shouldn't we use the airwaves to protect and strengthen Jewish culture so as to strengthen our resistance in the current dark historical days.

The Jewish Radio Hour brings a ray of hope and strengthens the cultural ties between our own brother Jews, and we must bring to bear all means and efforts to sustain the Jewish Radio Hour. We must strive so that our Jewish Radio Hour transforms itself in time into a Jewish Radio Hour for all Canada.

H. Weinstock, 164 Huron Street

Whether or not a Jewish Radio Hour was part of the solution, there was no question that these were dark days. Nazi Germany and Fascist Italy were already putting their war machines at the service of the Franco Fascists in the Spanish Civil War, provoking an editorial in the *Kanader Nayes* (August 12, 1936) ruminating on "Symptoms of a new world war," though without specific fears for the Jews: "Birds of prey, like Hitler and Mussolini, who look around for every opportunity to busy themselves with the duty of spilling human blood are already sharpening their venomous beaks." The paper had much more to say about these developments and we'll come to them shortly.

The six-month anniversary of the Radio Hour was obviously a time for reflection. In the next issue there appeared a full-length article by "P.M.Sh." assessing the show rather more objectively than Mr. Weinstock in his prize-winning letter. "P.M.Sh." was probably Moyshe Shapiro himself, given the theatrical references and, perhaps, the fulsome praise for some of the radio performers. But the references to "critics" and "criticism" were portents of another imminent shake-up:

A Few Words about the
Jewish Radio Hour, by P.M.Sh.
. . . as the Jewish Radio Hour has already entered into its sixth month of existence and counts already this week

its 22nd program, gradually establishing its presence ever more, the question poses itself: why has the Jewish Radio Hour had more luck than other Jewish radio hours and half-hours which we have had in Toronto before? Are the programs of the Radio Hour better than what we have had, or has the time perhaps come when a Jewish radio program has become a vital necessity?

From what I have been able to learn in seeking the answer, it has become clear that the Jewish Radio Hour can only thank its creator Mr. Greenfield for its existence to this point. It is true that a Jewish radio hour is really a necessity and Jews value it, so much so that, should the Jewish Radio Hour disappear, there would probably be a lot of regret; but until now nobody has taken it in hand to solidify its existence. *As for the criticism the Jewish Radio Hour has put up with from almost all Jews, the question is not whether the program is good or bad.* Either the radio show is a necessity or it is not. But as long as it is at least a Jewish undertaking and, indeed, an undertaking which bears a cultural character, must one certainly support it. The same thing can be said of Jewish Theatre and about all that has a connection with song or theatre performance, of which Jews are the greatest critics.

S.M. Greenfield, the creator of the Jewish Radio Hour is, for his part, a gentleman with a great entrepreneurial genius, and *he also has the virtue that he looks the critics straight in the eye. It's true that you have to concede that the Jewish Radio Hour has perhaps not yet reached such a high level, but you must not forget that this is just an experiment and, as such, has certainly been open to criticism. In comparison with the first programs, the latest ones have improved a hundred percent,* and the credit for that goes only to Greenfield who hasn't been afraid of anything and has seen to it that the Hour exists, applying throughout all means to set the course of the radio hour and to beautify and improve his programs. This has turned out so well that the Radio Hour certainly has every chance of remaining a permanent Jewish institution in the city.

I also want to take the same opportunity to say a few words about the talent that performs on the programs of the Jewish Radio Hour.

Isaac Swerdlow of the Morris Schwartz Art Theatre

is really a great prize for the Jewish Radio Hour and his artistic talent demonstrates itself in almost each program in which he takes part. The same can also be said about Max Mandel our talented Toronto singer and showman, who has contributed so much to the growth in stature of the Radio Hour from the first day on of its existence. Along with the above-mentioned singer, there is nothing to be ashamed of with singers such as Jack Barkin, Harry Jacobs and Saul Weinberg on a Jewish radio program. The musicians Maurice Turk and Joe Barsht are completely fine and often even beautiful. . . .

Taking into account the short time that the Jewish Radio Hour has existed and also that it has, in such a short time, been able to succeed in giving such programs as the last ones, one can safely predict a really good future for it.

This wasn't exactly faint praise, but one certainly gathers from it that the show had its critics. Very little of that could be found in the *Kanader Nayes* itself outside of some letters to the editor, and the *Yidishe Zhurnal* seems to have felt it safer to ignore the program altogether. The more refined English language weekly, the *Jewish Standard* finally got around to a brief review of the Hour in its August 1936 issue, and it, too, was largely favorable, to everyone but Greenfield himself:

ON THE AIR: Every Sunday between eleven and twelve you may hear the sweet voice of S.M. Greenfield announce in Yiddish the blessings of "Smetene", "oogerkes" or whatever happens to be advertised, and introduce some of the Toronto and Hamilton talent. Buffalo, Rochester and Syracuse are listening in while Cantor Stolnitz is master of ceremonies. This Yiddish hour has fine possibilities and often offers good talent. But it needs more careful planning and lovers of Yiddish would prefer that Mr. Stolnitz or somebody else more familiar with Yiddish than Mr. Greenfield make the announcements. [9]

---

[9] "Torontonesque," *The Jewish Standard*, August 1936, p.9. "Smetene" is sour cream, and "oogerkes" are pickles.

The Jewish Standard, August, 1936

TORONTONESQUE

NATIVE SONS: *Rabbi (Abe) Halpern* of St. Louis is summering at Roche's Point. The H. M. Goodmans, the (Dr.) Bill Stones, the Halperns and many other relatives are frequently to be seen on the Balfour Manor grounds. Rabbi Halpern, who came here to attend the Bar-Mitzvah of his nephew, Bernard Goodman, is renewing old friendships and acquaintances. . . . *Samuel Gerson Levy*, rabbi, Ph.D. (Semitics, Columbia), known as "Mookie", accepted a position in Montreal as educational director of the Shaar Hashomayim Congregation. "Mookie", who is now a father of a two-month-old son (how time flies!), is a scholar and a gentleman in the finest sense of the words, and we predict that he will soon gain the affection and admiration of Montreal. Mrs. "Mookie" is a lady of accomplishment and has been an excellent Hebrew teacher until she launched upon another career.

CONGRATULATIONS: *Trustee Ida Siegel* has been elected as the delegate of the Toronto women to attend the World Peace Conference at Geneva. . . . The organization consists mostly of Gentiles and Mrs. Siegel herself suggested that a church woman would be more in place, but she was drafted. . . . *Rabbi Lazarus Axelrod* of Hamilton is touring the Western States in the interest of the Zionist Organization of America. (Texas, Arizona, California, Oregon, Washington, Wyoming, Utah and Colorado.)

PH.D.: Besides Levi Jacob Jacober and Elsie Kaplan Palter, whom we mentioned in our last issue, the following received their Ph.D.'s at last convocation: *Saul Louis Cohen* (they say he is young and brilliant) and *Samuel Levine*. Saul is a graduate of a Brandon college. He is now going on a two-year scholarship to the University of Zurich, Switzerland.

THE ISLAND WITHOUT: Believe it or not, but you'll hardly find a Jewish face (or figure) on the "Main Drag" of Centre Island. The headquarters of Jewish "Bohemia" are at and around Shoreview Inn, Hanlan's Point, where Hye Bossin rules the roost. The Reds have almost faded away this year and the "balabattish" Jews are scattered here and there on Ward's and Hanlan's. But they are hardly seen or heard.

The Island is a place "where men are men and Jews play badminton". Ruth Schwartz, singing Jackie Lewis' new song, "Beautiful Bluff", was a high spot on the Lou Marsh memorial concert for the Star Fresh Air Fund at Ward's Island recently. Tommy McClure ran the show and Sammy Sales did the comedy. Lou Krugel stuffed things with his robust baritone. There was a remarkable preponderance of Jews in the audience on this Island Without, where the Bennetts, the Glasses and the Singers are among the few exceptions. . . . Lou Krugel will open a delicatessen downtown and it's bound to be the chief local port of call for transient and other thespians.

FRESSARNIA, FRESSETERIA, FRESSITORIUM, LA FRESSITEE: This is not Latin grammar. It is a classification of places where Jews meet over a delicatessen sandwich. It depends upon the *tone* of the outfit what you are going to call it. The tone depends upon the locality. You see, a place on Spadina or St. Lawrence Main or Rideau Street is a plain Fressarnia. On Park Avenue or on College, east of Brunswick, it is a Fressiteri. West of Brunswick Avenue or in Notre Dame de Grace—a Fressitorium. If and when on Meach Lake, we shall call it La Fressittee.

OUR WORTHY CONTRIBUTORS: We told you all about Hye Bossin. *Abe Klein* is doing a great deal of writing under his own and assumed names. Watch for that stuff in the American Home Journal and the Liberty. . . . Abe is especially busy on a sonnet in honour of *Sam Abramson's* proposed wedding and one for the "stag" in honour of the said Sam. Only the wedding sonnet wil be printed in the JEWISH STANDARD. . . . In case you don't know it, Sam Abramson is a famous litterateur and a man-about-town in Montreal. His literary contributions to the JEWISH STANDARD are published under a Latin pseudonym (you'll never guess!). Cactus's column has been quoted by foreign newspaper syndicates on several occasions. . . . Next to Sam's matrimonial career, the poetry of Bialik occupies Abe Klein's mind. A few excellent translations appeared in the *Opinion* and some are due to appear in the STANDARD. . . . Sam Abramson will have something to tell you about Abe Klein's poetry in the next issue. . . . *Marvin Gelber's* article in our last issue has made quite a hit.

THOSE WESTERNERS: *Murray Shapiro* of the Western Fur Company, London and Sarnia, young, handsome, dapper, sweet-mannered (and for all we know, rich!), spent seven days at Hotel Vermont, Ste. Agathe, after which he spent seventy minutes saying goodbye.

SYNAGOGAL: A new building is going up on *St. Clair, at Winona Drive*, which will house the new *Jewish Centre* of the Hillcrest district. The board of the Shaar Hashomayim Congregation (of which Mr. J. Kofman is president) contemplates an ambitious programme for the new centre: an educational department, consisting of a day school and a Sunday school, clubs, young people's societies, an auditorium, children's services, etc. The ground floor will be ready by the middle of September. . . . *S. Waperman* is the Canadian representative of Cantor Leib Langer, formerly of Moscow. Langer's appearance at the Jewish Centre of Brunswick Avenue caused a great deal of favourable comment. Langer was employed by the Soviet Government as a choir leader, but he did not approve of the system and skipped the Red Paradise. The daily press of Toronto devoted much space to Cantor Langer's visit.

ON THE AIR: Every Sunday between eleven and twelve you may hear the sweet voice of S. M. Greenfield announce in Yiddish the blessings of "Smetene," "oogerkes" or whatever happens to be advertised, and introduce some of the Toronto and Hamilton talent. Buffalo, Rochester and Syracuse are listening in while Cantor Stolnitz is master of ceremonies. This Yiddish hour has fine possibilities and often offers good talent. But it needs more careful planning and lovers of Yiddish would prefer that Mr. Stolnitz or somebody else more familiar with Yiddish than Mr. Greenfield make the announcements.

YOUNG JUDEA: Rabbi Morris Kertzer was the chief speaker at the Ontario Young Judea pow-wow. Morris had just returned from a trip to Palestine and inspired his listeners with his talk. The freedom of the city of St. Catharines was granted to the eighty delegates by Mayor W. J. Westwood. You've guessed it: Mark Zimmerman was re-elected president.

Eddie Gelber is in Haifa, enjoying

FAST DRIV
and
SLOW DRIV

This message is ad
to BOTH of Y

ALL OF US who drive motor cars have preferences as to the speed at which we of us like to drive slowly; others like to (I am not referring to the "speed fienc recklessly and dangerously, but to the of sane, sensible drivers.) There is a w in our preferred speeds.

When the road is clear and open, w reasonable right to give these preferen and travel at any speed which suits us legal limit. But I believe you will agr traffic is heavy, it is neither courteou travel faster or slower than the general s the traffic is moving.

At such times, the deliberately slow driv road for all who are behind him. It bec and wearying to those who have long tri of them — and finally induces them to take chances which they would never tak circumstances.

On the other hand, it is equally discour drivers to cut in and out of the traffic lan IS moving at a reasonable speed. It up nerves the more cautious drivers; increa dent hazard tremendously; and invariab a very FEW minutes of time in the en

I appeal to BOTH kinds of drivers to l be governed by the true SPIRIT of C consider the convenience and the safet motorists, as well as their rights. Let same courtesy to others on the highway, to visitors in our homes. It will go a long making our highways SAFER, and in mak still more pleasant.

Sincerely yours,

MINISTER OF
HIGHWAYS
PROVINCE OF
ONTARIO

TR
COURT
IT WO
BOTH

Of course, this article was just a little out of date, because, it will be remembered, Stolnitz quit in late July. Interestingly, Stolnitz's Yiddish is praised here, unlike in the letters column of the *Kanader Nayes*. But Stolnitz was raised in Vilna, where Yiddish is spoken very differently—more like German—from the catchment area of most of the Jews of Toronto. Where a Jew from Vilna (sometimes called the Oxford of Ashkenaz) would say "*gut*" for "good," a less refined Jew from the South of Poland, like most Toronto Jews would say "*git*." For instance, "*git*" abounds in "Music from the Jewish Hour." I had to break my teeth relearning a lot of my pronunciation when I performed for the purists at Yiddishland Café. It may be that Stolnitz's Yiddish was just a little too snooty for the Jewish Hour listeners, even though it evidently appealed to the writers of the English language *Jewish Standard*. As for Greenfield's bad Yiddish, or at least his bad pronunciation, this was confirmed by my Max's sister Sarah Kerzner who was a youngster of thirteen when all this was happening. She said that everyone made fun of the way Greenfield spoke Yiddish. She thought there was something terribly funny about the way he said "*nool*" for zero in telephone numbers. In fact, his newspaper ads for his bailiff business were far more Yinglish than Yiddish: "*Mir collectn rents un andere khoyves. Mir layen gelt ohf morghedzhes un oytomobilin. Mir manadjen properties.*" "We collect rents and other debts. We lay money on mortgages and automobiles. We manage properties."

It would be a matter of weeks before Greenfield and the *Kanader Nayes* parted company for good.

In the meantime, the show continued to hold its place on the front page. With Stolnitz gone, it was now being directed by Swerdlow "of-the-Morris-Schwartz-Art-Theatre," and the ritual aspects were being performed by Khazan David Glick. On September 13, two shows were announced, the regular Sunday show featuring the usual performers and a "Special Rosh Hashana Program" for the next evening from 9 to 10:30: "It will bear a religious character, with the participation of Khazan Glick, with a big choir, a big orchestra, Max Mandel, Albert Gamze, Hilda Rudnick, and Shirley Lieberman. Shana Tova greetings will be announced. S. M. Greenfield will announce both programs." (There's my mother again, using her maiden name Hilda Rudnick, though they'd been married more than two years by this time.)

Dubinsky's Jewish Radio Hour

But over the page from this announcement there was a big ad for yet another Rosh Hashanah Radio Hour that was even permitted by the editors of the *Kanader Nayes* to describe itself as "the most beautiful radio hour in Canada." What was going on?

> **"Dubinsky's Jewish Radio Hour"**
> Sunday the 13th of September, 4 until 5 in the afternoon
> Over the radio station CKCL Toronto 580 kilocycles
> The most beautiful radio hour in Canada
> Exquisite orchestra—program—eminent singers
> This is no amateur program, here you have professional artists performing. . . Mr. Dubinsky, who has the title "Bachelor of Music," is naturally himself a first class musician, with three years experience as teacher in the Toronto Music Conservatory and seven years as a radio artist.

There followed a very impressive list of no less than twenty-four sponsors of the hour, including, besides the usual creameries, bakeries, delicatessens, fish markets, etcetera, a couple of breweries as well, which might be surprising if you didn't know Dubinsky's father was in the brewing business.

Why was this portentous? Because, when the first Sunday after the holidays rolled around, Greenfield was gone, replaced by Dubinsky, whose photo appeared on the front page of the *Kanader Nayes* with this story:

> Starting Sunday the 11th of October, between 3 and 4 in the afternoon, the Jews of Canada will have a new Jewish Radio Hour, under the personal management of Mr. David Dubinsky, B.M. Mr. Dubinsky assures us that he will dedicate himself to making this Jewish Radio hour as rich in spirit as possible. Mr. Dubinsky told a representative of the *Kanader Nayes* that he is not content with the musical calibre that the Jewish radio hours—apart from a few exceptions—have until now presented to the Jewish world. "Jews have good music and also bad music," noted Mr. Dubinsky, "I cannot understand why the Jewish radio hours select the worst." Mr. Dubinsky believes that the cause of this is that the managers of the hours are themselves not artists. It is to be hoped that Mr. Dubinsky, who has the title "Bachelor of Music," will keep his word. The radio hour in question will be heard over the Toronto station CKCL.

So it seems that the *Kanader Nayes* editors took seriously the persistent criticisms of the Greenfield show that at least some elements of it were lacking in "refinement." And who was this David Dubinsky with the high opinion of himself? He was *not* the powerful American union leader of the same name (of the same era). The Toronto Dubinsky was a legitimate classical musician, a pianist who appeared on the English language radio. The same picture on the front page of the *Kanader Nayes* could be found gracing the radio page of the *Toronto Star*, of January 7, 1932 (p.24), advertising a recital series on CFCA (the *Star*'s own radio station), during which Dubinsky would play "clever interpretations of old and modern composers" such as Chopin and Manna-Zucca and even some of his own compositions. Dubinsky was clearly a class act, and CKCL was clearly an improvement over CKOC, with its studios in the sumptuous Prince George Hotel at the corner of King and York Streets in Toronto—*not Hamilton*, in other words.

The new Dubinsky Jewish Hour kicked off as promised on October 11. He brought over most of the regulars of the Greenfield show, "Toronto darling Max Mandel, the excellent tenor Saul Weinberg," as well as Maurice Turk and Joe Barsht, who, along with Dubinsky and H. Lanke (later "Linke") would make up "Dubinsky's musical quartet" (with two pianists!). Alexander Brown was the "master of ceremonies." Added to this group was classical singer Irving Levine. The presence at the inauguration of J. J. Glass, MPP, as with the first Jewish hour of six months earlier, attested to the importance placed by the *Kanader Nayes* on the event and, indeed, the paper's support for the show. Other guests who appeared in the next few weeks included Max's sister Rose Mandel (reputedly a decent singer), his wife Khayke (Jewish name), called Rudnick when she appeared with Rose—probably to diminish the number of Mandels—a Simon Guest and "the well-known singer Rose Schwartz," whose fame has not otherwise travelled down to us across the decades.

Swerdlow was a notable omission. He seems to have stayed with Greenfield, who carried right on with his own show on Sunday mornings on CKOC. All that the *Kanader Nayes* had done was switch horses. There was no mention of Greenfield, much less the turnover at the *Kanader Nayes*, in any of the other Jewish papers, so there was no newspaper sponsorship to fill the gap left by the *Kanader Nayes*. Greenfield didn't quit his day-job (the bailiff business), though. The February 7, 1937 edition of the *Kanader Nayes* had a big ad on page 3 for a bailiff's sale of the business of M. Cohen and Son, a slipper manufacturing firm. (Greenfield's Yiddish was as bad as ever: "slipper" in proper Yiddish should be *shtekshukh* "שטעקשוך," not "סליפער" which was the purely phonetic transliteration of the English that he employed).

Naturally, the *Kanader Nayes* thought the new Dubinsky show had been a colossal success:

> **Warm reaction to new Jewish Radio Hour**
> All Jewish radio listeners were surprised with the high level of the Jewish Radio Hour, which was for the first time heard last Sunday from 3 to 4 in the afternoon over the radio station CKCL Toronto. The new hour is under the personal management of Mr. David Dubinsky. Throughout the whole city, the new Radio Hour was the topic of conversation of the day. Without exception, everyone expressed great satisfaction both with the artists and with the character of the numbers that were chosen to be sung and to be played. The entire staff of the new Radio Hour was flooded with greetings and congratulations and with good wishes that the new radio program, which has had such a successful start, will also continue to maintain its success. Mr. Dubinsky has let it be known that he will try to make his program even more beautiful and better. [10]

Although Dubinsky's show started off with the same quasi-official status as Greenfield, its link to the *Kanader Nayes* became increasingly tenuous. The new show certainly did not own the front page the way Greenfield had. In a couple of weeks it was reduced to little ads on page 3, suggesting strongly that the *Kanader Nayes* had gotten out of the radio show sponsoring business. Dubinsky had his own sponsors, though, including a radio sales store, Himel's Toronto Tire and Radio Sales Co. and Peerless Bicycle Works. If you looked

---
10 *KN*, October 14, 1936, page 1.

close enough at the end of the ad for a spiffy new DeForest Crossley radio console from Himel's in the *Kanader Nayes* for October 18, 1936, you could find an ad for the show:

DeForest Crossley
No money down

5-TUBE CONSOLE —
FULL 7-TUBE PERFORMANCE —
BIG VALUE

Here you have an opportunity to purchase the best bargain. The DeForest Crossley ranks first overall in the category of popular-priced radios. It has three wave bands, standard broadcast, amateur, air aviation, police and all five recognized short wave and overseas reception bands. And your pocketbook will also benefit because you can buy this beautiful, brand new console radio for **$79.95** with just your old set for a down-payment.

We repair your old radio cheaply.

Bicycles, children's joycycles, automobile tires and batteries on easy weekly payments, 30 years in business, your best guarantee of honest dealing.
S. Himel, *manager*
**Toronto Tire & Radio
Sales Co. Ltd.**
and **Peerless Bicycle Works**
191-3-5 Dundas St. W.
Adelaide 3582

Listen to Himel's Program on Dubinsky's Radio Hour every Sunday from 3:30 to 3:45 CKCL

The Radio Stars on Stage

The popularity of the radio stars seems to have been at its absolute zenith. Towards the end of the first year of the radio experiment, the performers sought to take advantage of their popularity by putting on variety concerts at the Jewish concert halls. The first of these was November 29, 1936 at the Strand Theatre. For this concert, Max Mandel joined a group called The Modern Entertainers Group ("*Di Modern Grupeh Enterteyners*"), and headed up a list of artists which included Harry Harris, Philip Gurevitch, Albert Gamze, Michael Ziefert, Rivka Grad, Ada Singer, Sherman Gan, Maurice Ginsburg, Maurice Turk and his orchestra. Maurice Turk and Ada Singer we have already met. Sherman Gan was a very active blind accordion player and composer. Ginsburg was a by-now elderly Russian emigré classical musician who, in Toronto, had pursued a career as a conductor of musical theatre. But the really interesting name on this list is Harry Harris, hitherto an itinerant cantor and freelance entertainer, who would emerge as the main rival of Max Mandel in the Jewish Hour business, with plenty of bad blood as the years wore on. His stable of artists would include Gurevitch and Ziefert. By the time the concert rolled around, other

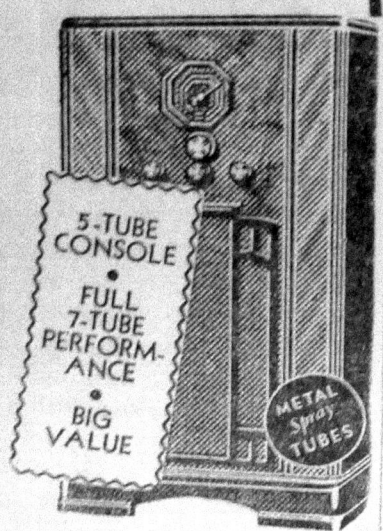

performers had been added, including Philip Kahn, Shirley Smith, Saul Weinberg and Sammy Shopsowich on accordian. Shopsowich was none other than the then-fifteen-year old future "Corned Beef King" of Canada, who lived just a few doors up from the Strand at 295 Spadina, where his parents had their ice cream parlour and (later) Shopsy's Delicatessen.

Dubinsky was not part of the Modern Entertainers Group but he quickly caught onto the idea and, with Max Mandel as his principle collaborator, planned a blockbuster "Concert-spectacle" at the Strand for the evening of December 27. The *Kanader Nayes* ran an ad and story with pictures of Dubinsky (in full conductor mode, with tails and baton) and Max:

The Linitzer Benefit Society
——presents a grand——
CONCERT SPECTACLE
Today, Sunday 8 in the evening
in the Strand Theatre
with the artists from **David Dubinsky's Radio Hour**
and other attractions
— 25 song and dance numbers —

David Dubinsky will direct an orchestra of 10 eminent musicians. Production of the Chelmer Assembly.
Come in Masses!
Reservations all day at the Theatre
Under the personal supervision of
David Dubinsky *and* **Max Mandel**

A review of the concert appeared in the January 10 edition of the *Kanader Nayes*. It was a triumph for the Dubinsky troupe, but most of all for Max personally, who had by now emerged as the "star":

> **1600 persons attend concert of Dubinsky's radio artists**
> Sunday evening, the 27th, when the Linitzer Society put on its concert in the Strand theatre featuring David Dubinsky's radio artists, 1600 people packed the theatre. Several hundred who wanted to get in and could not because of a lack of space went home disappointed.

Even though the concert was to have begun at 8:30, the theatre was already overflowing around 8 o'clock and the concert therefore started before the announced time.

The concert, which was made up of music, songs and short dramatic and comic pieces was put on under the direction of Max Mandel, one of the radio artists. The whole program was enthusiastically received by the public which loudly applauded the artists.

Taking part in the concert was David Dubinsky with an orchestra of ten persons in which Maurice Turk and D. Silverman played first and second violin.

Shimon Guest and Saul Weinberg, the popular singers from the Dubinsky Radio Hour, sang a good number of songs, which were strongly received and they were therefore called back several times. They also took part in several musical skits, such as "March, March, March" and "The Chelmer Assembly." Lilian Stambler, dancer, came on twice and was well appreciated by the audience.

The 10-year-old Ada Liberman was strongly received by the audience with her "Motl Peysi, the Khazan's son"[11] The little one declaimed like a trained adult artist and made an exceptionally good impression.

But the "star" of the evening was Max Mandel, who is already well known in Toronto both as a stage artist and as a radio singer. Mr. Mandel sang many songs, and put on several comic sketches, from which the audience got much enjoyment and laughed loudly. The last of those presented was "The Chelmer Assembly" in which Saul Weinberg, Shimon Guest, Philip Gurvitz, Khanina Englander, Michl Zeifert and Albert Gamze also took part; in a solo, Gamze also declaimed Kipling's "Boots" with a Jewish melody.

"Master of Ceremonies" for the evening was Alexander Brown. Mr. Eli Bok, president of the Linitzer Society gave a short speech. After a few hours of entertainment the audience departed a greatly satisfied one.

So, in the eight months between April and December of 1936, this twenty-eight-year-old shtetl boy from Apt had, through

---

[11] Sholem Aleichem's unfinished novel.

the force of his talent and the power of this new medium, been propelled from obscurity to stardom.

The radio artists sought to capitalize on their success with another concert at the Strand on February 14, 1937. "Diverse dramatic pieces will be staged, including Avrom Reisen's *Mai ko mashmalon*, a shoemaker scene of the song *Hemerl, hemerl klap*, a prison scene. Good jokes, several comic skits, beautiful music and songs will for sure not be missing." From the lack of any follow-up story about hundreds of people being sent away, we can assume that this concert did not do quite as well at the box office as the other one.

The radio artists also did a considerable amount of individual freelance concertizing at this time. In between the two Dubinsky concerts, Mandel once again appeared at the Strand, this time with Louis Kremer, the quixotic American labour activist turned Yiddish theatre star. The following Sunday's paper had "the beloved radio singer Max Mandel" and other radio artists at the Brunswick Avenue Talmud Torah. A few weeks later, the radio stars joined forces in a concert in honour of and for the benefit of impresario and *Kanader Nayes* friend Morris Shapiro, in the Strand. The concert included "the eminent artist Yitzhak Swerdlow who will put on *The Wise Men of Chelm* by A. Zeitlin, which was produced in Morris Schwartz's Art Theatre . . . Appearing in the musical section of the concert will be Max Mandel, who has recently made a name in Toronto as a very talented radio artist and stage artist, Saul Weinberg, noted as a singer of romances and folk songs and Moyshe Turk, young violin artist. Besides them, the Barsht Orchestra will also be taking part." The roster was later broadened to include "the two musical ambassadors, Sky and Daughtry," Chuck Miles and Ada Singer.

The Strand was a very busy place at this time and it wasn't

all Max Mandel and friends. Straddling these concerts were more politically-oriented events, though there was often a musical element to them, for example a "mass meeting and concert", with an address by Barukh Vladek and performances by Sam Stolnitz and the Workmen's Circle Mandolin Orchestra. Vladek's visit was a *Kanader Nayes* event and his meeting with Toronto's Mayor Robbins was front page news in the *Kanader Nayes*. Vladek, remember, was not only the *Forverts* manager but also a New York city councillor.

Moyshe Oysher Lifts Public to Ecstasy

The Dubinsky radio show itself carried on pretty much under the newspaper radar except when it had the occasional famous guest star, such as the "Wunderkind *Khazan* Shloymele Gomberg from New York" and, a real coup in March 1937, the sensational and controversial *khazan* movie star, Moyshe Oysher. The paper recounted the ordeal of prying him away from New York:

> **Moyshe Oysher comes to Toronto**
> Thanks to the efforts of M. Ginsburg, who had to drag his old Litvak bones to New York two successive times, the Londoner Shul will have the honour of hearing the greatest cantor of our time, the world renowned Moyshe Oysher. It is said that our Toronto Ginsburg (the former director of the Standard Theatre Orchestra) basically had to carry on a physical struggle with the New York rabbinate to compel them to let *Khazan* Oysher go for one *shabbes* to the provinces.
> Moyshe Oysher was attacked on s*likhes*[12] by a band of New York fanatics who claimed that he was not pious enough to pray at the cantor's desk. Now, however, they have become so in love with him that they don't ever want to let him leave them. According to the experts, Ginsburg

---
12 The High Holiday penitential service preceding *Rosh Hashanah*.

among them, Moyshe Oysher is the best cantor of our time. He possesses a rare, sweet tenor voice that, when it achieves the tenor crescendo, makes the window panes shake.

Moyshe Oysher, the Bessarabian born New York (via Montreal) cantor, recording artist and movie star lived from 1907 to 1958. One of his songs, *Unter Boimer* is sung by Irma Hasso on "Music from the Jewish Hour." His real life story of the struggles of cantorial secular singers was repeated many times, even in Max Mandel's case (according to Max's sister Sarah). Oysher made a huge splash in Toronto. The front page of March 7, 1937's *Kanader Nayes* had this:

> **Cantor Moyshe Oysher Lifts Public to Ecstasy**
> Jewish Toronto is now going through ups and downs. Hundreds are disappointed and upset. How come? Moyshe Oysher, the God-blessed tenor, davened Friday and *shabbes* and they didn't go to hear him.
> But it is not yet too late. The error can still be corrected. Today, Sunday evening, the same Moyshe Oysher will give a concert in the Londoner Shul, together with his esteemed wife, Florence Weiss. From what we're told, it will be a program that will outdo both the Friday and the *shabbes* ones.

You can just imagine what an audience they must have had for Dubinsky's radio show that day, as the *Kanader Nayes* announced:

> **Cantor Moyshe Oysher on Dubinsky's Radio Hour**
> Cantor Moyshe Oysher will be the guest artist on the Dubinsky radio hour this Sunday afternoon over CKCL. Also appearing will be Moyshe Steinhartz and the Dubinsky Quartet.

Steinhartz, was never heard from before or since and was probably the unidentified choir master that Oysher brought with him from New York to conduct Cantor Vladowsky's twenty-six-voice Londoner Shul choir. If this were the case, then the whole show was probably devoted to Oysher with the regulars being bumped. But you can bet the studio was pretty crowded that day, not only with the regulars, but also their wives. As the humour columnist wrote the following week: "They say that the *Londoner shul* has more trustees than *siddurs* [prayer books]...and that had the wives' gallery been full of wives [instead of trustees] Moyshe Oysher would have davened even better."

Moyshe Oysher was far from Jewish Toronto's only visiting talent at this time. Secular entertainers abounded. Maurice Schwartz brought his famous troupe to Massey Hall on April 8, 1937 with a musical comedy *The Water Carrier*, with music by Olshanetsky and words by Lilian. He returned two weeks later to the Victoria Theatre with a serious anti-Fascist piece, *The Border*. May 2 saw a Massey Hall concert by Esther Field, the "Yidishe Mamme" of New York radio. She returned to the Strand on June 6. Molly Picon's smash movie hit *Yidl mitn fidl* opened at the College Street Playhouse on May 7, with music by Abraham Ellstein and lyrics by Itzik Manger.

Another giant of the Yiddish musical stage, Joseph Rumshinsky, starred in two personally-directed productions in Toronto at this time: *Song of Songs*, with Samuel Goldenberg, Dora Weisman and Max Kletter at the Temple Theatre in May, and *The Galician Rabbi* starring Menashe Skulnick at the Victoria Theatre in June. This is probably where Max Mandel first heard the latter operetta's racy duet "*Shloymele-Malkele*" featured on "Music from the Jewish Hour."

Dark Days

There is plenty to make us laugh when we read the newspapers of these times. For instance, an ad extolling great advances in cigarette making:

> Now... a step forward in cigarette-making...
> A new and definitive improvement... apart from the fine varieties of tobacco which are used in Crown cigarettes, there is now the unique merit of a new kind of cigarette paper, free of odor and also impermeable to dampness. It doesn't stick to your lips, it maintains its freshness and the aroma from the tobacco in the cigarette. It keeps cigarette spit from getting in your mouth.

There was also a recurring ad for women with that Semitic facial hair issue:

> Women
> Beautify your appearance. Free yourself from hair on your face. Let it be taken off with electrolysis without risk and without pain. Results guaranteed.
> *M. Gorman, Electrolysis technician*

But the times were no laughing matter. They were very dark and getting darker. The Spanish Civil War raged on. In April, 1937, the German Luftwaffe, acting with impunity on the side of Franco's fascists, destroyed the Basque town of Guernica, an event portrayed in its full terror in Pablo Picasso's famous mural. In November, 1937, Hitler and Mussolini formed their Axis with Japan, which promptly invaded China and perpetrated the "Rape of Nanking." Naturally, the paper supported the Republicans in Spain, writing editorials and publicizing pro-Republican rallies and speeches by such luminaries as Norman Bethune, Emma Goldman and even Tim Buck, the leader of the paper's arch-enemy Communist Party.

The *Kanader Nayes*, of course, recognized Nazism as our bitterest enemy, and the paper railed against it at every opportunity. In March, 1937 the *Kanader Nayes* joined the German goods boycott movement called by the Canadian Jewish Congress with a recurring box on page 1: "We are boycotting goods that are made in Germany." In July, the front page endorsed an initiative by the Trade

Union Division of the Canadian League Against War and Fascism directed by J.B. McLachlan, which issued a "Boycott Stamp" against German-made products. The stamps, to be put on letter envelopes, would be sold at 100 for a dollar.

Nor was Nazism only a far-away thing. Page 1 of the June 13, 1937 edition carried a photo of the display window of the Public Library at College and St. George Streets showing Adolf Hitler on the cover of *Mein Kampf*, with the admonition, "It is to be hoped that, in public places, supported by taxpayer's money, one will not advertise this most shameful anti-Semitic tract." On June 23, 1937, a front page story headlined, "Toronto golf club doesn't want Jews," reporting that St. Andrew's Golf Club had posted signs announcing that only Christians would henceforth be eligible to be members, even though there was a long-standing Jewish membership. The story announced that this was part of a co-ordinated city-wide policy. Rabbi Sachs counselled Jews to play at the Jewish club, Oakdale, in Weston, which remains to this day the Toronto Jewish golf club of choice.

A lot of attention was paid by the paper to the plight of East European Jewry, whose situation was increasingly dire. The Yiddish writer Sholem Asch, recently arrived in the United States from Poland, gave a lecture at the Royal York Hotel on June 2, sounding the alarm bells about Polish Jewish poverty and the rise of Polish fascism. A regular feature of the paper was *"Kroyvim gezukht"* ("Relatives Sought") where letters that had arrived from Europe at Dworkin's office either directly or through the Immigrant Aid Society were published:

> The following are sought by their relatives in Europe and other lands...
> 1) Mr. M. Brenton, last address 261 Augusta Ave., Toronto Ont. is sought by Ita Heckl, known under the

name "Ita the Bubie's" from Morkhuletchky, Rumania. Her husband Khanan Meir is horribly sick and greatly lacks support. The Morkhuletchky Rabbi begs you to help...

61) Itche Mikhl Levine, coming from Rakov, White Russia, the name of his wife is Shoshe, of his daughters: Khana and Esther-Beyla, of his sons: Noah and Leyb. He left Russia about 25–30 years ago and finds himself in New York or Brooklyn. Sought by his niece, Gitl Levine, the daughter of Abraham the farmer from Nedrowecz–Skaryszew, Powiat Woloszyn, Poland, who must correspond with him about a very important family matter.

Mrs. Dworkin also encouraged her readers to send *"matza-peklekh"* (matzah packages for *Pesakh*) and *"peklekh alte kleyder"* (old clothes packages) to relieve the suffering in Poland and Russia:

> **Send them packages of old clothes**
> If your relatives live in Poland, we can send them over packages of second-hand clothing. This is a trifle for you, but for them it is a big thing. It will protect them from the cold.
> If they live in Russia we can send them new cloth for clothes, or already made clothes, shoes and underwear, according to "samples" which we will show you... Or you can buy these things yourself, just where you want, and we will equip you with the necessary documents needed for the transport. Come to us and we will give you all the information.
> *Dworkin's Shifs Kontor*

This was followed by a big front page picture of Mrs. Dworkin and a warehouse wall stacked high with boxes.[13]

The fundamental Zionist solution to the problems of the Jews in Europe, was, of course, to get them to Palestine, laying the foundations of a future Jewish state; so this was a period of especially intense Zionist activity for the paper. The year 1937 was the second

---

13 *KN*, January 9, 1938.

year of the Arab uprising against Jewish immigration to Palestine. The British Peel Commission made its recommendation in July for the partition of Palestine into a Jewish and an Arab state. Apropos, the World Zionist Organization was carrying on a special "Shekel Campaign," a recruiting and fund-raising device whereby annual membership dues were obtained by purchasing a shekel certificate. The *Kanader Nayes* supported the campaign with ads and articles ("Do you have your shekel yet?"[14]). An evocative cartoon in English, Yiddish and Hebrew shows book burning in Germany, university discrimination, and an Arab destroying a tree planted by a young woman pioneer, and exhorts Jews to "combat this and keep doors of Palestine open."

A *Kanader Nayes* editorial of February 21, 1937 shows the thinking of Labour Zionists on anti-Semitism, religion and Arab opposition. The title "Peace in Israel" was actually a double-entendre because its subject was peace between religious and secular elements in the *people* of Israel, i.e. the Jewish people. The editorial included the unpleasant but perhaps truthful argument that the more Jews went to Palestine, the fewer would remain in Poland, with the result that anti-Semitism would be reduced:

> Every Jew who will be saved from the Eastern European hell is not only a victory for himself, but, with his leaving, he makes the conditions easier for those who remain behind... [I]f we can succeed in, let's say, getting a million Jews out of Poland, this is not only a salvation for the million taken out but also an immense benefit for the two and a half million Jews who then still remain there. Herzl already knew it years ago, that anti-Semitism significantly grows in the same proportion as the Jewish community of the land grows. This explains why in fascist Rome there is less Jew-hatred than in the democratic lands.

---

14 *KN,* May 5, 1937, p. 3.

But the main point was the celebration of the recent contributions of the synagogues to the Labour Zionist campaign for Palestine as "one of the most pleasantly surprising phenomena of our troubled time:"

> But the importance of the new opening of our synagogues to the Land of Israel labour movement and its institutions lies not only in the value of the contribution itself. The new opening wipes away the artificial divisions between synagogue Jews and workers while our people are engaged in a life and death struggle. The synagogues Jews have begun to understand that "it is not study but the deed that is primary."[15] That it is of greater significance for Jewry that the Land of Israel should as soon as possible be occupied with young, energetic, ready-for-sacrifice pioneers, who even occasionally miss *mincha*,[16] rather than leave that holy land stand vacant in the fanatic, lazy, and exploiting hands of the *effendi*,[17] while millions of persecuted Jews long for an opportunity to plant and build.
>
> This is the reason for which synagogue Jews and freethinkers, bosses and workers, unite today to support the union campaign.

The paper missed no opportunity to glorify the achievements of the Jewish settlers in Palestine. It was bursting with pride when the Maccabee soccer team passed through Toronto on a North American tour in October 1936, playing an exhibition match against Ulster United Championship, proceeds to go for the Tel Aviv Maccabee sport organization and for Polish Jewry. *Kanader Nayes* readers were urged to "come see the 20 athletes from the Land of Israel demonstrate Jewish courage, skill, might, and sporting spirit." There was a big picture of the team waving American flags. To everybody's delight, the game ended in a 1-1 tie.

---

15 The quote is from the religious tract *Pirke Avot* 1:17.
16 The daily afternoon prayers.
17 The Arab land-owning class.

There was one question that could not be dealt with so easily, and would continue to nag at the editors of *Kanader Nayes*, and that was the question of Jewish revenge terrorism against the Arabs. The paper would return to this again and again. In 1937, the editors were full of understanding and blamed it all on British policy:

> **The terror must now be stopped**
> But what will come out of the continual [Arab] terrorist outbreaks? How long can a Jewish youth who is ready for struggle idealistic hold back from not answering terror with terror? Would it not be unnatural to hope that people who believe in the righteousness of their cause, and who feel their strength, should not let themselves be provoked by untold and unheard-of acts of murder?
> This really happened in Jerusalem last week, when, immediately after Arabs threw a bomb into a group of Jews, which wounded 17 innocent people, another bomb landed in an Arab café. It can truly be that both bombs came from Arab origins, which would not be the first time Arabs murdered their own people. From the other side, is it not believable that this was an act of revenge by the Jewish side, in which patience exploded? It is certain that, if England only wanted to, she could easily end the terror and bring a lasting peace to the land. But why will she not do it?[18]

Local Politics

Naturally, the paper was as immersed in local politics as it was in foreign affairs. It consistently took up local workers' struggles, especially on behalf of the Jewish unions, as in this militant ad in support of the Toronto Butchers Union:

> **Warning to all Toronto butchers**
> Take notice that our union which has the support of all Toronto workers organizations is now on legitimate strike against certain wholesalers.

---

18 *KN*, March 24, 1937, p. 4.

> You are asked not to deal with any scab meat exactly as the Jewish population will be asked not to eat any scab meat. Remember, whenever meat does not have a union stamp even if it has a hundred other stamps, it is as *treyf*[19] as pig.

But it often appeared that the paper's main enemies were not the bosses but the Socialist Zionists' communist rivals. One recurring example of this was the struggle within the furriers union over Max Federman's leadership. Federman was a Socialist Zionist and anti-communist just like the paper's editors. He fought a running battle with communists in the furriers union until he was expelled by the American (communist) leadership on a charge of misappropriation of funds, in which there was apparently some truth, though the use made of the funds was union-related and not personal.[20] When he was subsequently "acquitted" at a "trial" held by his supporters in the union, the paper published a full page ad:

> "FEDERMAN NOT GUILTY! is the verdict of the rank and file trial committee . . . All charges against Max Federman, our beloved leader, were a frame-up. (With "frame-up" directly transliterated into Yiddish as "פריים אפ".)

To the editors of the paper, the communists were guilty of many sins, including Moscow's anti-Zionism and the strong scent of anti-Semitism that found expression in the suppression of Jewish nationalism and the persecution of Jewish Bolsheviks in the show trials of 1936 and 1937. So, in any Canadian election, the paper's support for the CCF and Labour candidates was always second to its opposition to the communists. One example was the Ontario

---

19 Forbidden by Jewish dietary laws.
20 Joan Sangster, "Canada's Cold War in Fur," *Left History* 13:2 (2008), p. 10.

provincial election of 1937, in which the paper turned its attention to defeating the communists, even at the expense of the CCF party it usually supported. It gave very supportive attention to the ruling Liberals under Mitch Hepburn, and especially their Jewish MPP, J.J. Glass who was running for re-election in the Spadina Avenue riding, described by the paper as "the most Jewish neighbourhood of the most Jewish city in the whole American continent"—a clear exaggeration in the statistical sense, but perhaps not in the cultural sense, given the recentness of immigration compared to the big American centres. Support for Glass was no mere Jewish chauvinism; he was running against a roster of Jewish candidates: the communist J.B. Salsberg, the Conservative Nathan Philips and the CCF's Harry Simon (Max Federman's protegé). In its editorial of October 3, the *Kanader Nayes* expressed no support for any candidate, only opposition to the communists:

> **Don't let the Communists fool you**
> We're not dealing here with the individual personalities of the candidates. He might be the most honest and the best, but just by belonging to the Communist Party, he must be unfit and no conscious Jew and no freedom lover and no unionist must support him. In reality, deep in his heart, Salsberg, just like all Communists, is an enemy of freedom and a hater of democracy. . . . Salsberg, just like all Communists, sings hymns to dictator and freedom violator Stalin and bears responsibility for each and every one of his bloody crimes. . . . Since the unlucky day [when the Communist Party captured the government of Russia], innocent people have been imprisoned or sent to Siberia or even shot. Hundreds of men and women languish there in captivity just because they believe in a democratic socialism, or in Zionism, or because they have tried to teach children Hebrew. Salsberg, just like all Communists, says this is right.
> Because of a crazy idea, which the Russian Communists

call their foreign policy, the few Communists in the Land of Israel have been authorized to incite, support and help the dark, fanatic Muslims to make pogroms on our wonderful pioneers. This has already cost a couple of hundred holy Jewish lives and the pogroms and murders are still going on. The candidate Salsberg, just like all Communists, is in agreement with this bloody policy and he says that the pogrom-mongers are right.

The headlines screamed anti-communism: "Jewish Congress and Labour Zionists call for a struggle against Communists" and "Communism is the enemy of Jewishness, says Rabbi Sachs." The Liberals won a decisive majority over the Conservatives, with the CCF almost shut out. In St. Andrews, however, J. J. Glass only very narrowly defeated Salsberg 6481 votes to 6302, with the rest far behind. In the municipal elections of the same year, with more or less the same cast of characters, the paper backed the CCF, but, once again, the most passionate endorsements were the negative ones to not vote communist. This included a two-page anti-communist article by Professor Golecki, "Twenty Years of Communism" ("The Bolshevik regime has introduced the most confusing and horrible chaos into the socialist movement of the whole world") and a full-page back-page anti-communist diatribe in which readers were urged not to vote for any communist: Buck, Salsberg, Weir, Smith.

This time, however, when the results were in, it was the communists who were the winners. All the candidates backed by the paper lost. Salsberg had snatched the junior alderman's seat in Ward 4 by a healthy margin, and Stewart Smith won Ward 5 handily. John Weir got board of education in Ward 4 and Tim Buck came within a hair's breadth of winning the fourth city wide board of control seat, losing by a mere 44,402 votes to 44,248.

The Jewish Variety Radio Program

Meanwhile, our radio artists were having the time of their lives. They continued their intense blitz of concertizing, with three big spring concerts in the Strand. The first was the by-now annual benefit concert for the ailing M. Ginsburg on March 28. It included *The Two Matchmakers*, a "Jewish review" with the participation of then twenty-four-year old Hyman Goodman ("Hymie" in the story) —future concertmaster of the Toronto Symphony Orchestra—Max Mandel, Saul Weinberg, Jack Barkin, and Harry Yakubovitch, "first-class artists who are well-known to the theater and concert public." The Pasen sisters were on hand, "the best child artists on the American continent," all in honour of "the old Jewish musician M. Ginsburg."

The season ended with a mega-concert in the Strand Theatre May 16 involving all the local talent, including the rival Jewish hours, in a *Shavuos*[21] evening of theatre and song:

> To conclude this successful theatre and concert year in Toronto, there will be a celebratory farewell and Spring holiday evening this Sunday in the Strand Theatre with the participation of all the talent and artists from Toronto and singers from the Jewish Radio Hours. The successful melodrama of G. Menachemsohn "The Pushover Yisroel" will be staged with Max Mandel as "Little Itzik the Convert" and Shlomo Froman as "Our Shmelki the Rabbi." Fifteen musicians from the Toronto Symphony Orchestra will play and take part in the sensational music. As well, the singers from the Jewish Radio Hours, Albert Gamze, the two Pasen sisters, and Kahn and Gurevitch will appear in the brilliant comedy "Two Weddings" which is chock-full of humour, art, zest and pathos. Also

---

21 Jewish holiday commemorating reception of the Torah on Mount Sinai. Literally, "weeks" because its beginning is determined by counting seven weeks from Passover.

to be presented is "Jews Sing" by Tunkel[22] and the newest hit songs and marches. All Toronto Jews are invited to come to the Strand theatre and beautify the *simkha*.

Another Strand benefit on April 25, 1937 heralded a major shuffle in the Jewish Radio Hour deck. This time the "benefitees" were "the artist Isaac Swerdlow" and his wife Adele who were celebrating a "double jubilee," twenty-five years of marriage and of Isaac's career on the professional stage, which had started in his native Odessa. Among those taking part were "the singers from Greenfield's Radio Show," obviously, still on the air, "Max Mandel (Toronto darling), Maurice Turk with his fine violin playing" and a certain "Louis Herman with his fine tender singing." The theatre pieces on the program were Yakov Gordin's *Shloymke the Charlatan* and scenes from his *God, Man and Devil* directed by Yitzhak Swerdlow "with Toronto's finest talent."

This is the first mention in the *Kanader Nayes* of Toronto-born singer Lou Herman, who, though only twenty-six at the time, already had a substantial performing career under his belt. As a boy soprano in Cantor Shloyme Selsky's synagogue choir he had come to the attention of the legendary Cantor Yossele Rosenblatt, and wound up as a soloist in Rosenblatt's High Holiday choirs from 1925 to 1927, singing in Chicago, Detroit and other American cities to great acclaim. A story from the Toronto *Globe* of August 19, 1930, page 1, has Herman singing to help future Liberal MP Sam Factor's aldermanic election campaign in 1929, but missing a big picnic having been called away by Rosenblatt for the High Holidays. From there he went on to sing with various big bands in the United States and

---

22 Joseph Tunkel was a Russian Jewish humourist who escaped from France to America in 1941. He wrote for *Forverts*.

even sang under the pseudonym of "Eric Forbes the Irish Balladeer." From surviving cassette-tape recordings, it is clear how he pulled this off, being possessed of a very beautiful and well-schooled classic lyric tenor in the John MacCormack mold. As himself, he had appeared on one of those one-off Jewish Hours that preceded the *Kanader Nayes*'s "*ershte.*"[23] After serving in the army, where he performed in shows with the big Canadian comedy act, Wayne and Shuster, he ultimately settled down as a cantor in Camden, New Jersey.[24]

It was probably out of this collaboration at the Swerdlow benefit concert between Herman, Mandel and Swerdlow that the next new Jewish Hour was born, announced at the end of the summer in the *Kanader Nayes*.

> **New Jewish Radio Hour today from 5 to 6 over CKOC**
> Beginning today, a new Jewish radio hour, which will call itself the "Variety Jewish Radio Program" will be heard every Sunday from 5 to 6 in the afternoon over the radio station CKOC Hamilton. The hour will be under the direction of showman Isaac Swerdlow, the singers Max Mandel and Louis Herman and Khazan David Glick.
> Taking part in the program this Sunday will be Khazan Akiva Bernstein,[25] from the University Shul, the above-mentioned artists Mandel, Swerdlow, and Louis Herman, the Herman Sisters, Adele Swerdlow and the musicians Sam Silver, piano, Maurice Turk violin, and S. Wallace. Jewish listeners are invited to tune their radios to CKOC at 5 o'clock in the afternoon.[26]

---

23 See the *Mail and Empire*, March 24, 1932, p. 17, CFRB, 8:30 p.m..
24 His son, David Herman, an orthodox rabbi in Baltimore, directed me to a website dedicated to his father's career maintained by Phil Cohen, one of Louis Herman's many former bar mitzvah students.
25 In Yiddish the name was Borenshteyn, usually expressed in English as Borenstein, a name used by some of his famous cantor relatives; but later in life he settled on Bernstein in English, so we're using that throughout to avoid confusion.
26 *KN,* August 22, 1937, page 3.

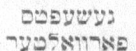

Khazan Glick we know already from the Greenfield Jewish Hour. The Herman sisters, Fayge, Golde and Miriam, were Lou Herman's sisters, students of Hyman Riegelhaupt, the director of Khazan Bernstein's choir, in which, of course they also sang. In fact, the *Kanader Nayes* of August 29 announced that "all the local radio singers" would be singing in the choir at that year's *slikhes* service. Sam Silver was the orchestra leader who had the (probably irksome) job of accompanying me in a few songs at my own bar mitzvah twenty-five years in the future. By that time I associated his name with the colour of his hair!

David Herman has kindly lent me the poster for the show, which shows that the multi-talented Sherman Gan was also to appear and reveals that Mr. Wallace played the cello.

The poster says that "guests in the studio are welcome" and a precious photo that came from the collection of one of the Herman Sisters shows a few of them behind the glass while the artists perform for the microphone.[27]

---

27 That's probably my mother, Hilda Mandel, third from the right.

The "Yidishe Gas" columnist was very excited about the new program: "May the new radio hour, which will be born today, have good luck. I hope that Swerdlow will see the better class of listener satisfied with things that have not yet been heard." Because Lou Herman was already a star on the gentile stage, there was even an announcement of the show in the Toronto *Star*:

> Lou Herman, local tenor, will head a new show to make its bow over CKOC, Hamilton, tomorrow at 5 p.m. The program, "Jewish Variety hour" will feature Lou's three sisters, Fay, Miriam and Goldie, who are something of a singing trio; Max Mandel, tenor; and Sherman Gan on the accordion. Gan is the blind musician who has mastered the violin, piano and organ as well as the accordion.[28]

Swerdlow, Herman, Mandel and Glick (calling themselves the "Jewish United Artists of Canada") had all gone down to lawyer Irving Weinert's Bay Street office on a summer's day—I imagine them all sweltering in their suits with no air conditioning—to sign a contract which has survived in the papers of Lou Herman. The contract makes delightful reading at this distance, but maybe less so for non-lawyers. It attests that they put down $50 each as "the capital" of the program; that they were all equal partners, except for Swerdlow, who was to "devote his whole time to the partnership business, acting in the capacity of announcer, continuity writer, and dramatic director and generally assisting in obtaining business and sponsors." He alone would get a weekly salary of "TEN ($10.00), but only during the weeks when the income exceeds all the expenditures by at least that amount and at no other times." David Glick would be the business manager, but also take an active part in the program

---

28 *Toronto Star*, August 21, 1937, p.22 ("Are you listening?").

whenever necessary. It was also "agreed and understood that the said David Glick shall be entitled and have his jewellery business suitably advertised every week over Radio Station CKOC during the radio hour, to a greater extent, if there is any part of the said hour unsold, and to a lesser one otherwise, without any charge." Herman and Mandel were designated as "artists taking part in the program as Singers, taking any part necessary on the program and shall act as musical directors of the programs whose duties it shall be to arrange and work out proper programs, subject to the approval of the other parties hereto. They shall also assist in obtaining business and sponsors for the radio program as much as possible." In recognition of the fierce competition in the radio hour business—Greenfield and Dubinsky were still operating—"NONE of the parties hereto may participate in any other Jewish radio hour or program in the city of Toronto, or in the city of Hamilton, or in the vicinity, not operated by the partnership, without the express and unanimous consent of all the parties hereto."

The *Kanader Nayes* clearly backed the Swerdlow show and not the others, morally if not financially (there was nothing in the contract). Anything seemed to be a good excuse for a story. A mere change in the time due to Hamilton's then-unique adoption of daylight saving time provoked a front page story complete with picture of Swerdlow.

> **Change in time of the Variety Radio Show**
> On account of the fact that in Hamilton this Sunday there will be a change in the time to Standard Time, the Variety Jewish Radio Hour will be heard this coming 2 Sundays from 6:30 to 7:30 in the evening, over station CKOC Hamilton. Very soon the variety show will present in episodes a life's picture under the name of *The Karps*, written by Samuel H. Cohn and directed by the noted showman Isaac Swerdlow.

However, before the year was out, the show had been relegated to the back pages and the last ad for it was on October 17, page 5, still with a picture of Max and the caption "Max Mandel today on the Jewish Radio Program."

> As always, also for today, Sunday, a rich program has been prepared, with the participation of Max Mandel, Lou Herman, the Herman sisters and Sherman Gan.

The Great Radio Show Debate

In January 1938, there were *three* Sunday Jewish radio hours being heard in Toronto. There was Greenfield's Jewish Hour on CKOC at 10:30, followed by the Variety Jewish Hour of Swerdlow–Mandel–Herman–Glick at 12:30 p.m., followed by Dubinsky at 3:00 p.m. on CKCL. What this meant was a fierce competition for sponsors, for listeners and for talent. And this led to an impassioned, no-holds-barred debate among the listeners about the relative and absolute quality of the shows, that, luckily for us, broke out in "The Readers Write" pages of the *Kanader Nayes*. It was kicked off on January 12, 1938 by a private op-ed article so scathing it could only be published with the editor's disclaimer **"Editorial Notice:** *The above article was printed in the name of free discussion."* The article was under the pen-name "אנכי" [*Anokhi*, Hebrew for "I"].

> **The Sad State of Jewish Radio**
> Radio has shown that, notwithstanding some of its negative sides, it has many positive ones. The peoples of the world have well understood how important it is to make use of the positive and unheard-of energy that radio possesses.
> With this wonder-instrument, one can now reach thousands and thousands of listeners, on an unlimited domain, exactly as in personal contact, and speak to them about whatever questions one wants. Through the medium of the radio, the words of the *goyim* penetrate

countless houses with the most edifying talks by the biggest experts, enlightenment on the best and most beautiful art. I once happened to hear a lecture on such a purely pedagogical subject as how to speak English correctly and to avoid the various incorrect words and expressions that have, with time, penetrated unnoticed into the English language.

There appears to be no such instrument as the radio to spread creative thought so far and wide, about whatever one wants. So it is doubly to be deplored that the field of radio is so badly cultivated with us Jews and that it is not thought worth making use of it in a way that serves Jewish potential. It is really a shame for ourselves and for the surrounding world that we have abandoned things to radio "specialists" who make the Jewish language and the Jewish word something to mock and laugh at.

Today's Jewish radio managers are irresponsible and uneducated people who have no inkling of Jewish culture or of art in general. They nurture the Jewish public with fairy tales and "jokes" which stick to the wall like a pea.[29]

We speak so much about the richness of the Yiddish language and about the great treasury of Yiddish literature. As for Jewish problems, the Jews of today are certainly not lacking in material. Why should we Jews neglect the mighty opportunity that radio provides to bring into every Jewish household everything that has a bearing on Jewish culture, enlightenment and knowledge in general, in a pure, cultured Yiddish language? Why should the Jewish home not benefit from our great artistic treasure, just because of the ignorance of the Jewish radio manager? Is the Jewish street really already resigned to this? Are we Jews agreed that such an important matter be left to incurably foolish people and those who want only that radio be a gold mine from which they can extract profits? Where is it written that the Jewish community must in fact put up with boors seeking honour at our expense on the Jewish radio? Something must be done to pull our community out of the dirt into which the Jewish radio "impresarios" have pushed it.

---

29 A folk expression meaning "of no lasting significance."

It's hard to conceive of a more blanket condemnation. You have to suppose that this was not an isolated viewpoint, given the decision to publish it. Certainly there were inklings of this sort of criticism in earlier discussions. Anokhi did not go unanswered, of course:

> **An Answer to the Radio Critic**
> . . . The article writer comes out with abusive words about the managers of the Jewish Radio Hours. He calls them: "irresponsible", "uneducated", "incurably foolish," "boors", and implores that something be done to bring a little culture and art into the Jewish home.
> Ask yourself a question: if the article writer has such an affinity for Jewish culture and art in general, why hasn't he found it necessary to talk about them before now instead of coming out with dirt which is not appropriate for such a culture preacher? Why, in fact, has he not turned to the managers and advised them on how to improve their programs?
> The article also says that the Jewish radio managers are aiming to extract profits. But would the writer be any more virtuous than this? Does he want that a person engaged in an undertaking that demands time and expense get completely nothing from it? The managers try to give the best that is possible. If we would help them with their programming instead of attacking them, in time we would have radio programs the equal of which would not exist on the whole American continent.
> Since the article writer has not given the advice he could to the radio managers directly, he has no right to come out with insults against them. In these circumstances, one wants to ask whether the article writer has something personal against the managers of the Jewish radio hours.
> With thanks,
> Z. Mandel

Although full of innuendo and *ad hominem*, the letter of Mr. Mandel (no relation) did not really address the substantive criticisms of Anokhi, which struck a chord with other listeners, one of whom raised the delicate issue of "what the goyim will say:"

A reader takes a word in the radio matter
Worthy editor of the *Kanader Nayes:*

I hope you will permit me to give my opinion about the article from Mr. Z. Mandel, "*An Answer to the radio critic.*" Mr. Mandel is far from correct with his objection against the writer of that article. And this is why:

Is it not true that the producers of the Jewish radio hours invite the Jewish audience to write to them on how they feel about the programs? If yes, so what's the noise? What makes Mr. Mandel so angry? Mr. Mandel brings up the question of profit. Is this really a puzzling question in these times? However, the key with which to solve it finds itself in the hands of the Yiddish speaking public. Only the Jewish listener can make the Jewish radio hour successful for the producer, and the "sponsors," too. Therefore, this public has a right to ask for nicer programs.

. . . Cheap and ignorant talent cheapen the Jewish radio hours. . . . Mr. Mandel says that the Jewish radio producer is doing the best under the circumstances. I categorically deny this. Does Mr. Mandel mean to say that Toronto does not have gifted Jewish talent that is looking to earn a couple of dollars? And, importantly, permit me to make another observation, that I want Mr. Mandel to take into account: Radio is one of the completely new discoveries that science has just created. Radio can be a blessing for humanity. However it may be, therefore, that those who possess a God-given talent are not forbidden to cultivate it with this apparatus, all others must remain outside the field.

Equally, it is also important to remember that we live among Christian neighbours who understand something about art. They probably hear from time to time what the "Jews" ["Jews" is simply transliterated and put in quotation marks as "דזשוס"] have contributed. Does Mr. Mandel think that we should be proud about what we have produced in the Jewish programmes?

Thus, "what the *goyim* will say" also has to be taken into account.
M. Landsman

This was followed by a letter from a Mr. Zelig, captioned "Reader answers two radio critics at once," which consisted mostly of a rambling summary of the debate so far, but finished with this:

And another thing. Mr. Landsman worries about "what the *goyim* will say." Let him ask himself a question, whether they have on their regular programs, other than the specials, better talent than, for example, Harry Harris, Khazan Stolnitz and his son, Mr. Barkin and so on? Let's hope that Mr. Anokhi will take that into account. Instead of attacking the producers of the Jewish Radio hours, he would do much better to advise them on how to improve their programs.
With respect,
M. L. Zelig

Landsman came back at Zelig with, among other things, an accusation of partisanship for naming some stars but not others.

What the goyim will say is also an issue
Worthy editor of the *Kanader Nayes*

I hope that once more you will give me this word to answer Mr. M.L. Zelig on his recent letter about me concerning the Jewish Radio Hour.

It seems to me that Mr. Zelig agrees with the objections from my last letter. It bothers him, however, that I am afraid of what the *goyim* will say.

I want to ask him if he truly thinks that a microphone or a radio is a *bimeh*[30] in a synagogue room in *Eyshishak* or in *Shnipeshak*[31] 50 years ago when a hoarse *bal tfileh*[32] stood davening a *shakharis*[33] or a *n'ila*?[34]

It's obvious that, in the old country, if the singing wasn't satisfactory, it remained within its own Jewish circle. Can he equate a microphone in the year 1938 with such a long ago parody? Can he equate our neighbours of today, among whom we are a minority, with the Russian "*muzhiks*"[35] of that time?

Consequently, in my opinion, for the sake of the Jewish community in general and the benefit of the producers in particular, the Jewish Radio Hour not only

---

30 Pulpit.
31 Invented *shtetl* names.
32 Leader of prayer.
33 Morning service.
34 Last part of the Day of Atonement services.
35 Peasants.

needs to have well qualified singers, but also requires that the manner of speaking into the microphone be pure and distinct, not drawled or mangled. Mr. Zelig asks further whether the people of the world have better ordinary programmes than the Jewish ones? Certainly—everybody knows what happened a short while ago when the actress Mae West did not give a good program. The newspapers stormed and protested until the broadcasting company apologized and announced later that this would never happen again.[36] Whether Zelig wishes it or not, "what the *goyim* will say" must absolutely be taken into account. Apart from this, we Jews also have a right to a good bit of music without having to apologize to the producers or the would-be talents.

With respect,
M. Landsman

Parallel developments in radio shed some light on this debate and suggest that, indeed, it had an element of a proxy battle to it. The kinds of criticisms that were being made were of course the sort that had been earlier made against Greenfield, and it was at this moment that Greenfield was making a push for dominance in the field that would drive out most of the competition. In early 1938 Greenfield started advertising not one, but *three* weekly shows all his own.

Beautiful Radio Program

This Sunday, from 7 to 7:45 evening, over CKOC Hamilton (1120 kilocycles) a beautiful Jewish radio program will be heard under the name of *A Khasidic Rhapsody*. Taking part, Sam Silver, pianist; Jack Barkin, baritone; Sam Stolnitz, baritone; S. M. Greenfield manager and announcer. Also Alexander Brown with important Jewish events from the week. Other Jewish programs over CKOC Shabbes night from 6:15 to 6:45 and Thursday evening from 6:30 to 7.

---

36 Mae West's appearance on ventriloquist Edgar Bergen's radio show, *The Chase and Sanborn Hour*, on December 12, 1937, was considered so scandalously full of sexual innuendo that it was condemned by the Federal Communications Commission, and West was banned from NBC and radio for more than a decade afterwards.

One important addition was Harry Harris in the role of producer of one of the programs. This was the launch of Harris's durable radio career.

March 6, 1938 seems to have been the last edition of the Swerdlow–Herman–Mandel–Glick Jewish variety hour on CKOC. Within a month, Greenfield had gobbled up the coveted 12:30 Sunday slot, as well as former Dubinsky sponsor Toronto Tire and Radio Sales Co. Max seems to have gone back with Dubinsky who carried on CKCL through to the end of 1938 and whose "radio artists" were reported to have appeared at an Apter Women's Association benefit after the Variety Hour went off the air. The evening raised $489 and seems to have been the first of many of Max's fund-raising concerts for his old *shtetl*, whose worst disasters lay not far ahead.

CHAPTER 5

War Years

THE YEAR 1938 WAS A VERY BAD ONE for Europe, but much worse for European Jewry. The Nazis took over Austria in March and immediately set about persecuting Austrian Jews the way they had been persecuting German Jews. A big international conference at Evian, France in July on relief for Jewish refugees from Germany and Austria was a big failure, in the sense that none of the major powers showed any willingness to accept significant numbers—even though Hitler had declared himself happy to be rid of "these criminals." In September, Italian Jews were subjected to an Italian version of the German Nuremberg decrees. In October, German troops were allowed to march into Czechoslovakia and annex the Sudetenland, leading to another flight of Jews. In November, came Germany's *Kristallnacht*, the "Night of Broken Glass," when, using the assassination of a Nazi diplomat in Paris by a Jew as a pretext, an officially authorized pogrom left Jewish homes, businesses and synagogues ransacked and destroyed. Ninety-one Jews were reported murdered and 30,000 Jewish men were taken to concentration camps where they were tortured and more than 1,000 murdered. More than 1,500 synagogues were vandalized and hundreds set on fire. The *Kanader Nayes*'s front pages spread the call for mass protests: "Congress and Workers Committee call Maple Leaf Arena protest meeting against Nazi decrees. Rabbis declare fast." Maple Leaf Gardens was filled to overflowing with 17,000 protesters.

The *Kanader Nayes* also carried on their war with communists, both international and local. The Moscow show trials, with their prominent representation of Jewish defendants, were relentlessly attacked by the paper. An editorial of March 9 on the question of whether the confessions of the accused could be believed, started with a critique of Canadian justice itself: "If in a free land, as ours where the law forbids not only forced confessions but where every police agent is duty-bound to warn an arrested person that everything they say can be used against them—even here—there can be forced self-incrimination, what then can happen in a land like Stalin's Russia, where violence and power have replaced law and justice?" The front page of March 13 announced an exposé by ex-Communist Party of Canada chair Maurice Spector: "Are the founders of the Soviet state guilty? Have the leaders of the Russian revolution transformed themselves into fascist spies? Mr. Spector will answer these questions in his talk, which will uncover the true facts about Stalin's savage blood purge." On March 20, page 1 announced a Massey Hall speech by former Russian Premier Alexander Kerensky, who had been ousted by Lenin and the Bolsheviks, and would speak on the Moscow trials and the "Trotskyist blood purges" in his lecture "On Behalf of Democracy." When a reader objected to the equation of Hitler and Stalin in the paper ("Please do not send me your paper anymore. When you equate Hitler and Stalin, I have nothing to read in your paper"), the editors' answer was full of sarcasm:

> Of course we will accommodate our sensitive friend and we will no longer send him our *bletl*.[1] Presumably, our friend is not one of the Great *Tovarish*'s orthodox followers, nor a reader of the Communist press, which has always called for a boycott of us. We must turn to all the anti-Stalinist Jews—and they are, *barukh hashem*,[2]

---

1 Little sheet.
2 "Blessed be the name." Traditional good-luck greeting/incantation of the orthodox Jew.

not a few—that they should come and help us get around the Stalinist boycott, if they believe in an unafraid press, even if it is, as the Stalinists call it, a *bletl*.[3]

As for the local communists, the *Kanader Nayes* carried on a running battle with them, too. After another blistering anti-communist year-end municipal election campaign by the paper in 1938, the editors decided to take a little credit for the heavy losses of communists Buck and Salsberg: "Mrs. Dworkin's *shmatte*[4] helps wipe out communists." On the other hand, Mrs. Dworkin continued to sell tours to the "Soviet Union," right up to the eve of the war, even if she no longer conducted them personally.[5]

As conditions got worse in Eastern Europe—during 1938 anti-Semitic riots broke out in Poland as well—Mrs. Dworkin's ads for food and clothing became increasingly desperate:

> The Cold has already shown itself in Russia and Poland!
> Your poor relatives have, therefore, a new addition to their sorrows.
> While you think about buying warm clothes, underwear and shoes for yourself or for your household, think also about them there.
> Remember that cold is a frightening companion to hunger and need!
> If your relatives live in Russia, you can, through us, send them new clothes, underwear, shoes and other things —if they live in Poland, you can send them packages of old clothes, shoes and underwear.
> D. Dworkin & Co.
> *Ship's cartons for all seas, money sent to all lands, radio licenses—"citizen papers."*

Things were looking bad in Palestine as well: "70 dead, more than 200 wounded in Land of Israel terror in a week"—"25 Jews

---

3 *KN*, August, 24, 1938, page 4.
4 "Rag." *KN*, January 4, 1939, p. 2 editorial.
5 *KN*, June 14, 1939, p. 4.

felled in Israel terror in 8 days. 43 Arabs dead from Haifa bomb explosion"—"20 dead, 74 wounded by bomb explosion in Jaffa"—"200 Arab terrorists dead in battles with British military"—"British Army takes Beth Lekhem, 11 terrorists killed."

With all the bloodshed, the paper now turned its face firmly against Jewish terrorism, even in retaliation:

> Terror is immoral and impractical.
> . . . [T]he only merit that the aggressive tactic can have is to give notice to an unworthy world that Jews are not sissies and, when necessary, are not afraid to strike back. Neither the Arabs nor, indeed, the Jews lack understanding of this. Both know that the Jewish pioneers are ready to give their lives for their right to the Land of Israel. . . . [T]he policy of revenge that the young people's groups are carrying out against the Arabs must immediately come to an end, and must once again concentrate only on defence. This will not only spare a lot of innocent Jewish lives, but also a lot of innocent Arab lives. No intelligent and just person can claim that every Arab is responsible for the vandalism and murder committed by the Arab terrorists. Every person of sense knows that the greater part of the Land of Israel's Arabs would want to live in peace with the Jews if the fanatical leaders would only let them. [6]

There was also a lot of worry over the British government's approval of the "White Paper" in early 1939 that tilted it steeply to the Arab side and, most importantly, severely limited Jewish immigration and curtailed the right of Jews to buy land ("Canadian Zionists Appeal to England against the New Decrees of the Colonial Office").[7] However, there were plenty of Zionist bright spots as well. There were successful fund-raising campaigns for the United Palestine Appeal and for the Youth Aliyah, the latter promoted by

---

6 *KN,* July 10, 1938, p. 2.
7 *KN,* July 23, 1938, p. 3.

a boxing match in Maple Leaf Gardens in February 1939 between two Jewish boxers, Sam Luftspring and Baby Yak, who had both famously boycotted the Berlin Olympics in 1936. Every year brought a Herzl *yortsayt* to be celebrated in an editorial such as "The Great Herzl" in which he was called "the modern Moses." "Comrade" Golda Mayerson returned for a "masterful talk" that held the audience in the Bellevue Theatre "as if magnetized by her wonderful descriptions of the life of the Jews in Israel."

Amid all of this political turmoil, of course, Canadian Jews got on with their lives and that included entertainment. In fact, the years 1938 and 1939 saw an incredible array of Yiddish cultural expression. This wasn't the calm before the storm; it was more like a riotous exuberance of fireworks before the darkness. Yiddish movies were coming on screen at breakneck speed. Moyshe Oysher's *Green Fields* and *The Cantor's Son* played, as well as the Polish productions *Al Khet* ("For the Sin") and *The Dybbuk*. American theatre star Jennie Goldstein made her movie debut in *Two Sisters*, alongside the sensational comic Michael Rosenberg.8 Two anti-Nazi films were promoted in the *Kanader Nayes*, *Professor Mamlock* and *I Was a Captive of Nazi Germany*, the latter a dramatization of the 1934 adventures of Isobel Lillian Steele, enacted by Miss Steele and an anonymous cast, with Ms. Steele on hand to present the movie in Toronto.

There were Yiddish concerts by such international stars as Sidor Belarsky, Leah Deganit, and Esther Field. There were "wunderkind" cantorial concerts (Khazan Avramele, the eleven-year-old Czech *khasendl*) and recording artist cantorial concerts, for instance by New York's Leibele Waldman who performed the davening-concert

---

8 Rosenberg's hilarious mock cantor audition of alter ego Shepsil Kanarek can be seen on YouTube.

routine at the Henry Street shul on shabbes morning followed by a concert at the Strand in the evening of folk songs, classics and cantorial compositions.[9] There were classical, but still Jewish, concerts. Jewish, pop singer turned operatic tenor Jan Peerce sang at Massey Hall in February, 1938, fresh from his Carnegie Hall debut under Toscanini. Also on hand was "Jewish violin virtuoso" Ephrem Zimbalist.

But above all there was theatre. Among many offerings was the politically virtuous *Pins and Needles*, put on at the Royal Alexandra Theatre by amateur players from the International Ladies Garment Workers Union. And Maurice Schwartz brought his Art Theatre (*sans* Isaac Swerdlow) to the Victoria Theatre in March 1938 to play *The Brothers Ashkenazi*. This was followed in May by *Semele's Bar Mitzvah* starring Herman Yablokov, Bella Meisel, Max Vilner and Max Kletter, with music by Ilya Trilling. The Victoria Theatre, located at Richmond and Victoria Streets (now graced by a parking lot), also hosted *Di Yidishe Bande* ("The Jewish Gang") from Poland performing in "the World Reels" along with Menashe Oppenheim and Lily Liliana, and an orchestra directed by Sholom Secunda. The rubber-bodied sad sack Menashe Skulnick played there in *Chaim Shaia Becomes a Father*. The Jewish Art Theatre from New York came back in April 1939 with Jacob Ben Ami, and Samuel Goldenberg performed in Leivick's *Who is Who*, and the Yiddish version of Clifford Odets' Depression drama *Awake and Sing*. Leivick himself came to the Strand to give a talk about the Land of Israel. "Red" Emma Goldman, newly returned from Spain, gave a series of lectures in the Labour Lyceum on the Civil War, which officially ended in February 1939. She would die in Toronto in May, 1940.

---

9 *KN*, January 16, 1939, p. 4

One innovation was an ambitious theatre season put on by Moyshe Shapiro and Isaac Swerdlow, who was now free of his Jewish Variety Radio Show duties. They had taken over the Spadina Concert Hall at 450 Spadina, one of those smaller theatre venues north on Spadina that had contributed to the Standard's demise. It occupied the old building still standing a few doors south of the famed El Mocambo Tavern. They booked Benny Adler and a troupe for a run of several months that included an astonishing number of different productions. Between October 15, 1938 and March 19, 1939 they put on, at my count, at least twenty-nine different productions, demonstrating, beyond doubt the indispensability of *repetiteurs* like Shapiro. In a lecture on the history of Yiddish theatre in 1979, Isaac Swerdlow's son Sydney attributed the number of plays to the small Jewish population from which the theatre-going audience was derived: "Here in Toronto, in the late 1930s, we used to play two new shows a week and a Sunday concert. Now, I wonder if you can appreciate the amount of work that is involved to put on a new show. How then can you keep the standard of quality and also quantity? The run started off with *The Road to Happiness*, a "joyful operetta with 15 song numbers, with a chorus of beautiful girls" starring Benny Adler and a mixture of imported and local talent: Celia Pearson, Isaac Swerdlow, Morris Bleiman, Florence Feinstein, Eleanor Kremer, Adele Swerdlow, Sidney Shaw, Hymie Feinstein and Sam Kravitz. Other productions included such titles as *Two Mothers-in-law, Homesick Souls, The Polish Wedding, Mirror of Life, Why Women Get Divorced, Lost Worlds, His Repentance, Song of Songs, A Man Without a Home* and ending, early in 1939 with *The Jew in Danger*.

The Spadina Concert Hall was really a scene for Yiddish theatre.

It followed Adler's long run with multiple productions starring Michael Michalesko (*His Great Love*), Misha and Lucy Gherman (*Women Who Men Forget*), Nelly Casman (*The Old Maid*), Sally Josephson (*The Happy Songstress*), and so on. But there were other venues as well.

As for radio, Greenfield's conquest was complete but short-lived. Dubinsky's show was gone by the end of 1938 and Greenfield was the only one left standing. By April 1939 he had expanded to four shows weekly, three on CKOC and one on the St. Catharines station CKTB. However, it wasn't long before challengers began to emerge. In May 1939, thanks to a Hamilton benefactor, Greenfield's star producer and performer, Harry Harris, was given his own show on CHML. According to a brief unpublished autobiography, Harris was then working for Greenfield for less than $6 a week. Harris' new show aired at 10:00 A.M. Sunday, in almost direct competition with Greenfield's 12:30 slot on CKOC—the old Swerdlow–Herman–Mandel–Glick time slot. Neither of the shows were affiliated with, or even supported by the *Kanader Nayes*. In fact, during the summer of 1939, the *Kanader Nayes* was preparing a new radio program which was to hit the airwaves on Rosh Hashana, but it did not say with whom or on what station: "For the holidays, the *Kanader Nayes* has prepared a few interesting radio hours. Professional people are now working on the preparation of a program, which will be aesthetically and spiritually appropriate for the time and the circumstances." The program never came off because, on August 23 everything changed, forever.

The Outbreak of War

There had been much sabre rattling and war preparation

throughout the year, and a lot of it played out on the front pages of the *Kanader Nayes*: "1,200,000 gas masks for British children; government calls for preparation of food"—"England takes up in earnest the organization of an anti-Hitler front"—"England is united and prepared for war, a warning to the Nazis." But what changed a tense and fearful mood to real despair was the Hitler-Stalin non-aggression pact, announced like a thunder-clap in the banner headline of August 23: "DEMOCRATIC WORLD SHATTERED BY STALIN-HITLER PACT." The *Kanader Nayes* editorial of August 27 makes chilling reading in light of what we know now as historical fact. These Jews, at least, were under no illusions as to what was at stake:

> **The Terrifying News**
> As we write these lines—Thursday evening—the radio has broken the news that Von Ribbentrop, the Nazi Foreign Minister who arrived in Moscow on an airplane, has already signed the "non-aggression pact" with Stalin. This means that the last preparations have already been made so that the curtain will soon rise on the bloody drama, which must now be played. Hitler's obedient troops are already on the border of Poland and wait only for the order of the MURDERER OF BERCHTESGADEN .... What will now become of the unhappy European Jews, especially the three and a half million Polish Jews?
>
> And we're not talking about Jewish nationalism or indeed chauvinism. When the world gets drunk with its own blood, all barriers between classes and races disappear. Today's military science has made "wonderful advances." Today, with one blast in one minute, you can kill as many people as you needed a week to do years ago. The cities and anything in the way of the campaigning military animal men will suffer terribly ....
>
> But, apart from the general catastrophe, the three and a half million Polish Jews will be afflicted with specific Jewish humiliations of which their Christian fellow countrymen will not know. Our elders remember what the unlucky Jews of Latvia and Lithuania suffered under the cruel Nicolai Nicolayevich in the last World War ...

More terrorized yet will be the Jews in the cities and towns who have the misfortune to fall into the hands of the Nazi storm-troopers. We know already how Hitler has dealt with his Jews in "times of peace," the way he has behaved himself with the Jews when his military triumphantly marched into Austria. There is no secret for anyone as to how the Nazi brigades deal with the Jews of Czechoslovakia—Hitler's protectorate. What then can the impoverished Polish Jews expect from the bands of German murderers when these bands are wild with the madness of war, with looting and plunder?

The outpouring of venom for the communists was unrestrained. Prof. Golecki, wrote on the same page, mockingly: "Stalin and Hitler in a United Front." Before long, the paper would refer to them, following *Time* magazine, as "Communazis."[10] In the next issue, with the headline "World Peace in the Balance," the page 2 editorial demanded the resignation of all communists from positions of authority in the labour movement:

> **Communist leaders must resign**
> ... As for the Stalinist "chinovniks,"[11] whether in the Labour League or in the unions, we must make it clear to these good men that we are in the middle of the eve of a bloody war that puts in danger the lives of millions of Jews and even more millions of other people, and that this unhealthy situation that currently torments people and their families is by act of their leader Stalin. And, further, we must make it clear that in such a tense time there can be no question about their continuing leadership. They must either immediately publicly dissociate themselves from the vile murderer-traitor of the Kremlin or they must immediately resign from their offices.[12]

When, at the end of the year, J.B. Salsberg had the temerity to run for

---

10 "Communazis make friends with Duplessis," *KN*, November 12, 1939, p. 2; "Peace, peace, call out Communazis" *KN*, November 19, 1939, p.2.
11 Russian state officials with various ranks during Tzarist times.
12 *KN*, August 30 1939, p. 2.

alderman again under the communist banner, the paper announced the news on the front page in the form of a death announcement with heavy black borders and the traditional death-notice heading "Sad News:"

> As we were going to press we learned that J.B. Salsberg has announced his candidacy for alderman of Ward 4 in the current elections. For Canadian Jews this is a threefold sad announcement: as British subjects we are enemies of each and every one who supports Hitler in this war; as downtrodden people we despise each and every one who endorses Stalin's violence against Polish independence; and as Jews we are enraged and shocked by Stalin, whose united front with Hitler has only strengthened Hitler's murderous power over the unhappy German, Austrian and Czechoslovakian Jews, and which has now newly oppressed three and a half million Polish Jews . . .
>
> Every Jew who votes for the Communist candidate or helps them in anything with their campaign, is, consciously or unconsciously, a terrible anti-Semite and Hitlerist.
>
> Jewish organizations must not let any Communist candidate in to speak at their meetings. Their British citizenship and their Jewishness forbid them. [13]

Naturally the paper pulled out all the stops for the annual municipal elections. A front page headline of December 31, 1939 read: "Don't Vote for Communists" and gave seventeen numbered reasons. The editorial on page 2, "The eyes of the land are on the Jews," underlined the importance of demonstrating patriotism at the polls:

> The eyes of the Canadian people, who are in a life and death struggle with dictators, are directed at the Jewish poll booths of Ward 4 and Ward 5. From the voting stations they will judge the loyalty of the Jewish citizens. . .

---

13 *KN*, December 17, p.1.

Not surprisingly, the communists were trounced in the elections, and the party was legally banned in May of the following year.

The Germans launched the war just nine days after the Hitler–Stalin pact with an attack on Poland on September 1. It didn't take long for the blood-curdling news to get out. In the first issue after war was declared, September 6 (the day the Nazis arrived in Apt), H. M. Kirschenbaum of the paper, and secretary of the Ontario chapter of the Canadian Association of Polish Jews, wrote "A Call to Toronto Jewry" addressed to "Toronto Jews, representatives of schools, societies, associations, unions, benefit societies and all who are interested in the existence of the Jewish people":

> With fire and sword, the Polish Jews are now being robbed, murdered and expelled from their homes. Never in the history of the Jewish people have enemies tried thus to exterminate the Jewish people as today. In just a few hours, the Hitlerites, the modern Hamans, have laid waste to the greatest Jewish communities in Poland.
> Nearly four million Jews in Poland alone are in danger every hour of fire and sword.
> At this dire moment, words are not enough to express the pain which has filled Jewish hearts from all over the world, who feel their agony personally, yet are powerless to help.
> Polish Jews have already gone through diverse epochs of terror and struggle since the day Poland became independent. But no era in history has so severely affected the existence of Polish Jewry as this bloody war.
> Our sisters and brothers, fighting back on battlefields, holding their positions, are being bombarded and killed daily.
> The Canada Polish Association is sending out a fiery call to all representatives of Toronto Jewry, to all presidents, vice-presidents, secretaries of all Toronto Jewish organizations and institutions to come to a conference Thursday the 8th of September in Radomer Hall, 210 Beverley Street, 8 P.M., to formulate plans on how to help Polish Jewry.

> We do not believe that the Jews of Toronto can watch indifferently as their brothers and relatives sink under, or that the local Jews will not unite and organize to fashion rapid assistance for our brothers and sisters who are suffering so terribly.
>
> May the conference be one of the biggest in the history of Toronto, and may it serve as an example of self-sacrifice for the unfortunate.
>
> May no representative of Toronto Jewry be absent from the conference Thursday night.

The war went very badly in the first year, with Hitler's armies going from success to success. The conquest of Poland was complete by October 6, 1939, with the country divided up about equally between Germany and Russia. In rapid succession, starting in April 1940, Germany conquered Denmark, Norway, Holland, Belgium, Luxembourg and France. The "Battle of Britain," the merciless Nazi bombing attack, threatened England with invasion throughout the summer and fall of 1940. Germany's Italian and Vichy allies were less successful in North Africa and the Middle East, but war raged there and even reached Palestine.

The *Kanader Nayes* faithfully reported all the important events of the war, of course, but it also highlighted the Jewish angle where possible: "Jewish quarter in London suffers from air attacks"—"112 Killed in Tel Aviv from Italian air attack"—"Jewish flyer, first Canadian Jew to be awarded a medal, lost." From the beginning the paper extolled the enlistment of Jews in the armed forces, backing the call of the Canadian Jewish Congress: "1,400 Toronto Jewish young people volunteer to join the military"—"David Croll, ex-Ontario Jewish Minister of Welfare enlists in the Army"—"Maurice Goldstick has enlisted in the reserves"—"20,000 Jews from the Land of Israel serve in British Military."

„היטלער װאלט
געהאט א הנאה
צו זען װי שײן דו
קוקסט אויס"

„יא, דו ביסט שײן ... אבער ביסט דו עם טאקע? איך
האב געמײנט, אז איך בין אויך געװען שײן, צוריק אין די
צװאנציגער, דאן איז געקומען דער קריזיס און האט מיר גוט
אנגעלערענט!"

„מיר װאלטען זיין פיל שענער אן קלײנער א י.ב מיר
װאלטען אויסגעגעבען װיגציגער געלט אויף אונזער אייגענער
אייסשטאטונג. און מער אויף דער אויסשטאטונג פון די
יונגעלייט, װאס באשיצען אונז. װי אזױ? דורך טאן זיך
א נאר אויסצוקומען אן א סך זאבען, כדי זיי זאלען האבען
פארפול אויף אליץ, װאס זיי האבען נויטיג!"

„װילסט דו דאך, אז זיי זאלען געװינען, א יא? אויב
אזוי, דאן קויף זשע װאר סײוױנג סטעמפס יעדע װאך ...
אזוי ארום קענסטו זיי העלפען. אבער א חוץ דעם, העלפסטו
דורך שפארען, צו האלטען די פרייזען נידעריג, און דערצו נאך
גרויסטו עפעס צו אויף אן עת צרה. לאמיר זיין באמת שײן
און קלוג!"

קורפס ווער סײװינג סטעמפס פון בעגק, פאסט
אפיסעס, דראגיסטען, גראסעריס און
אנדערע רמייל סטארס.

נעשאנעל וואר פינאנס קאמיטי

שפארען
הײסט
דינען

Like the other papers, the *Kanader Nayes*'s pages were full of ads for war bonds, the Red Cross and enlistment ads—only in Yiddish. For instance, a July 12, 1942 ad appealed to women to be less vain and buy more war savings stamps. The cartoon shows a mother standing over her daughter who is admiring herself in the mirror:

> **Hitler would get pleasure from seeing how beautiful you look**
>
> Yes, you are beautiful... but are you really beautiful? I mean, that I also used to be beautiful, back in the Twenties. Then came the crisis and it taught me well.
>
> We would be a lot more beautiful and smarter, too, if we would spend less money on our own equipment and more on the equipment of the young people who protect us. How so? By taking a vow to do without a lot of things so that they have plenty of everything that they lack!
>
> You want them to win, yes? If so, then buy war savings stamps every week.... That's how you can help them, but, apart from them, you help, by saving, to keep prices low and, moreover, in this way, to put something away for an emergency. Let's be really beautiful and smart!
>
> Buy war savings stamps from banks, post offices, druggists, grocers and other retail stores.
> National War Finance Committee
> Saving is Gaining

Or the ad by the Department of National War Services urging Canadians to save their fat and bones to make bombs: "Canada needs 40 million pounds of fat for exploding material. Here is your secret weapon. Save fats and bones and help smash the Axis." An accompanying cartoon shows "Adolph, Benito and Tojo" being bombed by the drippings of frying pans: "Out of the frying pan and into the line of fire."

Relief Efforts

Within a year of the war's start, desperation had set in about the situation of the Jews in the Nazi ghettoes of Poland and what, if anything, could be done to help them.

> **The Jews in Poland**
> The English press has recently been dedicating a lot of space to describing the sad situation of the Poles under Hitler's murderer bands in Poland. So, how then do we imagine the Polish Jews are now faring in Poland?.... We already have, more or less the general outlines of the situation under which our brothers and sisters live there. The Jewish press disseminated articles by people who have escaped from those places. In the September-October issue of the authoritative *"Contemporary Jewish Record"* there is an article by Abraham Weiss, who was in Warsaw until April 1940. He was also there during the siege. One shudders to read about the horrors that the barbarians are committing in this unfortunate city.
> The saddest evidence is that, despite their own situation under the Nazi tyranny, one even finds Poles who betray Jews to the Nazis, and this even worsens the terrible conditions of the unfortunate Jews of that unfortunate land. The writer recounts, among other things, how, if the Nazis distribute food, it is understood that the Jews are not allowed in the queues of the "lucky." Often, when the horrible hunger has driven a starving Jew to risk his life and enter the line, the Polish patriots have immediately denounced him to the "good-hearted" Nazi bread-giver.
> How our unfortunate sisters and brothers will be able to face another winter, without food, clothing or heating is hard to imagine. If we can do anything for them, we must do it as quickly as possible.[14]

But what could they do to help? A United Relief Committee was formed for Jewish War victims with a mass aid assembly in Massey Hall: "Not one Jew in the city is allowed to miss this assembly, which will be the first large demonstration by Toronto Jews against the great misfortune that has befallen our brothers in Poland." But

---

14 *KN*, November 3, 1940, p. 2.

most of this was, of necessity, directed to those who had escaped the Nazis, as was the campaign to donate clothes to Polish Jews who had escaped Poland to Lithuania at the beginning of the war, or Mrs. Dworkin's exhortations at the same time to people to send money to their relatives while there was still time through her shipping office to those parts of Poland and Eastern Europe under Russian control. At Passover, there was a food campaign for refugees who had made it to England, "Matza and meat for refugees." The paper asked Canadian Jews to open their homes to the refugee children from England during the Blitz, and it pleaded for immediate government help for refugees who sought to settle in Canada: "Will Canada open its doors?"[15]

From the very beginning of the war, the *Kanader Nayes* hammered away at the Zionist solution.

> **Help for the European Jews**
> The American and Canadian Jews are beginning to understand the colossal responsibility that circumstances have laid upon them in the current times. No other part of the Jewish people finds itself in such a favourable condition as the Jews who live on the American continent. Completely free politically, in a relatively good condition economically, the Jews here are today the most fortunate of their race. On the other hand, the East European and German Jews are the most unfortunate creatures of the world. Not only do they suffer equally with all other citizens from the chaos of war, from the spilling of blood and from the pillage that the Hitler–Stalin partnership has brought to their land, they also suffer from the distinct decrees that apply only to them as Jews. Nobody here knows yet accurately what has happened there in the land of grief and lamentation. Nobody yet knows the precise number of our unfortunate brothers who have fallen as victims of the Hitler–Stalin common front. We don't even know in what state the "fortunate" ones who remain alive now find themselves. . . .

---

15 *KN*, July 14, 1940, page 2.

It is truly good that our Toronto Welfare fund has pledged to contribute $80,000 to support European Jews
. . . We must not think only about provisional supplies, clothing and housing the poor people, we must at the same time think of solving great root problems, by emigration. We have on this same field now a wonderful opportunity to send thousands of Jews from Poland, Germany and Czechoslovakia, to the Land of Israel. Thanks to the war, the White Paper with its limits on immigration has become practically annulled. If we only had the necessary capital we could now do wonders in a relatively short time.
. . . The time is an extraordinary fluid one and nobody can say for sure how long it will last. It is not only a question now of creating an immediate place of repose for the persecuted in Europe, nor are we only dealing with the question of fashioning the Land of Israel into a Jewish land for generation after generation. The point is that as soon as we Jews succeed in bringing to the land of Israel a half a million Jews, just as quickly will all the hardship there disappear and the problems with the Arabs completely fall away.[16]

A big ad on April 21, 1940 read:

SUPPORT THE UNITED PALESTINE APPEAL!
How much will your contribution be?
The contribution of your
synagogue and organization?
Our answer is:
The number of Jews, your sisters and brothers, who you want to rescue from the Hitler hell in Europe and bring over to the Land of Israel.
That must be the measure for your donation to the current Land of Israel campaign in Toronto.

Nor did the paper scorn the traditional ways of confronting martyrdom. It published prayers (*"A special prayer for the victory of*

---

16 *KN* editorial, October 15, 1939, p. 2.

the kingdom of Britannia: Avinu malkenu!...[17]*)* and supported public religious mourning services, some in venues that had seen happier events, for example a Yiskor evening in the Strand Theatre: "All Jews know the fate of our sisters and brothers in Europe where Jewish life and possessions are arbitrary, and men, women and children are mercilessly tortured. The old ghetto wall has been put up around the Jews in Warsaw. In the more than 300 Polish cities and towns hunger and hardship rule. Tens of thousands of Jews have already been killed by Nazi hands" . . . .[18]

For those Toronto Jews from the *shtetls* under Nazi control, what more could they do? They could only hope and prepare for a time when they could do something. Apt was typical:

> **A call to all Apter landslayt**
> The time has come for us to do something for our sisters and brothers of our town Apt. . . . As soon as Hitler, may his name be erased, with his gang, are defeated, we must be ready with a great sum of money to help build up the ruin that Hitler's gangs have made. We must also help restore the spiritual and physical life of our suffering countrymen.
>
> Therefore, we, a group of Apter, have conferred and have decided to call a mass meeting of all Apter *landslayt*, young and old, to work out a plan for a big assistance action of a historical scope.
>
> Sisters and brothers, *landslayt*!
>
> The call of the suffering and exhausted is coming to us. We in Toronto must answer the call. We are a fortunate people to live on the American continent. We should kiss the earth every day when we go out in the street. Let us, therefore, know how to value our fortunate situation. Each of us must decide for himself that he should make a war contribution for our suffering war victims—our own blood and flesh. The time has passed when one could be indifferent and stay detached. Now, each and every

---

17 *KN*, September 8, 1940, p.1.
18 *KN*, December 15, 1940, p. 3.

one must volunteer in this important work. Who remains detached in such a bitter time commits a crime.

Calling you to this urgent work are your mothers and fathers, your sisters and brothers, your grandfathers and grandmothers, cousins and simply *landslayt*, who cry out in one voice: "Save us!" We are sure that you hear all of these cries of sadness and that you feel their pain.

Take up the call of the provisional committee, which calls you to the mass meeting to take place Sunday, the 17th December, *Parshat Vayihi*,[19] 6 o'clock in the evening in Radomer Hall, 210 Beverley Street.
Provisional Committee of Apter Landslayt

It was clear that the only real rescue would come from winning the war. So, very early on in the war, the *Kanader Nayes* withdrew its long-standing support for the CCF on account of the party's perceived pacifism and its initial equivocation about sending troops to fight in Europe. In September 1939, the CCF National Council voted 13–9 to support the government's declaration of war, though in the House of Commons, only one CCF MP, party leader J.S. Woodsworth, spoke and voted against the war.[20] In the federal elections of March 1940, the *Kanader Nayes* backed the ruling Liberals strongly: "The freedom of the Canadian people lies in the balance. See that Canada's war effort is united . . . . Forward with Mackenzie King." The paper went all out for the local incumbent, the only Jewish candidate this time around, Sam Factor: "Don't gladden Hitler, vote Factor." On election day, they had a *double page* advertisement with Factor's photo:

> Today is judgment day!
> Jews of Spadina riding
> Do your duty as free citizens in a free land. Do not

---

19 This is the portion of the Torah to be read in synagogue that week, a traditional religious way of designating a week.
20 "CCF should not be supported," *KN*, February 4, page 2.

> fail to vote!
> Send back to Parliament the only
> Jewish tribune of Ontario

Factor and the Liberals won by a landslide.[21]

Life Goes On

When we think of the early war years, we find it hard to think of anything but the Holocaust. Nor was it ever absent from the minds of the Jews outside of Europe during this time. But people have a way of coping with the worst personal tragedies. What cannot fail to strike you from reading the *Kanader Nayes* of this period, a Jewish newspaper as devoted to its people as any you could find, is that, after doing whatever little they could for the Jews of Europe, the Jews of Toronto got on with their lives. That meant not only making a living and fighting for their rights, but also entertaining themselves—which, of course, was the way the entertainers made their living. On the same pages as you have the *yiskor* evenings and the bombings and the desperate pleas, you also have the entertainment news. Would we have been any different? Look at any news broadcast of today, or any Israeli newspaper for that matter, or the *Canadian Jewish News*—one minute, or one page, tragedy, the next, what's on at the movies. Certainly, the scale of the Holocaust was exponentially worse than anything before or since, but so was the response of Canadian Jews before they got on with their lives. Such is life! It's only surprising when we look at it from a distance.

---

21 Just before the war was over, Factor was appointed a federal judge of the County Court, reported to be highest judicial office ever reached by a Jew to that time: *KN* April 1, 1945, p.1. Bora Laskin became Chief Justice of Canada in 1973. In 2011, four of the nine judges of the Supreme Court of Canada were Jews.

There were lots of Yiddish movies on offer during the first years of the war, all made in the great creative outburst before it started. The College Playhouse had *Tkiyes Kaf* ("Handshake Agreement") released in Poland in 1937; *The Mare* (US, 1939) and *Mirele Efres* (US, 1939). Moyshe Oysher was represented by *The Little Maestro of Vilna*, (in English, "Overture to Glory") (US, 1940). Also showing were *A Brivele der mamen* ("A Letter to Mother") (Poland, 1939), *Tevye the Milkman* (US, 1939) with Morris Schwartz, and *The American Matchmaker* with Leo Fuchs (US, 1940).

Real life Toronto matchmakers were busy finding nice Jewish girls for nice Jewish boys. A perennial advertiser in the *Kanader Nayes* was Morris Melamed, manager of Toronto Matchmakers Bureau, at 66 Spadina Street. This was the same Morris Melamed who owned Ontario Dry Goods and Dresses at 374 Spadina.[22] His ad, with his picture in profile read this way:

> Morris Melamed
> I make matches
> I often have boys and girls as well as men and ladies who
> seek acquaintance for the purpose of matrimony.
> If you are interested in this opportunity consult with me.
> Strictly confidential.

Besides movies, live theatre and concerts also abounded in the early war years. If anything, the war meant that more American stars came to Toronto more often because their previously frequent European tours had been completely cut off. The Victoria Theatre at Victoria and Richmond continued to be a popular venue. Maurice Schwartz brought his ensemble there in *If I were Rothschild*. Menashe Skulnick brought three shows there from New York: *Mazel Tov*

---

22 Where he was pictured with his daughters in Rosemary Donegan and Rick Salutin's *Spadina Avenue* (Toronto: Douglas & McIntyre, 1985), p. 152.

Rabbi, Lazar Eli Comes to America and *Little Goldie, the Baker's Daughter*, with music by Ilya Trilling, starring Skulnick, heart-throb Herman Yablokov and his wife Bella Meisel. This was followed by Olshanetsky's *Yossel the Musician* starring Michael Michalesko and "an international cast." In May 1941, with the Battle of Britain raging, the prodigious Aaron Lebedeff brought a New York cast to play in the musical comedy *Yoshke Becomes a Groom*, with music by Herman Wohl.

The Spadina Concert Hall had another full season for 1940–41, this time with more variety, opening with a "New York troupe" led by Sadie Sheingold, Sam Auerbach and David Popper, and including in the local talent none other than Isaac Swerdlow. In the classic repertory mode, they played a rapid succession of musical comedies, with titles such as *Mother's Eyes, A Heart that Longs, In a World of Sin, Sadie, Where are you Meddling?, Should You Have Children?, The Watchmen, Girls in Love, The Wedding Dress, A Gift for the Bride* (featuring a "large choir of beautiful girls! Many song numbers! Magnificent dances!"), *Shenyndelke from Poland, The Sinful Mother*. They were followed by a new troupe headed by husband and wife team Rachel Rozenfeld and Morris Novikov, who performed *A Wedding in Siberia* and *The Cabaret Singer*. Often, there would be a "Sunday evening big concert with the whole cast." This was due to the "blue laws" in effect in Ontario as well as many states of the United States which forbade theatre, but not concerts, on Sundays.[23]

There would also be frequent "benefit nights" for individual members of the cast. "Actors, like other performers, customarily contracted for one night a season to be played for their own benefit.

---

23 See Pesach Burstein, *What a life! The autobiography of Pesach'ke Burstein, Yiddish matinee idol* (Syracuse, N.Y.: Syracuse University Press, 2003), p. 70.

In this practice, not unique to Yiddish theatre, the performer picked and cast the play. On these benefit nights, the house might be filled with an actor's enthusiastic fans, and the box office take came to a significant yearly bonus. She might also receive gifts in addition to money profits.[24] There would also be benefits for other causes, as when, on April 27, 1941 Rozenfeld, Novikov and the whole troupe played across the street at the Strand in *Moyshe the Newcomer*, sponsored by the Pride of Israel Sick Benefit Society War Effort Committee. A concert in honour of the fortieth jubilee of the Arbeter Ring featured Menachem Reuben, Miriam Kressin and Sholom Secunda. These benefits not only guaranteed proceeds to the cause, but also, with their advance block-ticket sales, a pre-season intake for the companies to make productions possible.

There was material for the highbrow set as well. H. Leivick (born Leivick Halpern) would give a reading of his poetry in the Labour Lyceum, while at the Eaton Auditorium, the Jewish National Workers' Alliance presented a musical evening, "From Slavery to Freedom," with the prolific composer Maurice Rauch[25] at the piano and his wife, the Martha Graham dancer Lillian Shapiro, as well as the "character singer" Saul Meisels and Tsvi Skoler from the Schwartz Art Theatre ("all the proceeds going to the war effort"). In April, 1941, in the Margaret Eaton recital hall, Lou Herman, accompanied by Harry Adaskin on the violin and Leo Barkin on the piano gave a concert of "classic songs and modern Hebrew, Yiddish and English lieder." Herman had the honour of singing shortly afterwards in a kind of "command performance" at the huge

---

24 Nahma Sandrow, "Yiddish Theater in the United States," *Jewish Women: A Comprehensive Encyclopedia*
25 Rauch composed the music to *Yidish redt zikh azoy sheyn* on "Music from the Jewish Hour."

celebration on May 11, 1941 in Varsity Arena for Chaim Weizmann, Mrs. Weizmann and Sara Roosevelt, the President's mother, on the diplomatic visit to the US and Canada of Weizmann as President of the World Zionist Organization.

Radio

At the start of the war the Jewish Hours were thrown into considerable confusion by a decree banning broadcasts in non-official languages.

> **Foreign languages forbidden on radio,**
> **Jewish radio hours hit hard**
> By a decree of the Canadian censor, which has been introduced because of the war, the Radio Commission has forbidden the use of foreign languages on Canadian radio stations. Only English and French, the two official languages, will be permitted on the radio in Canada.
> The Jewish Radio Hours were hit hard by the decree. Already last Sunday they were compelled to do their commercial advertising for their programs in English. We are given to understand that they are preparing to conduct their Happy New Year programs in Yiddish.
> A person who is close to government circles told us that the decree is not just a whim, and most certainly not an expression of anti-Semitism or some other manifestation against foreign elements in the land. Of such a thing there can be no question now. It is the foreigners who live in Canada, apart from the Germans, who are concerned by blood that Germany suffers a defeat.
> The ban has been issued to prevent German spies from having any means to give military secrets hidden in an innocent Yiddish advertisement or in a Happy New Year greeting.[26]

Harry Harris reported being reduced to tears when he heard this news:

---

26 *KN*, September 6, 1939, p. 1. It's hard to tell whether this last line was written seriously or, as seems more likely, sarcastically.

> . . . the very first Sunday morning, September 3, 1939, the manager of the radio station was waiting for me. He let me know that he would not allow Yiddish to be spoken or sung. That my program would not go ahead. To be faced with such tragic luck, in that moment I felt as though everything was coming to an end. I don't know what came over me, but I remember very well. I started to cry in front of the gentile manager. This is my bread and butter, if you don't let me continue on with the show, I'll kill myself right here and now. I have a wife and children. This is my whole livelihood. I begged him further. I promised not to speak Yiddish, and we won't sing with words, we'll just hum the melodies. We quickly turned all the commercials into English.

The *Kanader Nayes* cancelled plans for its Rosh Hashanah radio hours, but soon turned the ban to its advantage in its front page advertisement for newspaper greetings— "A *Kanader Nayes* greeting is permanent. They even keep it in archives"—by including the reminder that "this year there will be no Yiddish New Year Hour broadcasts."[27]

But the decree was quickly lifted, at least as far the Jewish Hours were concerned, and they were back on the air in no time. Greenfield, however, continued only until January, 1940 when his CKOC show ceased production and his CKTB show came "under new management." The new management, who had the warm support of the *Kanader Nayes,* consisted of Mr. Itche Lieberman, a businessman who "has conducted for several years already a successful Jewish Radio Program in Rochester New York," and H.M. Kirshenbaum, not only an important figure in the *Kanader Nayes,* but also secretary of the Ontario Chapter of the Canadian Association of Polish Jews, and as such had written the stirring call in the paper of the prior September, which, I suppose, only goes to show how even the most

---

27 *KN*, September 10, 1939, p. 1.

committed Toronto Jews were able to get on with their lives and with the business of entertainment.[28] As I pointed out earlier, Itche Lieberman was no stranger to Toronto radio; his wife Shirley had already appeared as an actress on the early Greenfield shows along with my mother. Lieberman announced "that he will conduct the Canadian Jewish program at a first class artistic level. The program will have Jewish music, song, humour, drama and community news."[29] The CKTB show carried on faithfully throughout the rest of 1940. By the *Rosh Hashana* 1940 show, it had two hours going on Sunday and Max Mandel was back headlining, along with pianist Eydele Singer and other guest artists.

The *Rosh Hashana* show also saw the return of Isaac Swerdlow: "An extra attraction will be a sketch from Jewish life performed by a group of artists with the participation of Isaac Swerdlow, Belle Greenberg, Shirley Lieberman and others—directed by Irving Herman." In fact, it was only a matter of weeks before Lieberman moved back to Rochester to oversee what seemed to be an empire of radio shows, and Swerdlow took over management of the CKTB show.[30]

This was followed by repeated *faux* "news" stories that merely announced the time and station. In March, 1941, an evening hour was added with the unintentionally funny description, "The program will consist of better Jewish music. The usual program will be heard, as always, at 4:30 in the afternoon." It's from this time that the singing commercial for Blustein's Furniture Store on "Music from the Jewish Hour" dates.

---

28 Kirschenbaum did not survive the war, dying at age fifty in January, 1943.
29 *KN*, February 25, p. 1.
30 October 13, p. 4

> Listen to this sensation!
> The best ensembles
> Available to you
> At the absolute lowest prices
> The most beautiful furniture
> You can get everything
> In Blustein's Furniture Store
> Chesterfields and beds
> Kitchen sets and laundry machines
> All that you need, you get
> In Blustein's Furniture Store

We know that this is a wartime record, not from any dates on the disc itself, but from the fact that the record is made on a glass-core ("Presto") disc instead of the usual aluminum base, aluminum being in short supply due to the war effort, and from the fact that the flip-side is a rendition of *Varshe* (Warsaw), the lyrics for which clearly place it post-invasion but pre-liberation.

By this time Harry Harris was well-established with a morning Sunday hour at CHML, advertising in the rival *Yidisher Zhurnal* and this was more or less the picture throughout the war. Both Harris and Mandel devoted their talents to war relief efforts. Max always worked through the Apter society. The Apter *landslayt* in Toronto had no hope of getting help through to Apt under Nazi occupation, so the most they could do was to raise funds "to help our unfortunate sisters and brothers in the old home with a generous hand when the right time comes." In May, Max took advantage of the presence in the city of New York stars Rachel Rozenfeld and Morris Novikov, who were appearing at the Spadina Theatre, to hold one of the first of the Apter annual relief concerts at the Bellevue Theatre at 360 College Street:

BELLEVUE THEATRE
The Apter Annual Concert

This coming
Sunday the 25th May, 8 PM
in Bellevue Theatre
College at Brunswick
A very rich program produced
—by—
Max Mandel
with the participation
of the beloved stars
Rachel Rozenfeld
—and—
Morris Novikov
the wunderkind
Miriam Albin
and beloved "buff" comedienne
Sally Josephson
who have come specially for the evening.
Come in masses, you will amuse
yourselves greatly.

"Buff comedienne"? According to the politically incorrect Sydney Swerdlow in his lecture on "The History of the Yiddish Theatre" (1979), "Women who were fat and forty played soubrettes. Sally Josephson was forty-five when she played buff comediennes." Though "boff" is more usual, "buff" seems to have been the term used in Yiddish Theatre.[31] The word generally means riotously funny, which may come from the Italian "*buffo*." Others suggest it comes from "boffo," derived from "box office" to mean successful.

Max produced another Apter concert at the Bellevue the following June with front page support from the *Kanader Nayes*

---
31 See, for example, Burstein, *op. cit.*, pp. 81 and 277.

(June 7, 1942). Harry Harris, meanwhile, in association with Moyshe Shapiro and Isaac Swerdlow put on concerts in 1942 to aid the Red Cross and the soldiers. In June, 1942 they put on a production of *The Galician Wedding* in the "Victory Theater," as the Strand had just been renamed. It had closed and re-opened after major renovations as a "modern movie theatre," with Mickey Rooney in "Andy Hardy's Private Secretary "on October 9, 1941:

> **"Salute to Victory!" Grand Opening**
> Dedicated to the cause ever close to our hearts, the Victory Theatre opens its doors tonight.[32]

Obviously, "victory" was only a hope at this time, but Churchill had adopted the **V** sign in July 1941, with the *Kanader Nayes* picking it up immediately with a **V** on both sides of its masthead starting July 27, 1941, explaining in an editorial:

> **'V' Means Victory**
> The 'V' announces a new sunrise for bloodied and wounded humanity. People have a weakness for slogans and signs, so let's use it to free the world instead of enslaving it. Let's write over everything the letter 'V'.

According to the *Toronto Star*, Harris and Shapiro presented themselves at the *Galician Wedding* show in their reserve-army private uniforms and raised $300 for the Red Cross fund for British bombing victims.[33] In November, they put on a concert at the Victory, (the second of two), with Swerdlow, to aid the "cigarette fund":

> For the second time this year the Jewish Theatre Club which is managed by the well-known Maurice Shapiro will give a concert this coming Sunday in the Victory, the proceeds of which will go to the cigarette fund for

---

32   *Toronto Star*, October 9, 1941, p. 35.
33   *Toronto Star*, June 17, 1942, p. 35.

soldiers of the Canadian Army in England. Just as before, the artists will perform completely for free and a program has been put together so that the public will greatly amuse itself. Last time, the concert raised $252. . . . For soldiers on the battlefield, a little cigarette is one of the most necessary things. We, who find ourselves at home and contribute only money to compensate for the war's costs, must with the most satisfaction contribute to the cigarette fund.[34]

But by this time the war had changed direction. In June, 1941 Hitler gave up on conquering Britain and started Operation Barbarossa, his surprise invasion of Russia in which, with mind-boggling casualties on both sides, but especially on the Soviet side, the Germans smashed through Poland, Ukraine, Latvia, Lithuania and West Russia to within about twenty miles of Moscow before being beaten back by the Red Army and the Russian winter. The defeat of the Germans was a major turning point in the war, but their conquest of these lands was an unimaginable catastrophe for the millions of Jews who until then had lived under the relatively benign Soviet control. The political and religious persecution and the wartime deprivation suffered by Jews under Soviet occupation appear to have been no worse than what the Soviet citizen experienced during wartime. For instance, survivors among the Jews of my mother's city Bialystok recount discrimination against religion, exile to Siberia of dangerous elements, overcrowding, etcetera—in other words, the ideology and harshness of the Soviet wartime regime. But, those who remembered the Nazi occupation of the first three weeks of the war were relieved at the arrival of the Russians and actually found conditions improving until the second Nazi attack:

---

34 *KN*, November 22, 1942, p. 3.

The Arrival of the Nazi Murderers
Hell on earth for the Jews of Bialystok began on Friday morning, June 27, 1941, when the Nazis entered the city. Without delay, they streamed to the Jewish neighborhoods, throwing grenades into Jewish homes and wounding many. With unbelievable brutality the Nazis dragged Jewish men from their dwellings, beat them over their heads and forced them into the Great Synagogue. As this august house of worship filled with people, it was surrounded by Nazi vandals. Armed from head to toe, they hurled grenades into the synagogue, which immediately went up in flames. Crammed with more than 2,000 Jews, the synagogue burned for twenty-four hours until Saturday morning. Only then came the order to extinguish the fire.[35]

Operation Barbarossa brought with it the *einsatzgruppen*[36] and the gas chambers and the full horror of the "final solution" to all the Jews under Nazi power. It also immediately converted Soviet Russia from Hitler's co-conspirator into our prized ally. This caused considerable mixed feelings in the socialist Zionist circles of the *Kanader Nayes*. On July 13, 1941, two articles on page 2 blasted the communists despite their change of heart. Max Federman, who, as we know, had gone several rounds in the ring with the communists of his Fur Workers Union, rehearsed their misdeeds from the Hitler-Stalin pact on, in an article entitled, ironically "The Communists Become Patriots." Maurice Goldstick's editorial was more direct:

The communists should keep quiet
What actually do the communists want from us "bourgeois"? Everything must have its logic, even such a thing

---

35 *The Bialystoker Memorial Book—Der Bialystoker Yizkor Buch*, the Bialystoker Center, New York 1982.

36 SS units who accompanied the German armies as they invaded the Soviet Union, units whose sole task it was to round up and shoot all the Jews, as well as such other undesireables as 'gypsies' and communists. They murdered about one million defenceless victims without even the aid of gas chambers.

as communist politics. The "comrades" are making noise now that we "bourgeois" should forget about everything that has occurred so that we can help "Comrade" Stalin "destroy Nazism."

But where were these same "comrades" during the last 22 months? Apparently, during that time, he, comrade Stalin, was really trying to "destroy Nazism." Not only did "Comrade" Stalin not put one finger in cold water to "destroy Nazism," but he in fact ruled that "Nazism is a matter of taste" and that it is a "criminal foolishness" to destroy it.[37]

And what did the comrades do in our country before July 1941 to help "destroy Nazism?"

They devoted their entire organization-apparatus and spent hundreds of thousands of "Comrade" Stalin's dollars to prevail upon the Canadian people in general and the youth in particular not to take part in the war to "destroy Nazism" not even to buy victory bonds which bear a substantial percentage [in interest]. . . .

If the local communists really want to do what's best for "Comrade" Stalin, they should now be "quieter than water and as low as grass." They must assume the air of one who has suddenly awoken from a bad dream. Instead of speaking at mass meetings and making appeals for their Moscow rabbi, they should shut their mouths and keep them shut for the whole war. . . .

Every time the communists open their mouths to tell the Canadian people that Stalin leads a holy war against Hitler, the Canadian people should remember that up until three weeks ago Churchill was reckoned by them a gangster and Roosevelt a war monger, and that they called our war against Hitler an "imperialistic war."

The Canadian people will, on account of their own strategic reasons and military needs, and according to their own way, help the "father of all peoples." The most help that "Comrade" Stalin can get in Canada is when his local lackeys and followers will, at the right moment, truly and for a long time, be silent.

---

37 On signing the Hitler-Stalin pact, Molotov had famously tried to re-assure the Germans of Russia's friendship by commenting to journalists that "fascism is a matter of taste."

A year later, after the Russians had survived Operation Barbarossa and were facing a second major offensive, the paper was still wary of the enthusiastic support given the Soviets by British and Canadian leaders. The editor also took advantage of the opportunity to do a little philosophizing about capitalism.

A Salute to Soviet Russia
The great mass celebrations in all the cities over the whole British Empire and in all parts of the United States on the anniversary of Soviet Russia's entry into the war on our side is once again a confirmation that the Anglo-Saxons have an innate, deep political sense. No other people in the world who live politically free would be capable under the same circumstances of so warmly saluting the Russian people and their current political leader, as have the English, here and in England, and the Americans.

It is understandable that the people of the United Nations and especially the British would rejoice that powerful Soviet Russia has, completely unexpectedly, joined us in the life and death struggle with the Nazis. Thanks to the heroic Russians, our chances of winning the war have become a lot better. But one could not have predicted that the happiness should be expressed so spontaneously and on such an immense scale, especially when one remembers what our political leaders had previously said about this same Russia and about its political leader a year ago. . . .

Take for example the speeches that Mr. Brockington and Miss Dorothy Thompson made in the Varsity Arena. If you hadn't heard the same people on other occasions on the subject of Soviet Russia and the Communists, you could think you were being spoken to by members of the Politburo. If these speakers truly believe what they said in praise of Russia, it is a highly remarkable phenomenon, and if they have said what they said just for the sake of duty, that is also a very remarkable phenomenon.

One cannot, however, speak so ecstatically about the Russian political leader so as to make propaganda for communism, not only in Russia, but also here and everywhere. Would that mean that local capitalism is ready for a new orientation in relation to communism and the communists? In the nature of things, capitalists have hated to part with their favorable positions in society. And if that is so, they have had to understand that communism and socialism will always remain bloodily opposed to capitalism. Can it be possible that the capitalists are now ready to make concessions?

But, however this turns out, it is a joyous event. It is perhaps unwittingly an expression of remorse on the part of the capitalists for their terrible sin of bringing Hitlerism into the world. Without Hitlerism this relentlessly horrible war would not now be raging.

Perhaps the capitalists will yet come to their senses. Perhaps they will yet realize the foolishness of their own rule. Perhaps they will yet understand that in a mortal world it is not worthwhile simply, day in and day out, to squander this short human life just to die rich.[38]

With the Americans in the war after Pearl Harbour in December 1941, the ultimate defeat of the Nazis was felt to be not only achievable but inevitable. ("With the great Roosevelt, we believe that we will win the war and achieve peace.") However, until the Battle of Stalingrad, which ended victoriously for the Soviets, the more assimilated Montreal-based leadership of the Canadian Jewish Congress, led by liquor magnate Samuel Bronfman, seems to have tried to keep a low profile, to stress the patriotism of the Jews and the fact that Hitler was a common enemy. They evidently feared provoking latent anti-Semitism, especially endemic in Quebec, by making this a war to save the Jews.[39] After the war, some Congress leaders would express remorse for being "too damned polite":

> When the survivors blame the Jewish communities of the free world for not having tried to force the hands of the Roosevelts, Churchills, MacKenzie Kings, etc., they're probably right. Actually, I don't think we could possibly

---

38 *KN*, June 28, 1942, p. 2.
39 Max Beer, "The Montreal Jewish Community and the Holocaust," *Current Psychology* (2007) 26: 191.

have even if we had marched on Ottawa every hour on the hour. But we can't have an easy conscience because we didn't try to the extent that we should have. We were too damned polite about it.[40]

By 1942, one can sense the growing frustration of some activists with this approach, for instance Gershon Pomerantz, secretary of the Toronto based United Jewish Relief Conference. In a *Kanader Nayes* op-ed of March 8, 1942, he wrote:

> **For Our Martyrs**
> This Sunday evening Toronto Jews will assemble in Massey Hall, en masse, to give honour to our martyrs, the fallen, and to send a word of comfort to the living who are carrying on a stubborn struggle against the Hitler-murderers of the world.
> 　It's truly hard, very hard, to live such a sacred moment. It is hard because nobody among us knows, if among them, those who we want today to remember, who we want to honour with "*yizkor*," is not included our mothers, our fathers, our sisters and brothers. Who knows? Who can know which infants the Hitler-murderers have slaughtered in Kiev; who they have burned in Kharkov; who they have drowned in the water of the Dnieper, Volga and Bug. Who can know that? Can it be that my own have been hanged in the slaughter rooms of Romania to wait for the butchers with their knives and their hands to slaughter them "kosher." Who knows? And is it, after all, better that we should know about those things? Hard to grasp, hard to endure, what is going on there, "there," in the cities and the towns of Poland, Lithuania, Ukraine, White Russia and Ruthenia, what has happened there, and what is being done there today, while we, the Jewish residents of Toronto are going to come together and spill a tear for the dark fate of our people.
> 　Hard to keep calm in such a time. Hard to keep quiet and not cry out so the world will hear our rage, our protest and our pain over the 760 Jewish souls who banged on the doors and towers of the Land of Israel

---

40　Saul Hayes, executive director of the Canadian Jewish Congress from 1940 to 1959, quoted in Tulchinsky, *op. cit.*, at p. 237.

and found their peace and rest in the stormy waters of the Black Sea. Who can stay calm? Who can keep quiet? Who can forget?

The reference to the "760 Jewish souls" is to the incident in February 1942, in which a ship, the *Struma*, carrying refugees from Romania to Palestine was set adrift by Turkish authorities while the refugees were trying to overcome British objections to their entry into Palestine. The ship was then torpedoed by a submarine, much later revealed to be Soviet, under secret orders to sink all neutral shipping entering the Black Sea in order to reduce the flow of strategic materials to Nazi Germany. All but one of the 769 men women and children on board were killed.

The accompanying *Kanader Nayes* editorial congratulated the conference for the *yiskor* initiative, but barely concealed its impatience:

> **Yiskor and still more**
> Our mourning and our weeping will only be an external manifestation of inner hard-heartedness if we don't make use of this opportunity to organize all our energies to help the thousands of suffering ones to whom we can yet come with our aid.

By May, impatience with the lackadaisical approach of Canadian Jews to the suffering in Europe boiled over in a scathing article by Pomerantz that makes bracing reading today:

> **The Call of the Suffering Ones**
> We have already become used to the words "war victims." In the beginning, when Hitler's attacks began, the words "Jewish war victims" were so moving and burning. Every time one remembered the Jews who had fallen under Hitler's regime a shudder ran through us. With every new bit of news we were shaken. Recently, however, we have become apathetic. We read about "tens of thousands of Jews killed in Minsk, tens of thousands of Jews shot in Kharkov; thousands of Jews murdered in Lomza"—

and—we go ahead with our day-to-day activities. We do our business and—there, ruin, holocaust and death carry on, every moment of the day, every minute of the night. Thousands of Jews die month by month in the Warsaw Ghetto; tens of thousands of Jews are suffering in slave-camps under the whip of the cruel ones. Jewish children suffer from disease and hunger—almost a million Jews find themselves in Soviet Siberia, Jews who escaped from Nazi–Poland and—they need clothes, bread, medicine, bandages. Jewish children, infants, need a little milk—We have, however, already became used to the daily descriptions in the newspapers and—we pass by as if nothing had occurred, as if nothing had befallen.

Is it good, thus, while a people is perishing? Is it good, thus, to go along our way—sitting in our armchairs, giving a sigh, or an "oy" and sinking into apathy? Is it good, thus, that we, the satisfied, the free, the happy of our nation, that we have been worthy that our fate should lead us out of Egypt—shipped us overseas to freedom—is it good, thus—that we should forget? Is it good, thus, that we should not raise ourselves up as a great people to make it our mission to be the saviour, the bringer of good tidings to our downhearted and suffering, to our martyrs and heroes, who are carrying on such a stubborn struggle with their tormentor? Is it good, thus, that we make ourselves forget our bond, our connection with our sisters and brothers on the other side of the sea? Will history forgive us that we are satisfied just with sighing, that we give not any portion of our every morsel of bread for our brothers whom FATE HAS DECREED that the horrors of Hitlerism shall be visited on their bodies?

Some of us argue that the relief work is fragmented. Everybody does *shabbes* for themselves.[41] Societies establish relief associations and collect for the war. What more is there that an organization can collect for relief for our "poor sisters and brothers on the other side of the sea"? Everybody tends their own little garden. Others maintain, "Can you really send them relief? Since there's nothing we can do, why do we have to collect?" Then they say, "the best way to help is the Red Cross." And, when you come together and you put a couple of dollars together for the

---

41 In this case, Sabbath celebrations, meaning people celebrate on their own and not with others.

Red Cross, you get a "picture in the gentile newspapers" and all the Christians see that Gnendel gave a dollar ... what could be better?"

Is it really not possible to do more? Is it not possible to build a central body which can, day-in-day-out, awake, call and remind, that not with pennies, certainly not with sighs, will one rescue the Jews in Europe? Is it truly not possible to awake the consciousness of local Jews to the responsibility that history has laid upon them? Are we, the American and Canadian Jews, to be the ones to rebuild a new life from the ruins; are we, moreover, to be the ones who will not let the Jewish flame be extinguished from the world before our very eyes? Is it possible that we have such a sacred privilege?

Since the outbreak of the war, Canadian Jews have collected a half million dollars for the Jews in Europe. This is the money that has been collected from ALL the Jews. From this half million dollars, two hundred thousand has gone for refugees in Canada. Three hundred thousand has gone for war victims. Is this enough?

Can anyone say of a three-year war—and such a war for the Jews—that it is enough that the one hundred and sixty-five thousand Jews in Canada can justly acquit themselves by giving THREE AND A HALF DOLLARS PER CAPITA to cover both the war victims and the refugees who have settled in Canada? Can anyone say that that is the proper tithe for our satisfied life and our freedom? [42]

But people continued to "make *shabbes* for themselves" and the paper continued to promote these actions as well. An ad for donations to the Red Cross appeared on page 4 the same day Pomerantz's article appeared on page 2: "$900,000,000 is immediately necessary. Every dollar you give to the Red Cross will be multiplied three times." The paper also showcased the annual campaign of the United Toronto Jewish Welfare Fund (the pre-cursor of the modern United Jewish Appeal) which collected during the High Holidays for a myriad of Jewish causes, including the United Jewish Refugee and War Relief

---

42 *KN,* May 3, 1942, p. 2 (emphasis in original).

Agencies, the Jewish Family and Child Welfare Bureau, the Toronto Old Folks Home, Jewish education, the Mount Sinai Hospital, the Canadian Jewish Congress, Canadian Friends of Hebrew University, Jewish summer camps, and more.[43]

The Canadian Jewish Congress continued throughout the war to hold memorial events as a form of protest against the unfolding Holocaust. It held a *yiskor* demonstration in Massey Hall on October 11, 1942 and, during Khanukah 1942, it declared a "Khanukah of Mourning:"

> Canadian Jews, together with all the other Jews of the world, mourned Wednesday, December 2 over the catastrophe of European Jewry. The mourning proclamation of the Canadian Jewish Congress was communicated through the press and over the radio.

---

43 For example, the illustrated double-page spread on pages 4 and 5 of the *KN* for September 20, 1942 (reproduced above).

All religious leaders and the *Poale Tsion* movement took part. In Montreal, mourning assemblies took place in 9 synagogues. Several schools where the number of Jewish children is large brought together the Jewish and non-Jewish children in assemblies and heard speakers on the situation of the Jewish children in Europe.

The rabbinate declared that people should fast and should refrain from every sort of amusement during the day and should cover the mirrors in Jewish houses with black.

In Massey Hall, Toronto, a large mourning assembly took place that was addressed by Mr. A. B. Bennett, president of the Jewish Congress, Central Division, Rabbi S. Sachs, Dr. I. Shatsky, and Reb. Kamenetsky. An impressive children's meeting in the Victory Theatre in the morning was addressed by I. Rabinovitch, culture director of the Jewish Congress and Alexander Brown. Rabbi Sachs was chairman and Cantor A. Bernstein sang the memorial service. S. Rapaport read from the book of *Selichot*.

Jewish workers paused in their work for 15 minutes from 11 until 11:15 in the morning and Jewish businesses remained closed during that time. Many assemblies also took place in Ottawa and in Western Canada.

The day of mourning was also observed in Windsor, Sault Ste. Marie, Cobourg, Belleville, Pictou, Trenton, Simcoe, Stratford and other Canadian cities.

But Khanukah 1942 was also a huge turning point in the war. The battle for Stalingrad, the culmination of the second German offensive against Russia, was reaching its decisive weeks. In February 1943, after mind-boggling losses of life—estimates run as high as two million dead soldiers and civilians—the German forces were destroyed and the Russians emerged victorious. By the summer of 1943, the Russians had gained the upper hand and had begun their counter-attack, driving the Germans out of Russia and ultimately out of Eastern Europe. In tune with the times, the anti-Communism of the paper softened considerably. In the next Ontario provincial election in 1943, the *Kanader Nayes* threw its weight heavily behind the CCF, which made a huge breakthrough, going from third-party status to official opposition. This was a period of a strong leftward shift in Canadian politics. Because of war production, the years 1942 and 1943 saw an unprecedented number of strikes and major victories for the unions, especially in the auto industries. The Communist Party was still illegal, but it managed to run two candidates as "Labour Progressives," J.B. Salsberg and A.A. Macleod, both in ridings with heavy Jewish concentrations. Some *Kanader Nayes* correspondents bridled:

> They have betrayed Canada, they have betrayed the Jewish people and now the communists are crying that all that should be forgotten. Why? Can one forget such a thing? What guarantee have we that the communists won't once again be traitors to Canada and traitors to the Jewish people? And another question I have for the communists. Why are they running, in fact, in the two Jewish ridings and not in others? Do they want to give material to the anti-Semites who can say: look, the Jews are Bolsheviks![44]

The pro-Soviet tide was, however, very strong. In July, a mass rally in New York was held in honour of a Soviet Jewish fundraising delegation led by Solomon (Shloyme) Mikhoels, a Russian Jewish actor, and Itzik Feffer, a Soviet Jewish poet; both would be murdered by the Soviets in the postwar era. The 1943 rally, which was chaired in New York by Albert Einstein, would be repeated under the auspices of the Canadian Jewish Congress in Toronto's ice hockey shrine, Maple Leaf Gardens, on September 8, with singing by my friends from the Freedom Singing Society, the presence of

---

44 Sh. Lieberg, "The Toronto Jewish community and the election" *KN*, August 8, 1943, p.2.

SUNDAY, SEPT. 5, 1943 — CANADIAN NEWS — "קאנאדער נייעס" — 2 — זונטאג, סעפטעמבער 5, 1943

די שטימע פון סאוועטישן אידנטום וועט רעדן צו אייך
דורך די אידיש סאוועטישע שלוחים

פערזעכלער אין דעם נאמען פון אונזער העלדישע שותפמ'דיגע אין ברידערשע פארבאנד וועלכע זיינען אין ברענן. או עקשנות'דיגן קאמף מיט דעם היטלער ריצח'ים

מיטוואך, דעם 8-טן סעפטעמבער
8.15 אזונט

פאלקס קבלת פנים

לכבוד די אפיציעלע שלוחים פון די מיליאנען קעמפנדיגע אידן אינעם סאוועטן פארבאנד צו די אידן אין קאנאדע

פארזיצער
שלמה
מיכאעלס

פארזיצער שלמה מיכאעלס, פאלקאוניק איציק פעפער, שלום אש

פאלקאוניק
איציק
פעפער

אין
מייפל ליף גארדנס

קאנטאר מענדלסאן	פארזיצער אלברט איינשטיין	שלום אש
פון דער שערי שמים שול אל מאנטרעאל, וועט זינגען דעם מיזכור אלע מיליאנען אידישע קרבנות וועלכע זיינען פון אום געקומען	וועט רעדן בנוגע די מיסיע פון די סאוועטיש-אידישע שלוחים אין מייפל ליף גארדנס	וועלכער באזוכט איצט שיקאגא, קומט מיט דער דעלעגאציע קיין מאנטרעאל און זאגט אן דעם ראיפ-הויפטשטאט'דיגער פארזאמלונג
	דזשי. טיאמקין	אידישער פאלקס כאר
	שרייבער דאפטער, פון דער קארפאנטרער אמאטסאציע אן אדיעסלער פאר די סאוועטישער אידן	זינגען אין ספעציעל צוגעפאסטען לידער אראנזשירט פון מאוסמטעל דירזשענט, ע.ט.א גארטענע

דער פאלקס קבלת פנים ווערט דורכגעפירט פון דער
צענטראלער דיוויזיע קאנאדער אידישער קאנגרעס

פאר מער אינפארמאציע פארשטענדיגט זיך מיט נוסן פאמעראנץ, קאנאדער אידישער קאנגרעס, 150 בעווערלי סט. AD. 5455

writer Sholem Asch, and 12,000 in attendance. Einstein did not make it in person, but sent greetings by telephone feed:

> **12,000 greet Soviet-Jewish delegation in Maple-Leaf Gardens**
> The talk by I. Feffer, which was often "peppered"[45] with fine humour, and the more dramatic talk by Prof. Mikhoels, brought forth big applause. Describing the horrible massacres that the Nazis have committed against the Jews in Europe, in which they have killed four million Jews, more than a quarter of the Jewish people, and the heroism of the Jewish fighters in the Red Army, both speakers called for a ceaseless struggle until fascism is wiped off the earth. The well-known writer Sholom Asch praised the heroism of the Soviet struggle against the Nazis. He affirmed that Hitler's declaration that his two greatest enemies are the Jews and the Russian people, is a compliment to the Jews, because the Russian people are now striving for social justice.[46]

In November, 1943 the Tehran conference would see Roosevelt, Churchill and Stalin meet for the first time to plan the joint strategy for the defeat of Germany.

So the paper's news reporting and editorials leading up to the 1943 election steered clear of their usual anti-communism and there were no personal attacks on J. B. Salsberg. Both Salsberg and Macleod won their Jewish ridings for the communists and this drew no adverse comments from the paper. From then on, Salsberg, who would not leave the Communist Party until 1956, acquired the status of a respected community leader. He was featured with

---

45 Feffer and "pepper" are the same word in Yiddish.
46 *KN*, September 12, 1943, p. 1. The *Toronto Star* of September 9, 1943, p. 8 reported that Pfeffer and Asch, but not Mikhoels, had declared that anti-Semitism had been eliminated from Russia. The *KN* evidently felt that reporting that would be too much for its readers, who knew better. September 8 was also the day that the new government of Italy announced that it had switched sides, which was cause for great celebration at the rally.

other "prominent Jewish leaders" including Sam Factor and Rabbi S. Sachs (who had denounced Salsberg in 1937) to appear at a war relief meeting at Massey Hall on November 28, 1943. Why not? The *Rosh Hashana* edition for September 17, 1944 even featured a New Year's greeting in Yiddish with picture from none other than Tim Buck, "national leader of the Labour Progressive Party."

Even during the darkest days of the war, Toronto Jews sought to entertain themselves. As the *Kanader Nayes* humour columnist put it, "You're allowed to laugh," even though his particular jokes weren't all that funny. For example:

> A village mother, who had a son in the Yeshiva in the city, sent him a coat and in the inside pocket placed a letter with the following contents:
> "My dear son, look in the inside pocket of your coat and you will find this letter."

The lack of Yiddish movie production after 1940 and the lack of European outlets seems to have resulted in far more live theatre and concerts than might otherwise have been the case. All the big American stars paraded through Toronto, usually in war benefit shows: Molly Picon in a production by her husband Jacob Kalich of *Oy is this a life*, with music by Rumshinsky; Esther Field (the "*Yidishe Mame*" and star of *Eli* (1940); Herman Yablokov with his wife Bella Meisel and the husband and wife act Pesakh'ke Burstein and Lilian Lux. Maurice Schwartz and his famous troupe performed often during the war in fare by Sholom Asch, Sholom Aleichem, and I.J. Singer.

מאלי פיקאן.

Jacob Ben-Ami appeared in a Yiddish version of Ibsen's *Ghosts* and Gordin's *God, Man and Devil* with a cast including Stella Adler, and *A Miracle in the [Warsaw] Ghetto* by Leivick, with music by Sholom Secunda. Other Adlers, Frances and Celia appeared along with Max Bozik in the *Kreutzer Sonata*, the Tolstoy novella turned Yiddish play by Jacob Gordin. Bozik also appeared with Michael Michalesko in *His Great Love*. Even the most serious of these pieces had music by the Jewish operetta giants, Sholom Secunda, Joseph Rumshinsky and Alexander Olshanetsky who often came along to do the conducting honours. The Victory Theatre was the busiest venue, but there were many others as well.

There were even blockbuster spectaculars like the June, 1942 production of the folk opera *Bar Kochba* for the 100th anniversary of Goldfaden's birth at Massey Hall, with a dream cast including

> **EATON AUDITORIUM**
> Yonge & College   TR. 1144
>
> דער אידישער פאלקס כאר
>
> עמיל גארטנער, דיריגענט
>
> פירט אויף צום ערשטען מאל אין קאנאדע
>
> „גאלדפאדען ספעקטאקעל"
>
> טעקסט און מוזיק לויט אברהם גאלדפאדען   מיטן אנטייל פון „איטעס"
> א קאסט פון 50 שפּילער   א כאר פון 100 זינגער
> אויפגעפירט פון אונזער גאסט־רעזשיסאר און בינע קינסטלער פון ניו־יארק
>
> יעקב מעסטל
>
> פרייטאג און שבת, אוו., 26 און 27 מאי
>
> בילעטן: 50 סענט, 75 סענט, $1.00, $1.50 שוין צו באקומען אין
> 7 בראנוויק עוועניו און אין 501 קאלעדזש סטריט (ווארסיטי בארבער
> שאפּ) און בא אלע מיטגלידער פון כאר

Moyshe Oysher, Ludwig Satz, Michael Michalesko, Tsili Adler and Rumshinsky conducting: "The greatest combination of artists in the history of Jewish theatre—100 people on the stage in honour of the 100th jubilee. The following year, the Victoria Theatre held a similar, if less high-brow star-studded extravaganza, *Sing America Sing*, a musical revue with Aaron Lebedev, Michalesko, Jennie Goldstein, Hymie Jacobsen and Leo Fuchs: "Litvaks and Galitzianers, Poles and Americans in the laugh-revue."

The local talent also kept busy. Isaac Swerdlow presented a concert at the Victory Theatre of the Jewish Actors Club for the benefit of Russian Jews in February, 1942. The Freedom Singing Society, renamed the Jewish Folk Choir, presented a *Goldfaden Spectacular* in the Eaton Auditorium conducted by its new permanent director Emil Gartner and guest artist Jacob Mestel, the acclaimed New York actor and director. The Choir also performed a benefit concert at the Victory Theatre in April 1943, for the Red Cross, and, ironically, for Gershon Pomerantz's United Jewish Relief Committee, just as Pomerantz was criticizing Jews who gave to the Red Cross! On May 1, 1942, there was a "mass meeting and concert" with a socialist bent in the Labour Lyceum. The socialist party had speakers from the *Arbeiter Ring* and *Poale Tsion*, as well as union (Max Federman) and CCF speakers. The concert side featured the Children's Choir of the Farbund Folk Schools and the Brooch School under the direction of S. Riegelhaupt, joined by "the esteemed young artists trio," M. Kornerman, Victor Feldbrill, and Albert Pratz, all Toronto Symphony players with long careers ahead of them. There was a concert by Lou Herman, now Private Lou Herman, at the Victory Theatre with Molly Fruitman and Leo Barkin on the piano.

The Jewish radio hours stayed pretty much pat through to the end of the war, with Harry Harris at CHML in Hamilton and Max Mandel at CKTB in St. Catharines. In March 1942, Swerdlow left to return to Montreal and Max teamed up in what would be an enduring partnership with Lublin-born Winnipegger Sam Yuchtman to take over management of the CKTB show, which continued its special relationship with the *Kanader Nayes*. The announcement of the first show under new management was treated as a news story on the back cover with Max's old wedding picture:

A New Jewish Radio Hour
Beginning this Sunday March 1, a new variety radio hour will be heard over Station CKTB 1550 kilocycles.
   The hour will be heard every Sunday from 4:30 to 5:30 afternoon and will be managed by the well-known

> singer Max Mandel and Sam Yuchtman
> The blind musician Sherman Gan and other artists will take part in the first program.
> Lovers of Jewish music are invited to listen to the program.

The CKTB show would broadcast from the Merrittt Mansion on Yates Street in St. Catharines, dating from about 1850, and still used by CKTB as I write. St. Catharines was almost twice as far as Hamilton, so the fees much have been much reduced. While Mandel's show was supported by the *Kanader Nayes*, Harris advertised exclusively with the *Yidishe Zhurnal*. There might even have been some animosity involved, because, when Harris's show was referred to in the *Kanader Nayes* it was always without Harris's name. For example, when Gershon Pomerantz was announced as appearing on CHML Sunday between 2 and 3 to speak in Yiddish, no mention whatever was made that this was the Harry Harris Hour.[47]

Not that the coverage of the show in the *Kanader Nayes* was anywhere near what it had been in the early days. Usually, there was just the small ad that I had first seen thumbing through the paper in the archives. But there was still clearly a loving relationship, as shown even by front-page announcements of cancellation of the program for religious holidays or the apology for the shortened show on May 17, 1942: "Last week because of unavoidable reasons that have to do with the war effort, the program was shortened by a half hour, but this Sunday and every week the program will once again last a full hour." Actually, the show had been partly pre-empted by the historic broadcast of "I am an American Day," the most massive rally in American history, with more than a million people in New York's Central Park, with the show featuring Irving Berlin leading

---

47 *KN,* July 30, 1944, p.4.

the singing of his "God Bless America," the broadcast of a live message from Charles de Gaulle, then leader of the "Free French," and Lily Pons singing "The Marseillaise."

The Last Years of the War

After the stunning victory at Stalingrad, the Canadian Jewish Congress took a more activist stance, initiating a petition to the Canadian government to protest the Holocaust and to admit Jewish refugees into Canada. A *Kanader Nayes* article of May 16, 1943, by Gershon Pomerantz, now petition committee secretary of the CJC Central Division asked, "How much longer must we be silent?"

> The Canadian Jewish Congress is preparing now to intervene, to send our cry to the world about the atrocities which are taking place against our sisters and brothers in Europe. A petition that every Jewish soul who lives in Canada must sign and demand of our government that it intervene with help for the suffering and with protests against the butchers. The petition will be a historical document that the Canadian Jewish community was not silent and did not renounce its bond to the millions of Jews who have fallen into the butcher's hands. We must mobilize ourselves to take part in all the war efforts of our land and help in all the war actions of the United Nations, because the quicker the war is ended, the more opportunity there is for our brothers to be freed from their imprisonment.

An ad for the petition read, "Jews, sign the petition to allow refugees into Canada. Every Jew, man or woman over 18 years old must sign the petition to allow the victims of Fascism and Hitlerism into Canada." A dramatic *yiskor* appeal by the Canadian Jewish Congress in the *Kanader Nayes* on October 8, 1943, had a tombstone and many religious invocations:

> **YISKOR**
> Remember the millions of Jewish martyrs who
> have died in sanctification of God
> Help the living Jewish heroes in their holy war with
> the worst enemy of our people—stretch out to them a
> brotherly hand in their hour of hunger and hardship.
> On *Yom Kippur* it is the duty of every *shul*, every
> house of prayer, to make appeals and pledges
> for the sacred *Yiskor* fund....
> No Jew, no Jewish family is allowed to separate
> from the community of Israel.

But besides memorials, petitions, and protests, some groups went on the offensive. One was the Jewish Labor Committee, a New York organization led by *Forverts* luminary Adolph Held, like Baruch Vladek a socialist alderman in New York City. In the Canadian branch of the committee, the various union and political groupings close to the *Kanader Nayes* were strongly represented, for example, the Workmen's Circle, the Amalgamated Clothing Workers Union and the International Garment Workers Union. Dorothy Dworkin was one of the three Toronto delegates. Another was N. Neslen of the Workmen's Circle, who wrote the following article for the *Kanader Nayes* on October 17, 1943, trying to dispel the widely held belief that nothing could be done for the Jews under Nazi occupation. [48]

> **How one can help the European Jews**
> There are people who think to themselves that the Jews in the Nazi-occupied lands have already been murdered and therefore there is nothing to do to help. And they also believe that, in the event there are, nevertheless,

---

[48] In fact, there was much armed Jewish resistance, not only in the famous ghetto uprisings, but in the many partisan groups operating in the forests of Nazi-occupied Europe. There were also elaborate rescue operations, such as one that saw my dear friend, Dutch Jew Harry Glasbeek, clandestinely united with his family in a farm in the South of France where he spent the war masquerading as a French farm child while his parents were hidden in the barn. "Jewish Resistance," Holocaust Encyclopedia, United States Holocaust Memorial Museum.

some still remaining alive, one cannot anyway get to them with help.

Such ideas are false and harmful. It is true that the Hitler-murderers have killed a huge number of Jews, but, according to all the information, there still remains a great number who are looking for our help.

Secondly, it is not impossible to send help into the Nazi-occupied lands. Help has been and will be sent to those lands. It is true that in order to bring in the means of life to our unlucky brothers, people must risk their lives. But it is a fact that it is being done. Thanks to this, it was possible for the Jews in the Warsaw Ghetto to put up the heroic resistance against the murderous Nazis, about which we have heard and read so much.[49] The time of miracles is already long gone. Nothing happens by itself alone. When we speak of help for the Jews in Europe, it is useful to look a little at the reports which are coming out of there. From these reports we can learn how our unfortunate brothers and sisters live and struggle and die. . . .

So, what should we Jews in America say already! True, we have pity for the Jews in Europe, but with pity alone they will not be made better off. We must give them real, substantial help with whatever we can. And here I come back to what I wrote at the beginning. It is not true that under Nazi control no help can be sent in. I, as secretary of the Jewish Labor Committee, am well-acquainted with it. More than once have receipts been issued for things which we have sent to the Jews in those places. . . . When a fire is burning one does not think, one just rescues, and so I am certain that in the coming campaign of the Jewish Labor Committee which begins the 14th of November, everyone will not only contribute, but they themselves will be collectors.

We here will not be the ones to express thanks to those who help in the campaign, but they, there, the suffering and victimized Jews, will bless the hand that goes out of its way for them.

A December, 1943 ad for the Jewish Labor Committee went like this:

---

49 The reference is to the Warsaw Ghetto uprising of April–May 1943.

> Have you read about the heroic battles of the Polish Jews against the Nazi-bandits? With what have you helped the fighters? For three years the Jewish Labor Committee has been helping the Jewish underground fighters in the ghettoes on the other side of the sea. How much has your organization, your union, your *landsmanshaft* given to this year's campaign of the Jewish Labor Committee? The heroic fighters are being killed, but everyone who has survived is sending their call to the Jewish Labor Committees that we, American and Canadian Jews, give them the means for their continuing struggle.
> Are we going to remain indifferent?
> *Landsmanshaftn* of Polish Jews, on you lies an especially great obligation!
> Help the Jewish Labor Committee rescue the last survivors of the Polish Jews.

By the end of the year, the tide had turned definitively against the Axis. The Americans, British and Canadians were battling their way up through Italy and the Russians had re-conquered Russia and parts of the Ukraine. The year 1944 started on a note of optimism. A war-stamp ad in the *Kanader Nayes* on January 9 read: "Hitler must have the same end as Mussolini! Buy war saving stamps." (Mussolini had been overthrown and arrested in July, 1943, but he had been rescued by the Germans in September and set up as head of a mini-state in the north of Italy, so this stamp was perhaps a little out of date by January 1944.) It was around this time that Max Mandel recorded *Neyn, neyn s'iz keynmol nit geveyn* ("No, no, it has never been") on "Music from the Jewish Hour," with this optimistic stanza:

> The evil Hitler . . . got afraid of Russia . . .
> Because he was given a whiff of the powder of the Red Army . . .
> Once Nazism has been annihilated, and this has already been determined,
> America, Russia and England will build a new world!

June 6, 1944 was D-Day, the allied invasion of Normandy. By the end of the year, on the Western Front, most of Europe had been liberated and the invasion of Germany had begun. The Eastern Front saw a relentless push-back that drove the Germans out of Russia, Ukraine, Romania, Hungary and half of Poland. This meant the liberation of some of the death camps, for instance Majdanek in July 1944. A *Rosh Hashana* edition of the *Kanader Nayes* included a summary of the year's events in English:

> **Milton Brown, It Happened Last Year**
> ... the advance of the Russian armies brought gloom also, as their liberating armies confirmed the fears that Hitler had gone through with his extermination of the Jews. In city after city liberated by the Russian armies—Odessa, Minsk, Vilna, Lublin—scarce a Jew was to be found ... Confirmation of the merciless and wholesale slaughter of Jews in all Nazi-occupied regions came from a Christian body—the International Church Ecumenical Refugee Commission—which reported that their information showed that in just two of the German "death camps" for Jews, a total of 1,715,000 Jews had been put to death.... In the same "gas chambers" in Poland, tens of thousands of Jews of the Netherlands, of Greece, of France, of Belgium and of Germany, the old and the young, men, women and babies, had been deliberately led to their death.

Relief to the survivors now became a concrete reality:

> **Concerning helping our war victims**
> Thanks to the heroic recruits of the Red Army in the East and the Allied armies, including our Canadian Army, in the West, we can now get to our brothers and sisters in the war lands. One can now reach the Jews in Lithuania, a part of the Jews in Latvia, almost all the remaining Jews in Poland, the Jews in Romania and in Bulgaria, almost all the French, Italian, Belgian and Dutch Jews who were not slaughtered, or who did not die of hunger can now be helped by us. ...

A big *"yizkor"* ad for a "great peoples' assembly" in the Victory Theatre proclaimed, "Remember the millions of Jewish martyrs, rescue the Jews who remain alive!" Canadian journalist Raymond Arthur Davis who had just returned from a mission to the liberated towns of Eastern Europe and the concentration camps of Majdanek and Treblinka brought "a living greeting from the freed Jewish communities" to Massey Hall in November 1944. Warsaw was liberated in January 17, 1945 and Auschwitz on January 27. By April, the fate of Nazi Germany was sealed. A front page *Kanader Nayes* editorial on April 1 could not help but proclaim:

> **Nothing to rejoice about**
> Unfortunately, as Jews we have nothing to rejoice about this *Pesakh*. Since last *Pesakh* we have discovered, to our horrible pain, that not only has that occurred which we so greatly feared, but the tragedy has exceeded even the fantasies of the most pessimistic prophets of doom. Hitler killed almost all the Jews in the lands he put under his yoke.
>
> The only consolation that we have, equally with all the other people of the world, is that we can clearly see the end of his devilish government. Hitler's hordes, which have already been for a substantial time in a desperate defensive battle are, thank God, on the verge of a complete collapse. Every new day can make an end to the resistance of the "super men." The catastrophe which the Germans brought to the world in general and to Jews in particular will not, however, disappear with them. The many people of our generation who live in the fortunate lands that the enemy did not succeed in penetrating will never recover from the blow that the war has dealt them. They are prevented from doing so by the living witnesses in the war lands. They are condemned to carry to the grave the shock that these cursed war years have brought to their consciousness.
>
> There is no consolation for our sinful generation. Nothing can make amends for the catastrophe. The best that people from our generation can wish for is that the little children, who have, happily, not yet developed

enough intellectually to understand the horrible events, and the not yet born generations—that they will not be devastated by our disaster.

It is to be hoped that something substantial will be impressed upon the foolish world of human society. Perhaps, perhaps, we will succeed in maintaining peace twice as long as after the First World War. To hope for an everlasting peace is not now possible. Such a thing would be too good and too simple, so why would the foolish people embrace it?

If we are going to have an age of peace it will only be because humanity is now terribly exhausted and broken and not because it has realized, let alone remembered, the absurdity of the atrocities of wars. The best of us and the smartest will know how to use the circumstances to educate our children in an atmosphere of hatred and struggle against everything which could lead to new wars. Unfortunately, there is no guarantee here that we will succeed in realizing our objective.

Let us be happy, this *Pesakh* at least, that we are finally on the verge of the end of the war.

Two weeks later, on April 15, the front page featured a big picture of U.S. President Roosevelt:

We Mourn
Franklin Delano Roosevelt
January 30, 1882 – April 12, 1945

Together with all freedom loving people the whole world over, we mourn the sudden death of President Roosevelt.

He was one of the greatest persons of our time. Not only did he strive to free the millions of slaves in his own country, but he also made possible the liberation of all humanity from the bloody Nazi tyranny.

Roosevelt, the great brother of the oppressed, will always be remembered by all good people from our generation and from all future generations with gratitude and veneration.

Russian troops reached Berlin on April 23. One week later,

Hitler was dead. On May 7, 1945, Germany surrendered. There were exultant headlines in all the daily papers, but, in sober reflection, the by-now weekly *Kanader Nayes* said this instead:

> **Let us rejoice and mourn**
> Now that the European war is officially completely won, we can, together with all other civilized and free peoples around the world, be happy with our whole hearts. There is, indeed, here something to rejoice about. The world has, indeed, as if by a miracle been saved from doom.
>
> But immediately afterwards, when we will have finished the greatest historical celebration of all times, let us sit down to *shiva* to mourn and lament our innocent children and brothers who have paid with their holy lives for the incomparable victory which we have won. Let us mourn and lament the millions of innocent martyrs in the war countries whose lives have been extinguished.
>
> In the final tally, there can be no compensation for the victims who have fallen; for the suffering, both physical and spiritual, of those who remain alive; and for the mutilated bodies who will be forced to carry on a war against their physical condition until they are in their graves.
>
> Yes, let's rejoice and shed tears, rejoice at the victory we have won and shed tears for the unbearable price we have had to pay for this victory.[50]

---

50 *KN*, May 13, 1945, p. 2.

מיר טרויערען

פרענקלין דעלאנא רוזוועלט
יאנואר 30, 1882 -- אפריל 12, 1945

צוגלייך מיט אלע פרייהייט־ליבענדיגע מענשען איבער גאר דער וועלט, טרויערען מיר אויפ'ן פלוצלינגען טויט פון פרעזידענט רוזוועלט.

ער איז געווען איינער פון די גרעסטע מענשען פון אונזער צייט. ניט נאר האט ער אנגעשטרענגט צו באפרייען די מיליאנען שקלאפען אין זיין אייגען לאנד, נאר ער האט אויך מעגליך געמאכט די באפרייאונג פון דער נאגצער מענ־ שהייט פון דער בלוטיגער נאצי טיראניי.

רוזוועלט, דעם גרויסען בירגער פון די אונטערדערריקטע, וועלען אלע גוטע מענשען פון אונזער דור און פון אלע צוקונפטיגע דורות, מיט דאנקבארקייט און יראת הכבוד, אייביג גערענקען.

CHAPTER 6

Post War Years

THERE WERE THREE major themes dominating the *Kanader Nayes* in the post-war years. The most urgent one was dealing with the disaster that had befallen the Jewish people. This included not only material relief to the survivors but also an attempt to come to some kind of moral, spiritual and psychological grips with the shock of the deliberate murder of two-thirds of the Jews of Europe, ninety per cent of the Jews of Poland and about one-third of the Jews of the whole world. The second theme, not unrelated to the first, was Zionism and the fight for the establishment of a Jewish state, which turned out to be a stunning victory. The third theme, not unrelated to the first two, was the fight to save Yiddish, a losing battle if there ever was one.

Relief and Making Sense

The most urgent need was to provide relief to the Holocaust survivors in Eastern Europe and Jewish charitable enterprises were mobilized quickly. The Canadian Jewish Congress started a campaign calling for the donation of used clothing. ("Many of your brothers and sisters are going about today in Nazi prisoner clothes with the yellow patches. In all the European countries Jews are going in rags because they have nothing else to wear.") The annual *Yom Kippur yiskor* charity appeals and *Pesakh's* traditional *moes chitim* collection of food and clothing were earmarked for the survivors. ("Will they sit at a Seder?") The Council of Jewish Aid Organizations welcomed a fund-raising delegation from the Central

Committee of the Jews of Poland at a big gathering in Varsity Arena ("Delegation of Polish Jews Takes City by Storm") and the *Kanader Nayes* published a list of all the names and addresses of the various *landsmanshaftn* of the city: Ivansk, Ozhorov, Apt, Bendin, Beizitchin, Byalistok, Dombrover, Drylz, Viszhvinik, Zoloshitz, Tchenstochov, Patchiniv, Chmelnik, Lublin, Lanov, Lipsk, Stashev, Stopnitz, Tsoyzmir, Kielce, Kapshivnitseh, Klimentov, Radom, Radomsk, Rakov, and Shidlov.

The various *landslayt* tended to the needs of their *shtetl* survivors. An Apter emergency conference, in coordination with the Apter of

New York and Montreal was immediately held. It was unknown at the time how shockingly few they were, a scant 300 out of a 5,200 pre-war population. "Rescue banquets" were held, where survivors were the guests of honour:

> The rescue banquet of the Apter Aid Association was a success. Almost three thousand dollars were collected for the Apters on the other side of the ocean. The evening was distinguished by a very nice program." The speakers listed included famous Apters Anshel Weiss and Max Mandel. (Mr. Mandel, in an exemplary way, appealed for specific and necessary concrete actions and the audience warmly applauded). The main speaker, Mr. S. Waverman, warmly greeted the martyr Mrs. Rivka Weissblum, who had recently been standing on the threshold of Hitler's crematorium . . . . Mrs. Weissblum, the evening's guest of honour, moved the audience with her descriptions of the suffering which the Jews endured before the Hitlerist murderers killed them and the public cried and sobbed at the indescribable catastrophe.

Heroes of the resistance were feted at fund raisers, for instance Joseph Ziegelbaum, an underground fighter from the ghettoes and the forests, son of the famous Polish Bundist Shmuel (Arthur) Ziegelbaum, who committed suicide in 1943 outside the House of Commons in London to protest the inaction of Allies in the face of the Holocaust: "Only by helping the people for whom they fought—the impoverished and suffering Jews—through taking care of the orphans of our holy martyrs can one best honour the heroes."

People tried their best to make sense of what had happened. An article by Hersh Shishler of Johannesburg entitled "Graves of the Fallen Butchers" imagined speeches at the gravesides of Mussolini, Hitler, Goebbels and other Fascist beasts, ridiculing them and revelling in their fall. The renowned New York Workmen's Circle writer Joseph Opatoshu spoke in the Victory Theatre on the theme

"The future of the Jews in Poland" and read from his "Ghetto stories." Apropos of a *yiskor* evening for the fallen martyrs of Galicia, an article by A. Fridman, "Our debt to the Galizianer Jews," attempted to understand why the Nazis, who dreamed of empire and exploited everyone and everything were so profligate with the Jews as not to enslave them but to exterminate them. The author's answer was that the Jews represented a truth that the Nazis could not tolerate:

> The Nazis knew the Jews and they knew that a people who gave the world a Moyshe Rabeynu, a Rabbi Akiva, a Baruch Spinoza, a Karl Marx, could not be brainwashed. . . . The lie never feels secure as long as the truth exists. So long as there lived the people who gave the world the first principles of the spirit and of freedom, the Nazis did

not feel secure in their power. They were afraid of the Jewish spirit! And the Jewish people, too, believe that their spirit is their pride and their power! "Because they are our life and the length of our days."[51] Our spirit is the stuff of our life and the secret of our survival.

Mostly, however, Toronto Jews just mourned.

> And when I was sitting weeping in *shul* and, with a grieving heart, heard the cantor cry out, "Remember, God, the martyrs of the city Apt," I did not just cry for my beloved parents, brothers and sisters, I also shed tears for all of Polish Jewry, as well as for my capital city Apt. And so ended, with all our crying, that dark *yiskor* evening.[52]

Zionism

The *Kanader Nayes* never lost sight of the Zionist struggle even during the war years. It celebrated the twenty-fifth anniversary of the Balfour Declaration in 1942, the Bialik-Herzl *yortzayts*, and mourned the death of the Zionist leader Menachem Mendel Usishkin (1943). It promoted Zionist events in the city, such as an address by American Zionist leader Louis Lipsky, or a talk by the Russian born Yiddish playwright Peretz Hirshbein on Israel and the Soviet Union. A lot of emphasis was placed on the Youth Aliyah as a practical solution to the European Jewish refugees. In 1943 a complete list of the names of Polish Jewish refugee children who came from Russia and were sent via Tehran to Israel was published. The 1944 campaign kicked off with a speech by "Judge Jennie"—Jennie Loitman Barron, the first full-time woman judge on the Massachusetts bench and, later, the first woman judge of the Massachusetts Superior Court.

The paper hardened its stance against Jewish terrorism in

---

51 A quote from the evening synagogue service, "Because they [the Torah and your laws] are our life and the length of our days." כִּי הֵם חַיֵּינוּ וְאֹרֶךְ יָמֵינוּ.
52 S. Waverman, My City Apt, *KN*, January 6, 1946, p. 2.

Palestine after the Menachem Begin-led Irgun declared a revolt in February of 1944 and started a bombing campaign against the British:

> **Concerning the Terror in the Land of Israel**
> "Dear God, save me from my friends, from my enemies I can save myself." If it's true what the British administration in the Land of Israel says—namely that the bombs that have exploded in certain places in the Land of Israel were placed by Jewish terrorists—then this clever folk saying is applicable to the group of Jewish youth who have put their lives at stake to force the stubborn British government to fulfill immediately their solemn promise to the Jewish people.
> These young people, the terrorists, if they are, in general, without doubt sincere—although a little fascistically inclined—children of our people, are using an un-Jewish weapon, with the bomb, to achieve their end. To use such a weapon is not only a murderous crime but also the worst danger to our cause. It is a crime because all of the victims of the bombs are innocent people. None of the policemen or other officials who were killed by the bombs had any scrap of connection to the foolish and unjust policy of the British government, which has tried to estrange their sincerest friend, the Jews, and to embrace the whims of the Arab exploiters, the *effendis*.
> It would not make sense from either a moral standpoint or from a practical one. . . . No intelligent person could believe that even with the greatest and the most powerful terror by our Jewish terrorists—if such they be—could one go so far as to weaken the British administration so much that they would give up. . . . Terrorism holds the greatest danger for us, because it will give a new pretext to the opponents of a Jewish state in the Land of Israel, both in England and in America, only to justify keeping a bigger army in the Land of Israel, at Jewish expense, after the war, and it will even justify keeping the ban on immigration. How can one let people into the land who use bombs?[53]

---

53 *KN*, April 23, 1944 p. 2 editorial.

Once the war ended, the Zionist cause was the paper's main preoccupation. At every step of the way, the paper emphasized that the real solution to the plight of the Jews of Europe was to get them to Israel. The Youth Aliyah was a big focus. The paper urged vacationers of the summer of 1945 to put something aside:

> Remember the unfortunate homeless Jewish war orphans while you and your children enjoy your vacation.
> Remember the Youth Aliyah which is concerned with these young refugees.
> Make a collection for this holy objective in your cottages and send the money to the Youth Aliyah Office.

Likewise, the first Yom Kippur after the war became an occasion for an appeal to support Israel. Apart from appeals for money, there was constant political activism, the objectives being open immigration to Palestine and the establishment of a Jewish State. Here are two ads from October 7, 1945, a union ad and a Zionist Council ad, for the same demonstration:

The Jewish Unions Call!
All Jewish workers in Toronto to come to the big
Peoples Demonstration in Massey Hall
Monday October 8, 7:30 p.m.

> *to demand of the English Labour government*
> 1) to open the gates for freer Jewish immigration to the Land of Israel
> 2) to repeal the shameful White Paper
> 3) to carry out immediately the Balfour Declaration and establish an independent, free, secure National Jewish Home in the Land of Israel
>
> The fate of the Jewish people lies in the balance! None of you should stay away from the demonstration Monday evening.
> Be in solidarity with the whole Jewish people in this critical moment in our long, martyrful history.

אידישע יוניאנס

אויפגעוועקט!

אלע אידישע ארבעטער אין מאראנטא
צו קומען צו דער ברייטער

פאלקס
דעמאנסטראציע

אין מעסי האל
מאנטאג, דעם 8-טן אקט.
7.30 אוונט

ווען דער
טויט דען ווארמען!

ארץ ישראל איז גרייט צו אויפצונעמען
אבער דער פארעמפטעריִשער זשוויסער
פאפיר דערלאזט ניט

עפנטליכער ארץ ישראל
נוים-פאר
פארזאמלונג
מאנטאג, דעם 8-טן אקט.
8.30 אוונט
אין מעסי האל

[*Zionist Council Ad*]

Let Death wait!

Thousands of our Jewish brothers and sisters are standing face to face with death by hunger and emaciation in the horrible concentration camps of Europe.
Israel is ready to take them in but the traitorous White Paper does not allow it. Your moral support is needed.

Attend the public
**Land of Israel
Emergency Assembly
Monday 8 o'clock in Massey Hall**
Every Jew—young and old—is duty-bound to come and demand that the gates of the Land of Israel are opened for the suffering survivors of European Jewry and the Land of Israel is decreed a democratic Jewish Commonwealth.

The speakers for this event included a broad spectrum of such luminaries as future Conservative Prime Minister John J. Diefenbaker, CCF leader M.J. Coldwell, Liberal Senator Arthur V. Roebuck and David Croll ("Lieutenant Colonel"), though the only rabbi on the list was Reform's Abraham Feinberg. The union speakers were the usual suspects from the non-communist unions: Federman, Langer, Simon, *et al*.

The demonstration was a huge success, packing Massey Hall with 10,000 people. One of the speakers, Arthur Roebuck, was a committed Christian Zionist. In the *Kanader Nayes* edition showcasing the twenty-eighth annual convention of the Zionist Organization of Canada, the English pages reported a fiery speech he had made to delegates as a member of the Christian "Canada-Israel Association" arguing that a Jewish state would be an agent of the West in the Middle East, and that this was the reason the Arabs were opposed to it.

> **"Insure Peace through Jewish Palestine"—Roebuck**
> The Palestine question is a matter of world politics. By that I mean that the Arab rulers are opposed to the location of a community on the shores of the Mediterranean industrialized beyond their own capacity and bound to Great Britain by ties of sentiment and material interests. It is easy for the Arabs to spark up some anti-Semitic sentiment to cloak their real designs, but their motives in attempting to block Jewish immigration are obvious.

Rabbi Jesse Schwartz put the same message in more moderate terms:

> In reminding the British government of the pledges assumed under the Balfour Declaration and the Mandate, the delegates will speak as loyal citizens of the British Commonwealth and Empire, who believe in common with many understanding non-Jews, that the best interests of the Commonwealth and Empire will be served by a Jewish commonwealth in Palestine. Such a commonwealth will, we know, be democratic and will deal justly with all the citizens thereof in keeping with the great ethical traditions of the Jewish people.

The convention kicked off the Land of Israel Appeal with a quota of $375,000. In February, 1946, a "Grand Peoples' Demonstration for the Land of Israel" was announced in the Tivoli Theatre. At the end of March, there was a gala kick-off of the twenty-second Annual Palestine Histadrut campaign in Massey Hall. Along with the speakers, the featured artist was the fine classical singer Emma Shaver, just returned from her famous six-month tour of the displaced persons camps. Another high-class end-of-campaign concert for the Youth Aliyah featured Hyman Goodman, Sara Barkin, Joe Litman, and Feygl Gartner.[54] In April, the Shekel Campaign was revived:

---

54 Feygl Gartner was a wonderful pianist, wife of the Jewish Folk Choir conductor Emil Gartner, and the choir's accompanist for many years.

> **Buy a Shekel**
> Everywhere Jews still live, from Oslo in Northern Europe to Johannesburg in South Africa, among the free, happy and rich American Jews and among the locked up, downhearted and hungry Jews in the concentration camps—everywhere—there is now going on a diligent action to distribute the Zionist shekel—the symbol of belonging to the World Zionist Organization.[55]

Besides the Youth Aliyah, the paper also supported so-called "Aliyah B," a world-wide movement to get Jews to Palestine by boat in defiance of the White Paper, still enforced by the British government with naval blockades. On September 15, 1946, p. 3, there was a photo of one of these boats, with the caption "Illegal Immigrants" and the story:

> A picture of the ship *Colonel Wedgewood* which is taking Jewish refugees to the Land of Israel. As one can see from the picture, the unfortunate people are packed together on the ship like herring. This is, however, all fine with them as long as they are not in the dark, accursed Hitlerish concentration camps or among the pogrom victims in Poland.[56] And of these unfortunate people, Atlee, Bevin and company had the *khutzpah* to say they are "illegal immigrants" and therefore must be put back in their concentration camps on the island of Cyprus.

Zionism and the UN

On February 18, 1947 the British, no longer happy with their 1922 Mandate to administer Palestine, declared they would hand over the question to the newly founded United Nations. For the whole year the *Kanader Nayes* and Maurice Goldstick in particular, got to exercise

---

[55] *KN* editorial, April 29, 1946, p. 2
[56] The reference is to the Kielce pogrom of that summer, in which forty-two Jews were murdered and fifty seriously injured.

their considerable analytical and polemical skills dissecting developments as they occurred. It makes for very exciting reading today.

At first the British declaration that they wanted to wash their hands of the Israel problem was regarded by the *Kanader Nayes* as "having no greater worth than Germany's guarantees of the independence of Belgium."[57] When it turned out that the British were in earnest, the paper's mistrust of the big powers did not diminish in the slightest:

> **We haven't lost yet**
> As we write these lines, it looks as if the "friends" of the Jewish people at the UN are determined not to allow any representative of the Jewish Agency into their sessions. When the Arab representatives designated three consecutive days to pour out their bitter *effendish* hearts to their friends at the UN, everything was kosher and constitutional. As soon, however, as the Polish representative proposed that they should invite a representative of the Jewish Agency to enlighten the gentlemen of the UN, the "sensitive" members of the U.N., especially the representatives of England and the United States, raised an uproar that this was in violation of the constitution. And our Canadian representative, Mr. Pearson, who had appeared as if he were even a Zionist, went so far as to declare, that he, as chair of the Political Commission, would not allow any debates on the part of the Jewish Agency at the sessions of his Commission.
>
> It is clear that the big three, England, America and Russia, are striving to ingratiate themselves with Ibn Saud and the other Arab satraps, exactly the way their predecessors in the various administrations strove, in the years before the terrible war, to ingratiate themselves with Hitler and Mussolini . . . .
>
> One should not be too disheartened by this. In the meantime, the UN has not yet given any verdict against the Jews. In the worst case, Lake Success[58] has given the

---

57 *KN*, February 28, 1947, p. 2
58 Lake Success is the small town on Long Island, New York, that was the temporary headquarters of the United Nations from 1946 to 1951.

American Jews a warning, that, if they do not take a stand against Mr. Truman, an aroused anti-Jewish movement might be brought to bear against the latest position. If the American Jews want to know how to improve their situation, even the anti-Zionist Truman, regardless of the cooperation of Mr. Lessing Rosenwald and the other "prophets" from the "Council of Judaism,"[59] is constrained to recognize the cold truth, that on the day of judgment of the election, millions of Jewish and Jewish-friendly votes will be as important as millions of barrels of Standard Oil, pumped out of Ibn Saud's wells.

Mr. Truman's counsellors will have to make him understand that it not now even at all a question of him having to balance the Jewish vote against the influence of Standard Oil. On the contrary, if he is smart he can have both. If only we Canadian Jews were in such a position with respect to our Canadian government as the American Jews are with theirs. In Canada, we are missing many thousands of Jewish noses. If we had tens of thousands of Jewish voters in the various provinces of the country, our friend Mr. Pearson would perhaps be less constitutional and more decent. [60]

In fact, when the United Nations Special Commission on Palestine (UNSCOP) was set up by the General Assembly in May, 1947, the decision was, indeed, to hear from the Jewish Agency. Ultimately, it was the Arab states who refused to participate.[61] Not only that, in a speech to the United Nations General Assembly on May 14, the Russian representative surprisingly came down strongly on the side of the Jews, opting for a single, bi-national state if possible (a position favoured by many in the Zionist movement,

---

59 Lessing J. Rosenwald, chairman of Sears-Roebuck and Co. from 1932 until 1939, was a prominent Jewish advocate of American neutrality in World War Two before Pearl Harbour and then president of the American Council for Judaism, an association of anti-Zionist Reform Jews.
60 *KN*, May 9, 1947, p.2.
61 Official Records of the Second Session of the General Assembly Supplement No. 11 United Nations Special Committee on Palestine Report to the General Assembly, 3 September 1947.

including the *Kanader Nayes*), and partition only if necessary. This speech marked a radical change of attitude by the Soviet Union and produced consternation among the Arabs, but was warmly received by the Jews, for example in a fascinating editorial in the *Kanader Nayes* of June 13, 1947, that expressed a strong preference for what we might now call a "one-state" solution. On the other hand, the positions taken in favour of partition by Zionist luminaries such as (future first President of Israel) Chaim Weizmann and (future first Prime Minister) David Ben Gurion, drew nothing but scorn from the paper's editors.

The summer of 1947 was a particularly tense time for the Zionist movement. While UNSCOP was meeting in Palestine, the "Sergeant's Affair" broke out, during which the Irgun[62] kidnapped two British sergeants and threatened to kill them if the death sentences passed on Irgun militants arrested by the British were carried out. UNSCOP was even petitioned during its Jerusalem hearings for the release of the militants but it refused to intervene, saying it was beyond its competence. Two days after UNSCOP packed up and left, the militants were executed and the sergeants were killed in retaliation. The *Kanader Nayes* was against the Irgun executions, but it bristled more at the suggestion, for example from a certain Dr. Rabinovich, that "political Zionism" was to blame:

> **A bad diagnosis from a good doctor**
> . . . If Dr. Rabinovich were really learned, he would know that Moses and the other prophets and sages of the Talmud were "political Zionists" or even better, that they were "religious Zionists" at the same time as being "political Zionists" . . . .
>   No one expects either Dr. Rabinovich or any other peaceful Jews to approve of the terror that a number of

---

62 The paramilitary wing of the Revisionists.

desperate young Jews are carrying on in Palestine. Of course and of course not. On the other side, however, is it proper for a Jew like Dr. Rabinovich, who follows the Jewish Torah, not to rebuke with a single word the most recent fiery threats against the Jews? Does he not know that representatives of mighty England have concluded an agreement with representatives of the weak Jews about strengthening and helping the building of a national home for the Jewish people? Does the 'righteous' Dr. Rabinovich mean that the mighty are not bound to keep their word? If so, is that in accord with the philosophy of the Jewish prophets? His two sad published statements against the Zionists cast doubt on Dr. Rabinovich's devotion to Jews and to Jewish interests, as he himself clearly shows.

At the end of the summer, when UNSCOP, by majority, did recommend the partition of Palestine into two independent states, the *Kanader Nayes* held it "of doubtful benefit to the Jews, both from the point of view of the current situation and the hopes of the Jewish side."

On the front page of the September 5, 1947 paper, an unsigned editorial attempted to draw up a balance sheet for the year. After all we had gone through, it was yet another very dark one for the Jewish people. However, the editors were able to find some "bright spots."

> **The year ends with bright spots**
> The year 5707 was one of the darkest years in the long, melancholy history of the unfortunate people of Israel. Our desperate sisters and brothers in Europe did not find any relief during the year from their unbearable situation. The population of the concentration camps did not diminish during the year. On the contrary, for each one who died there or who had the good fortune to flee from there for good, others entered, leaving the number of that population much higher today than on the day when Hitler made an end to his eternally-cursed life.
> The liberated Eastern European peoples, on the morning after their liberation, as everybody knows, took

to persecuting the unfortunate Jewish survivors whose flesh and blood had been so mercilessly handled that today in Europe there are missing six million Jewish souls, the toll from the war. Six million Jews were burnt without ceremony in Hitler's lime ovens or killed in some other horrible manner.

Unfortunately, the black prophesies of the pessimistic modern Jewish prophets have been fully realized: the Hitler poison has remained in all the eastern lands that fell under Hitler's yoke, even after the bloody madman breathed his last polluted breath. And Jews were forced to flee from the 'liberated' Eastern European lands so as not to be annihilated by the new wave of pogroms. And that explains the increase in the population of these concentration camps.

However, the deathly atmosphere of these camps has led a small part of the desperate to risk their lives and set out for the land that was promised to the Jewish people. They have wandered hundreds of miles over mountains and valleys, through heat and cold, through rain and snow, hungry and in rags, so that they could reach the Land of Israel. They have journeyed there by sea in leaky, unsanitary ships, on guard against every eye as if they were criminals escaped from jail.

Well, for British Jews it is doubly hard to describe the welcome that these unfortunate refugees have met on behalf of the representatives of the government of our mother land, England. Instead of receiving them, the first victims of Hitlerism, as dear relatives who have undergone the most severe losses in a common struggle, they went after them like their worst enemies. Very few of these unfortunate refugees managed to save themselves from the 'protective' English fleet or from the murderous raids of the troops set upon them. A number of the refugees have been killed in cold blood because they wouldn't believe that the men of the 'socialist' government of England—which had for years presented itself as the constant friend of the persecuted Jewish people—were simply hoaxers.

The sad results of the experiment of sneaking into the promised Jewish land are already known to everyone. The *Exodus 1947* is the latest witness of this apparently unbelievable turn of events, that the British Labour government would scoff at the entire solemn obligation made to the Jewish people and would take these horrible, indeed Hitlerish, steps.[63]

All this stands on the darker side of the Jewish balance sheet for the year 5707, together with the criminal complicity that the leaders of the American States have so clearly shown in keeping their gates *de facto* locked to the displaced Jews.

However, thank God, the same 5707 ended with a few really bright spots of hope. A committee was established more than three months ago through the United Nations to investigate the Jewish claim to the Land of Israel, the legitimacy of this claim, the suitability of the land to receive Jews and to serve their needs, the desire of the homeless among the Jewish people to start a new life in the Land of Israel, and the readiness and resolve of the free Jews in the democratic countries to support the needs of the Land of Israel. This committee, thoroughly studied the question and, by the end of that otherwise particularly sad year 5707, put forward a report to the United Nations that recommended, among other things, that the larger part of the east of the Land of Israel should be given to the Jewish people to establish a Jewish state; that steps should be taken to allow one hundred and fifty thousand Jewish refugees into the Land of Israel in the interim period; and that free peoples should open up the locked gates of their countries to take in the remaining Jewish refugees.

We Jews could have expected no better outcome for the situation under the circumstances. Against us stood the American and English oil magnates who supported the dark Arab exploiters and fanatic reactionaries. On our side, further, stood our own timid and fearful leaders, who were ready to accept as significant the littlest thing the committee recommended.

---

63 In the summer of 1947, the ship *Exodus 1947* with 4,515 Jewish passengers, including 655 children, on board, was on its way from France to Palestine when it was attacked by British destroyers and boarded. Two passengers and a crewman were killed in the ensuing battle and thirty were wounded. The ship was forced to return to France and then, after a stand-off of twenty-four days, taken to Hamburg, Germany, then in the British occupation zone. The immigrants were forcibly taken off the ship and transported to two camps near Lubeck.

Experts have commented that, in that part of the land that the committee recommended for us, we can rescue all the Jews that now languish in the concentration camps and all those who feel a need to live in Jewish surroundings. This alone is the most important event of more than two thousand years of history, even though it is a lot less than what Herzl and the first political Zionists had planned for the Jewish people.

One must point out that the *effendis*, both Arab and British, do not yet want to give in so easily! That our 'friends' Ernest Bevin, Herbert Morrison and Creech Jones and the other 'kind gentlemen' in the current British ministries will apply all means to delay the matter as long as they are allowed.[64] And, that our own people, the Lessing Rosenwalds on one side and the extremists on the other side, will also oppose the recommendations of the majority of the committee and in this way help the Jewish enemies in the U.N. to delay their intrusive plan.

They will not decide anything, however. No one is going to give in to even the least of their demands. In the worst case, they might succeed once again in delaying for a while the valid solution to the problem. As long, however, as we Jews keep control over our own Weizmanns, Goldmans, Ben Gurions and their devotees, the modest plan of the committee can be realized.

So that is what the sum total of the year 5707 has brought us. Let us only remain stubborn and determined, let us only support with all our energy the collection of money for the Land of Israel—the Combined Land of Israel Appeal—and in the coming year, some of our hostages in the concentration camps will be freed.

A full page ad for the Combined Palestine Appeal, as it was called in English, appeared on the back page of the paper for September 26, 1947, with the symbol of the campaign: a circle with the letters CPA and "1947" and a drawing of refugees crossing into Palestine, with writing around it in English "*Palestine is still the Answer!*"

---

64 Ernest Bevin was Prime Minister of England, Herbert Morrison, Deputy Prime Minister and Arthur Creech Jones, Secretary of State for the Colonies.

פראקלאמאציע

דאס טאראנטער אידענטום
שטײם פאר אן ערענסטען ארויסרוף

די "יו. ען." קאמיסיע רעקאמענדירט:

אז 150,000 אויסגעװארצעלטע אידען זאלען אריינגעלאזען װערען אן ארץ ישראל

אז אן אידישער סטאט זאל עטאבלירט װערען אין ארץ ישראל

אונזערס, װעם זײן די ערשטע שטימע צו דעמאנסטרירען אױף א ממשות׳דיגען אופן א
בריטהארציגער שטיצע פאר דעם 1947 קאמביניטען ארץ ישראל אפיל קאמפיין. אן מיר גע־
מען אױף דעם ארויסרוף און די גרויסע היסטארישע פאראנטווארטליכקייט װאס שטײם פאר
אונז.

מיר קענען ניט פאראכלעסיגען אונזערע שוועסטער און ברידער. מיר טארען ניט.

די װארטען שוין צו לאנג און טארען ניט אנטוישם װערען

• בלויז דורך געבען דעם פופטעל מיליאן אידישע
אויסגעװארצעלטע מיליאן פון דיימשלאנד, עסטרײך און
איטאליען א געלעגענהײט צו נעפמען הײמען אין
ארץ ישראל. װאו זיי מוזען װעלען זיך באגעגען.
װעט דער קאפ װערען פארנעמדען אין זייערן לעבען.

• צװײ לעבענסװיכטיגע פאראנטווארטלעכקייטען א ליבע פון
האפענונג, פאר די אידען פון אייראפא, די האפענונג
אױף פאלעסטינע — פאר די מיטגעזט פון דעם שער.

סעל מיליאן אידען װאס װיגען פארשפארט אין די
אויסגעװארצעלטע לאגערען — אן פאר די איבער־
געבליבענע אידען פון אייראפא, דעם קאטאסטריװי
אז זײערע ברידער אידען אין קאנאדא װעלען צו
שפילען די חלק װאס איז אױף דרענגליך גיטיג
צו ברעטגען אן עסטי איופולונג."

דר. ראשעדע ם. חײמאן.
ווירגלפרעוידענט פון הוטטער יארק.

ניט בריטהארציג, ניט װי א קרבן צו דעם
1947 קאמבינירטען ארץ ישראל אפיל
העלפט אויסלייזען דעם פאלק ישראל אין דעם לאגר פון ישראל

ארץ ישראל איז נאך אלץ דער ענטפער

Palestine is still the Answer!

Campaign Headquarters:
651 SPADINA AVENUE
Kingsdale 2153
TORONTO, ONTARIO

Proclamation

TORONTO JEWRY
faces a GRAVE CHALLENGE

The UN commission recommends:
That 150,000 displaced Jews be admitted to
the Land of Israel
That a Jewish State be established in
the Land of Israel

Ours will be the first voice to demonstrate in tangible form through all-out support of the 1947 Combined Land of Israel Appeal campaign, that we accept the challenge and the great historical responsibility facing us.

WE MUST NOT FAIL OUR BROTHERS
AND SISTERS. WE DARE NOT.
They have waited too long to be let down now

- 'Only by giving the quarter million Jews made displaced persons by Germany, Austria and Italy the opportunity of finding homes in Palestine, where most of them wish to settle . . . will chaos be prevented in the camps.'

- 'Two beacons of light offer hope to Europe's Jews, the hope of Palestine—for most of the quarter million Jews trapped in the displaced persons camps—and for the remaining Jews on the continent, the knowledge that their brother Jews in Canada will provide the help so desperately needed to effect a genuine revival. . . .'
Dr. Joseph C. Hyman, *vice-president of the Joint.*[65]

Give Liberally, Give Sacrificially to the 1947 Combined Land of Israel Appeal
Help Redeem the People of Israel in the Land of Israel

[In English] *Palestine is <u>still</u> the Answer!*
National Objective $2,000,000

---

65 Short for the Joint Distribution Committee, the American Jewish aid institution formed during the First World War and still operating today.

Back to the UN

After the UNSCOP recommendation of September 1, a period of diplomatic suspense followed, with no government declaring their intentions. This was ridiculed by the *Kanader Nayes*, with some fine, old-world Jewish humour:

> It is highly probably that these and other statesmen don't even know themselves, right now, how they should vote when the time comes, or how they'll have to react when they can no longer hide behind diplomatic chicanery. The stance of these diplomats reminds one of the 'tramp' who was brought before the judge on a charge of robbery. When the judge asked whether he was guilty or innocent, he replied that he himself didn't know and had to wait until he heard the evidence....

On October 11, 1947, the Americans, following Soviet-bloc Czechoslovakia and Poland but preceding the Soviet Union's own pronouncement, declared themselves for partition. The British, on the other hand refused. Until shortly before the vote, it was unclear how Canada would stand. Nevertheless, the *Kanader Nayes* expressed gratitude for the role Canada and Canadians had played thus far:

> **You Reap What You Sow**
> ... the Canadian government is to be thanked, first because it gave a free hand to its genial representative in the UN Land of Israel Committee, Judge Rand, to deal according to how his mind and conscience dictated. And second, because it exhibited an extraordinary uprightness when it recognized that the people, starting with organized labour and ending with the elite of the Canadian community, supported the modest demands of the Zionists. The government, through Justice Minister Ilsley and its representative on the UN Committee, Assistant Minister of Foreign Affairs Mr. Lester B. Pearson, took the courageous position that it pursued through the compromise between the United States and the Soviet Union. Thanks to this compromise, one can

expect that something substantial will be accomplished in the current session of the United Nations Association.

One must keep in mind that the Canadian pro-Zionist policy did not fall from the sky. It called for a colossal amount of courage and work to plow and seed the grounds of Canadian public opinion, to be able to overcome the unwilling part of the powerful Canadian non-Jewish press, which tried hard to justify the deceitful actions of the anti-Semitic Ernest Bevin.

The Zionist workers movement in the United States had already converted the presidents of the American Federation of Labor and the CIO and their comrades to Zionism years earlier. This made it possible for the Canadian Labour Zionists to persuade the Canadian labour leaders that justice demanded that the Jews shouldn't be overlooked in the establishment of world peace.

The Canadian Zionist Organization, under the leadership of Mr. Sam J. Sacks, has earned recognition for its great work in waking up the conscience of our Christian fellow citizens in the country's cultural, spiritual and political leadership circles. Mr. Sacks's administration dedicated a lot of time, effort and money to organize our Christian friends in Canada and to win new friends for the Christians for Zionism. The faithful Christian Herbert Mowat was prevailed upon to become director of the Christian Council for Palestine. The dedicated Sir Ellsworth Flavelle undertook to serve as chair and, with the cooperation of such a liberal spirit as Senator Arthur V. Roebuck, has succeeded over the last four or five years in winning over these leadership circles, and with them also dear Lester B. Pearson, for Zionism.

Without this friendly public opinion it would have been impossible for our government to take a position at the UN which opposed the position of the British government. This was a real diplomatic revolution. Not only did this diplomatic revolution directly help the Zionist cause at the UN, it also helped improve the standing of Canadian Jews in the eyes of the local Christian community. They took very great care to see to it that the events in the Land of Israel did not create an anti-Semitic atmosphere in Canada.

Canada did indeed vote for the UN partition resolution on November 29, 1947, which barely passed by the necessary two-thirds majority. The editors of the *Kanader Nayes*, who had long abandoned their earlier skepticism over partition, also declared that they now believed in miracles.

The Victory at Lake Success
These lines are being written immediately after the radio has brought us the historical happy message that the United Nations has by an over two-thirds majority approved the Land of Israel partition plan, which nearly all the Jewish people supported and which nearly all the Arabs opposed.

This joyful event has once again confirmed that determination, based on courage, is hard to defeat. Again it has been shown that the age of miracles has not yet passed into eternity.

Thanks to the heroic persistence and idealistic boldness of the first groups of modern Zionists and their determined and heroic followers in all countries of the world, the Land of Israel has more than forty percent Jews in its population; and has, in certain regions, a great majority of Jews; and two hundred thousand souls in the nearly all-Jewish city, Tel Aviv; and a Jewish business class; and a Jewish Parliament with a Jewish administration...

Nobody should doubt any more the genuineness of the miracle of the great Moses standing on the edge of the Red Sea and dividing the water with his staff so that the Jews could cross over and in that way escape Egyptian servitude. And nobody should have any doubts about the second miracle of feeding a people for forty consecutive years with *manna* which fell from heaven. And nobody needs to wonder at the collapse of the walls of Jericho and about the hundreds of other miracles and wonders which happened to our fathers.

In our own day the great Herzl has divided the sea of Jewish indifference and disbelief and led his followers to the other side; and the Zionists have nourished themselves on the *manna* of their faith for not only forty years, but for a whole fifty years; and the towers of scorn and opposition in our time, which were a lot stronger than the brick towers of Jericho, were made to dissolve and the fortresses of assimilation were conquered.

Only a naive person could take it for a natural event, when such non-Zionist groups as the American Jewish Committee, Agudat Yisrael,[66] the Jewish Workers Committee and the communist organizations threw themselves body and soul into the struggle to get a Jewish state in the Land of Israel for the people of Israel. No, this was not a natural event; it was a supernatural event, which means, in the language of our fathers, a miracle.

Of course, one can find logical reasons to explain the changed attitudes of these groups, exactly as one can find logical reasons for the above-mentioned miracles in the times of our forefathers. . . . In our case one can find the key to the mystery in three main elements that led to redemption: (1) the three-quarters of a million strong community in the Land of Israel with all its mature, democratic governmental institutions; (2) the indescribable hardship of the survivors in the Hitleristic and Bevinistic concentration camps; and (3) the overwhelming political power of the five million strong united Jewish community in the United States which literally forced an anti-Semitic American government to support a one hundred percent Zionist project. . . .

Unfortunately, we have in our time already seen how peoples have become self-governing and then once again lost their self-governance. Not only is there going to be a need for colossal capital funds to build our country, but there will be a need for a lot of patience and persistence and understanding both with the until-now independent fighting groups and with the deluded Arabs.[67]

War of Independence and Declaration of the State of Israel

The Arab resistance began the day after the partition resolution passed, with an attack on a bus that left five Jewish civilians dead. The War of Independence had effectively begun and would continue for more than a year. The British announced on December

---

66 Literally the Union of Israel, a political movement of the ultra-orthodox, originally opposed to the Zionist project.
67 *KN,* December 5, 1947, p. 2

11, 1947 that the Mandate would end on May 15, 1948 and began an increasingly chaotic withdrawal. As fighting intensified in 1948, Canadian Jews, along with Jews throughout the world joined the fight by sending money, material and even volunteers. In April, 1948, the United Jewish Appeal kicked off with some star-studded events, one an evening at Toronto's Royal York Hotel with I. F. Stone, then editor of *The Nation* as the keynote speaker, and another at a local yeshiva with heart-throb Herman Yablokov, fresh from entertaining the refugees in the camps. A big ad on April 9 had Yablokov pictured in uniform, with this text:

> CANADA IS ALSO ON THE WAR FRONT
> Nobody is shooting at us.
> On our streets one doesn't see any barbed wire.
> We sleep without suddenly being awoken by machine gun fire which deafens the silence of the night. Our houses are not fortified and we can peacefully travel from Toronto to Montreal or from Halifax to Vancouver. Death does not lie hidden behind every tree.
> HOWEVER, WE ARE ON THE FRONT...
> Just like every hero in the hills around Hebron or in the Negev who keeps a vigil at night or who takes aim at the hateful snipers.
> WE ARE ON THE FRONT AND WE MUST NOT FORGET IT
> They depend on us, the young heroes who lack equipment, the fighters who lack penicillin, the *yishuvim* [settlers] who lack in raincoats, firewood, cement, defense kits, the new settlers who lack in aid and rehabilitation.
> The whole building, struggling, war front community turns to us.
> WE HAVE A WAR FRONT...
> Let us make a donation to do our duty through the $1,800,277 United Jewish Appeal—Combined Land of Israel Appeal—combined Jewish Welfare Fund.

Some Jewish youths took the war front idea more literally, and enlisted in the *"Machal"* [foreign] brigades to fight in Israel.

At first there were fears that the Canadian government would ban participation as it did during the Spanish civil war, but this never happened, and 232 Canadians joined about 3,300 other volunteers from around the world. Then, on May 14, 1948, a big front page banner headline:

> Celebratory Demonstration in Maple Leaf Gardens For the Proclamation of the Jewish State in the Land of Israel

This was followed by pictures of Baruch Zukerman, Dr. Chaim Weizmann, Dr. Binyamin Ze'ev Herzl, Dr. Abba Hillel Silver, Ha Rav Meir Berlin all under the heading, "The former and current captains of the Zionist ship who have guided it to the hope of triumph." And beneath that, the following unsigned article, in which, with an exuberant generosity, all contributions were given due recognition, including, surprisingly, those of "the so-called terrorists in the Land of Israel":

> **A Dream Becomes Realized**
> That to which all Jewish generations since the destruction of the Second Temple have looked forward with the greatest longing will be officially realized in the coming week on May 16 through the proclamation of the Jewish state in the Land of Israel.
>
> The unceasing two thousand year-old prayer of our religious sisters and brothers has now been answered. By giving back to the Jews their stolen land, they are also given back their stolen honour.
>
> Starting from the 16th of May, 1948, the ancient Land of Israel will be recognized once again—even though for the present by only a few peoples—as the homeland of the ancient people of Israel. From that day on, that land will be the protector of all persecuted Jews and the home of all homeless Jews. For the first time in the long, exile history of our suffering people, the Jews will like all other people have a voice, as a people, to call for justice for

themselves and for others.

Every Jew must take this same historical opportunity to remember with love, gratitude and honour all those who helped bring closer this historical day. The free thinkers, equally with the religious, must not for one moment forget that we have to thank first of all our religious fathers and mothers who incessantly and under various circumstances kept holy and fundamental the longing for Zion and Jerusalem as a redemption for the Jewish people. And we must also not forget our modern Zionist leaders, from Moses Hess, Pinski, Herzl and Nordau through to Weizmann, Ben Gurion, Neeman and Silver, who dedicated their rich lives to their people and their land.

It would, however, be no dishonour for the mentioned and unmentioned glorious geniuses to put at the head of the table all those young and old men and women in the Land of Israel who fought for the liberation of their land and who fell, and those who fought and remained alive. In the final analysis it is not very important if their holy struggle was certified as kosher by the official groups or not, and if the methods they employed were acceptable to all ethical people. Unfortunately, many righteous people employ unrighteous methods to achieve righteous results.

Let us now confess, that after all the great headaches that the so-called terrorists in the Land of Israel often caused us, they must be thanked for the fact that Bevin's England was forced to leave the Land of Israel. That step was bound, naturally, to lead to the proclamation of May 16. And let us also take comfort that we Jews were not the only ones with righteous ideals who sinned against divine and human morality. All fighting people have had such impatient souls. Even the stately English have had idealists who have cut off the head of their own king.

And we, who will have no direct opportunity to defend with our blood and life the newly born Jewish land against the attacks of the Arab exploiters and their European accomplices, will not be absolved of our responsibilities by our deeds of the past. Let us, on this solemn day, swear anew that we will not rest until the existence of the new-born Jewish nation-state is completely assured.

Long live the newly born Jewish independence in the ancient Jewish land!

The acknowledgement that Jewish terrorism had made the English leave Palestine stands in stark contrast to what the same editorialist had written four years earlier: "No intelligent person could believe that even with the greatest and the most powerful terror by our Jewish terrorists—if such they be—could one go so far as to weaken the British administration so much that they would give up . . ." Circumstances change, of course, but maybe the "headaches" they were referring to were the obvious embarrassment the terror acts had caused Christian Zionists such as Senator Roebuck who had written in the paper just eight months earlier:

> I am disturbed and annoyed. If I could get my hands in the hair of the terrorists of Palestine, I'd wring their necks. . . . These men have done more harm to world Jewry and to the national home cause than the most anti-Semitic of non-Jews are capable. . . . In the meantime, the wonderful Zionist cause is under a very dark cloud, and one must look elsewhere for the good cheer one likes to note at New Year's season.

But the time for embarrassment was past. It was a time for celebrations and demonstrations and practical action. The great celebration that was advertised for Maple Leaf Gardens was, according to the *Toronto Star*, the "greatest rally ever" in Toronto: "Recognize Israel, Rally of 20,000 Jews Asks Canada. Greatest Rally Ever in City Urges Canada Permit Arms for Israel."[68] The march of Jews and Christian Zionists and their supporters started at Bathurst and College Streets and proceeded along College to Maple Leaf Gardens, gathering adherents along the way with Israeli flags and Hebrew songs, ending in a rally inside with many speeches and prayers (including one by Senator Roebuck).

---

68 *Toronto Star*, May 17, 1948, p.1

But now there was a war to be fought. The *Kanader Nayes* soon confronted the question of accepting military aid from Soviet-bloc countries despite the disapproval of the Americans, the English and the Canadians:

> Every sensible person must admit that the strongest resolutions of the Zionist federations, the Canadian federation included, will not be strong enough to hold back the Mufti and Abdullah and Ibn Saud and the other Arab rulers from their criminal adventures against the Jews. Without a doubt, an airplane with a machine gun that comes from Rumania or Bulgaria will have a better effect on the attackers than such resolutions.
>
> One understands that the anti-Semites in the United States, in England and in Canada will strive to exploit this element to corroborate their claim that all Jews, the Jewish millionaires included, are secret Bolsheviks, who lie in wait to change the American or the English or the Canadian "way of life" into the Soviet way of life. And it can possibly be that this element will turn out unfavourably for the Jews in certain circles, and that some Jews will feel discomforted by it.
>
> Only what significance can this discomfort of the few Jews have in comparison with the decisive gains in favour of the Land of Israel that can come from accepting help from states that are not in step with Truman's America, Bevin's England and St. Laurent's Canada? The Jewish leadership has come to be entrusted by circumstances of destiny to protect the present and the future of the Jews in the Land of Israel.

The entire collection of the United Jewish Appeal for 1948 went to Israel:

> One does not need to explain anymore what a contribution to Israel means now. In all recorded history so far, no group has surpassed the achievement of the heroes now fighting in the Land of Israel. With bare hands, they have succeeded in turning back the Arab hordes, which have been so well armed and equipped by Bevin and his anti-Jewish friends. Not only have our heroes been able to hold

> all their positions, they have also managed to capture large tracts that belonged to the enemy.
>
> However, even the greatest battlers must eat, and when they are wounded, their wounds must be bandaged. . . . If we do not equip them with their irreducible necessities, then regardless of their incomparable heroism, Bevin and the Arab bands will overwhelm them and triumph. . .
>
> It follows that anyone who begrudges Bevin and the Arab bands victory over our heroes must immediately contribute once again just as much as he can to the United Jewish Appeal. The whole collection, as already announced, goes completely for the Land of Israel.[69]

There were also many independent aid efforts, including a "food shower" organized by the United Toronto Jewish Women's Division, a coalition of several disparate women's groups. They asked for "canned"[70] kosher meat, salmon, other fish, condensed milk, cheese, coffee, sugar, and all kinds of food for children. The paper called out incessantly, "Help for Israel" and "Israel needs skilled people." As the war reached its decisive stage, the editors of the *Kanader Nayes* called on Canadian Jews "to help Jewish victors instead of Jewish victims."

> **Help for Israel**
> Of course, it would have been more comfortable and a lot healthier for all of us if the Jewish state would come to be without a war and without the violence and tragedy of the holy Jewish victims, who have already been offered on the altar of the Jewish state, and—may we be allowed to say—who will yet be necessary before the eternal Jewish wish will be completely fulfilled.
>
> But what can one do? Our sinful world has been cursed with a horrible curse—that no good event can occur without sweat and blood. It is already miracle enough that we have grabbed the possibility, through heroic struggle

---

69 *KN*, June 25, 1948, p. 1
70 Spelled both properly and in Yinglish: "געבלעכעלטע (קענד)"—"*geblekhelte (kenned).*"

and hard work, of building a Jewish nation-state. And even greater is the miracle that, after two thousand years of unceasing persecution and unbearable suffering, the Jewish people is strong enough to take gun in hand and go out and make war with enemies who are incomparably more numerous than us and immeasurably better armed. In the meantime, our heroes have triumphed on all fronts in a way which none of us, not even the optimists, could have imagined, not even in their wildest fantasies....

It is our minimum duty to provide them with the things which, if they were not forced to fight their war and our war, they themselves could construct and provide. We must provide them with food, with clothes, with medications and with all the other things that our government permits us to give them. In this moment let us do what the Aid Committee desires of us. Let us fill up the bags with food for the food train that Canada promised the heroes of Israel.[71]

Let us remember that this is now the first time since the period of the Second Temple that we turn to the fortunate and rich part of our people to help Jewish victors instead of Jewish victims. That this is the first time in two thousand years that we ask the fortunate and rich part of our people for a contribution to a triumph and not for a defeat. Let us understand the greatness of the moment and open our hearts and our pockets, so that the heroes who have endured the Arabs' spears and bullets do not fall victim to hunger and disease. Let us help them as brothers and sisters![72]

In the same issue, the paper included a report from Max Federman, one of the stalwarts of the *Kanader Nayes* and its anti-communist champion in the labour movement, bursting with pride from his twelve-day visit to Israel, over a picture of him with "a group of Haganah fighters at the front" that looks rather more like a group of Jewish gentlemen in khaki shorts carrying rifles in front

---

[71] In September, 1948, the Canadian government made train cars available to collect food items for Israel, which were gathered by volunteers from householders all across the country.

[72] *KN*, September 17, 1948, p.2.

of a hotel but in this case, the thousand words is worth more than the picture:

A Joyful Greeting from the State of Israel

... I want now to report that the Jewish state is a fact, that the state has come to life and stands on solid foundations. I say this with the fullest conviction. And I encountered the community full of hope and confidence. I must add that I myself did not expect such wonderful development in all domains, and especially in the military domain.

... I have, in my life, encountered various types of soldiers from different peoples, but this is the first time I have seen such a soldier as the Jewish one. In him is embodied so much spirit and intelligence, such a great moral energy! Thus did the Haganah smash the legends about the mighty Arab powers.... The army, all things considered, is the purest symbol of a people's army. The soldier is a worker and the worker is a soldier. The Jewish army is also the most "international" army in the world. I saw fighting men from all parts of the world—even a few "countries" such as Auschwitz, Majdanek and Bergen-Belsen have their representatives there. It's not only once that you see an armed hand holding a gun and on that naked arm there peeks out the number that Hitler branded him with. From among them, too, some have already fallen victims on the front, and one sees also the veterans of *Exodus* on the front who take part in the fight and in the building. One tells me that there are already victims among them, too. A great experience for me was when I encountered our youth from Canada on the battle fronts. Our youth from all countries are on the front, and a great moral lesson is calling out from them that the whole Jewish people over the whole world must now stand in full mobilization to look after the interests of Israel...

From the first minute, as soon as I had put my foot on the ground of the Land of Israel, I sensed the great experience of happiness and deep joy to be in the State of Israel and to breathe the air of freedom and creativity that one feels in every corner of it. It is simply impossible to explain what it means now to spend day after day in our homeland, in our old-new land, which has risen up after two thousand years to a robust and strong life. You feel

> that this is yours and that you are a part of it. One can experience this especially in Tel Aviv. There, you have a great city that can compete with all the great cities of Europe. You feel turbulence and confidence in everything and in everyone, in the whole land in general. Men and women go about with confidence, especially the young people—free citizens! Nowhere in the whole world can you see such Jewish youth! . . .
>
> It was a shame for me that my visit was for just twenlve days, but what a great feeling I got from it.

By the end of the year, the war was over. Canada had recognized Israel, but had abstained on the failed vote for admission to the UN—the *Kanader Nayes* bitterly remarked, "Canada has disappointed us. . . . [its] non-vote had exactly the same value as Syria's *khutzpadike* [brazen] vote to reject the application."[73] However, once the armistice agreements had been signed with Egypt, Jordan and Lebanon, Israel was admitted, on May 11, 1949, by a healthy margin, with the UK still abstaining, but Canada voting in favour.

Post-war confidence and renewal

These great Jewish struggles of the post-war period seem to have invigorated Canadian Jews. Our standing was certainly increased by the common struggle against Hitler and the establishment of the State of Israel. An increase in confidence could be seen in the involvement of Jews in the immediate post-war civil rights and anti-racism movements. At least the *Kanader Nayes* had no shame jumping into these debates. One of these was the immediate post-war treatment of Japanese Canadians. It is well-known today that, during the war, Canadians of Japanese descent living in British Columbia had their property confiscated and were sent to internment camps.

---

73 *KN*, December 24, 1948, p. 2.

What is less well-known is that, after the war, they were forbidden by the federal government from returning to British Columbia and given the option of dispersion elsewhere in Canada or deportation to Japan. These decrees, passed under emergency powers during the war and renewed after it, were upheld by the Supreme Court of Canada and the British House of Lords, and only lifted in 1949. When the measures were renewed in 1947, a major debate ensued in Parliament. The *Kanader Nayes* had no hesitation in condemning these measures in the strongest terms available:

> **Nuremberg Laws**
> Last week a harmful and shameful law was passed in the federal Parliament: the ban on Canadian Japanese from returning to their homes in British Columbia has been newly approved. . . .
>
> In wartime one could hide behind the fig leaf of wartime necessity. One could convince naive Canadians that, because the Japanese must certainly be disloyal to the country, and could thus be spies for the bloodthirsty Japanese government that was making war on us, they must be expelled from British Columbia. The claim that the Japanese must be traitors was justified simply on the premise that, for people who had been so badly handled as the Orientals in Canada, it must be hard to be loyal.
>
> At that, it's worth remarking that Canadian Germans and Italians, whose countrymen also shot Canadian sons in battle, were not expelled from anywhere unless they were discovered to really be spies. Can there then be any doubt that, regarding the Japanese, their guilt lay in their racial origin and not in their disloyalty? . . .
>
> It should be noted, for the eternal praise of the CCF party, that its members of Parliament—and a great number of them come, in fact, from British Columbia—used all means to prevent this law from passing. And it should also be noted that our Jewish Member of Parliament, David Croll, this time as always, let it be known that he was against this ugly law. Among other things, Mr. Croll stated that there was already enough unofficial discrimination in Canada against decent people because

of their race or religion without creating new official discriminations.

The other Liberals who spoke and voted against the law were Bona Arsenault from Quebec, Benidickson and Michaud from Ontario. Among the Conservatives who fought strongly against the law were Diefenbaker and Hackett from Western Canada—two truly progressive men. [74]

However, reaction won out and, to the shame of our land, modified Nuremberg laws have been introduced. Today these laws are aimed at the Japanese, but tomorrow they can, with the same logic be turned against other 'undesirable' races or nationalities. Only the Eternal knows where this can yet lead.[75]

The paper's anti-racism was also on display in the 1949 federal elections when it gave a favorable front-page story to William White (brother of the famous opera singer Portia White), the first black federal candidate, who ran for the CCF in Spadina ("CCF nominates negro in Spadina"). However, the paper did not go so far as to actually support him. Its continued and increasing antipathy to the CCF over World War Two, Zionism and the coming Cold War, led it to back the Liberal candidate David Croll, whom the paper supported very strongly as a Jew, Zionist and war veteran. Croll won easily. While opposing racists such as municipal politician Leslie Saunders, and supporting liberal-minded politicians such as Alan Lamport (a veteran and an opponent of the Sunday closing laws, which were seen as discriminating against Jews who could not shop on Saturday either), the paper tended to support Jewish candidates, whatever their politics, for instance future mayors Nathan Phillips (and his son Howard) and Phil Givens (who, early in his career, would send in his Rosh Hashana greetings to the *Kanader Nayes*

---

74 Michaud was actually from New Brunswick and Hackett from Quebec.
75 *KN*, May 2, 1947, p. 2.

with the alternative name of "Pinchas Geverts").

This was also a lively period for Yiddish-language entertainment. There was an endless parade in the immediate post-war of famous names from America and even from Europe. Performing at the Victory, Victoria and Temple Theatres and at Massey Hall, were Eyza Kremer ("the international balladeer"), Yehuda Clyde ("the eminent showman"), Michael Rosenberg ("the comic of a thousand charms") and BenTsion Witler ("an artist with a huge repertoire from the other side of the sea"), all appearing together with "a cast of good New York artists" in *The Happy Brothers*; Esther Field, ("the *yidishe mamme*") in a "Victory Concert" under the sponsorship of the *Alle far eynem* ("All For One") sick benefit society; Molly Picon in both Toronto and Hamilton venues; the husband and wife team of Pesach'ke Burstein and Lilian Lux with a New York troupe in

Sholom Secunda's *Honest is Hard*; Hannah Hollander and Max Vilner; Khayele Luxemburg and Mordechai Rothstein and Menashe Skulnick in the Abe Ellstein musical *What a guy!* (in Yiddish, "The Real Guy"). On May 9, 1948 there was a concert at the Victory Theatre for the *Farband* School of "the greatest surviving Yiddish artists of Europe," Jonas Turkow, his wife Diana Blumenfeld, and Didye Epstein. These were celebrated Warsaw artists and Yiddish movie stars who had survived the Warsaw Ghetto (where Blumenfeld was a famous performer) and toured the world after the war.

The higher class entertainers also came. The workers' poet Leivick brought his poetry to the Labour Lyceum, apropos of which the *Kanader Nayes* published selections in the paper. The great tenor Richard Tucker appeared in Eaton Auditorium in January 1949 in a program of opera arias, Yiddish and Hebrew songs, including the march song of the Hagganah.  He returned a year later accompanied by Jewish soprano Regina Resnick. Also appearing at the Eaton Auditorium were more local talent, though with a larger spread if they happened to be related to the Goldstick-Dworkins, like the huge ad that appeared for a piano recital by Sylvia Goldstick-Kamin with the whole story of her musical education and career.

The Jews were adjusting quite nicely indeed to post-war Toronto. One typical ad that caught my eye was from June 2, 1946 p. 4:

Khazan Akiva Bernstein Summer Hotel [76]
Everybody needs and must take a pair of weeks' summer 'vacation.'

If you want to spend this summer in a place that is the best and most beautifully prepared for your pleasure, with delicious, strictly kosher meals prepared by the best chef under the personal direction of Mrs. Bernstein and her sister Mrs. Lipshitz, then put yourself in contact with Khazan Akiva Bernstein. . . .

Khazan Bernstein was, of course, one of the stars of the Swerdlow-Herman-Mandel-Glick Variety Radio Hour of 1937, but

---

76 In Yiddish the name was "Borenshteyn," but became Bernstein in English.

that's not what caught my eye. Rather it was the memory of his resort on Lake Couchiching in Ontario where we used to rent a little cabin when I was a child. It was memories of milk and cookies by the lake while *zaftig* [buxom] Jewish matrons in black one-piece bathing suits shampooed their hair in the lake sighing "*mekhaye!*" (pleasure), next to the recreation hall where I made my singing debut at the age of six or seven, singing (at the urging of my older sisters) "A Woman in Love"—not so well as I wanted to, as I remember, but probably as good as Marlon Brando in *Guys and Dolls*. But most of all it was that *name*, "Mrs. Lipshitz," a common Jewish name with no inappropriate Jewish meaning, of course, but the mention of which never failed to send us kids giggling uncontrollably.

Things were good for Toronto Jews in those years. Everything seemed possible. Everything had a new start. The radio shows, too. In the summer of 1946, Sam Yuchtman announced that he would be bringing the St. Catharines show back to Toronto. The *Kanader Nayes* front page story read in part as follows:

> **New Jewish radio program**
> ... Mr. Yuchtman has produced radio programs for a long time on the St. Catharines Radio station. However, that station had the disadvantage that it had become hard to find talent to travel there. One had to substitute records. This also became a disadvantage because the best records could not replace a live voice. On the new hour, not only will live talent appear, but they will also be the best that can be found ...[77]

The opening was announced for September 15, and, on the appointed day, Max's wedding picture (of fifteen years earlier!) graced this brief announcement:

---

77 *KN*, July 14, 1946 p. 1.

טאָראָנטער אידישע ראדיאָ שעה

היינטיגען זונטאָג 10.30 אין דער פרי־
פאנגט זיך אָן די טאָראָנטער אידישע ראדיא
שטונדע אויף סטיישאָן „סי. אייטש. יו. עם",
1050 אויף אייער ראדיא. אונטער דער לייטונג
און מיט דער באטייליגונג פון די באוואוסטע
אידישע ארטיסטען, מעקס מאנדעל און סעם
יוכטמאן. א צאָל אנדערע ארטיסטען וועלען
אויפטרעטען אויף די פראָגראמען פון דערדא־
זיגער ראדיא שטונדע. די באליבטע זינגערין
דאראטי נעיל און געסט ארטיסטען. אינפארמא־
ציע ביי סעם יוכטמאן, לאידברוק 0375, אדער
מאקס מאנדעל, רענדאלף 7453.

Toronto Jewish Radio Hour
This Sunday at 10:30 in the morning begins the Toronto Jewish Radio Hour on station CHUM 1050 on your radio under the direction and with the participation of the eminent Jewish artists, Max Mandel and Sam Yuchtman. A number of other artists will appear on the program of this radio hour, the beloved singer Dorothy Gale and guest artists. For information Sam Yuchtman, Lloydbrook 0375 or Max Mandel, Randolph 7453.

CHUM had started broadcasting less than a year previously. It was Toronto's first new post-war radio station, founded in 1945 by a group that included Al Leary, who had been the station manager at CKCL for fourteen years, where he knew Max from the Dubinsky show in 1936–37. The studios were at 21 Dundas Square, and then, in 1947, they moved to 225 Mutual Street at Granby in Toronto, a state-of-the-art building that, after CHUM moved out, continued as a recording facility up until 2005 and still exists. Before CHUM became a pop music station in the Elvis Presley era, it was a station with a strong ethnic bent. This is where Max crossed paths with Johnny Lombardi, who got his start there on the "Italian Hour."

There was fierce competition between the new CHUM show and the Harry Harris show on CHML, with duelling pictures of Max and Harris, and big ads for the new Mandel–Yuchtman show, in the *Yidisher Zhurnal*, otherwise Harris territory.

The competition with Harris even extended to their benefit concerts. In the *Yidisher Zhurnal* of December 1, 1946, p. 3, beside Harris's usual radio ad, there was an ad for a concert in the Victory Theatre for a week hence that he was directing for the Daughters of Israel Charity Society. An even bigger ad right below that one advertised Max Mandel's "Grandiose concert" for that very evening in the Victory Theatre on behalf of the Toronto Independent Benevolent Society under his direction and with his participation, as well as a host of other performers including the "Joe Barsh orchestra" (Joe Barsht from the original Greenfield hour): "A splendid evening of song, music, dance and entertainment awaits you. . . ."

The new CHUM show advertised "the best Jewish artists," but, except for Dorothy Gale, a local Toronto singer, they were never named. We have some idea who they were from a *Kanader Nayes* ad [78] for a week of movie theatre concerts featuring the "entire cast" and a movie to boot:

---

[78] *KN*, November 28, 1947, p. 4.

KINO
College and Manning
Lloydbrook 3711

From Monday, December 1
A whole week — until 6th Dec.
Premier Entertainment Film Dist.
presents
On our stage
2 presentations every day
7:30 and 10 in the evening
Entire Cast of

Toronto Jewish Radio Hour

Sam Yuchtman, Manager
with **MAX MANDEL**
Irma Hasso – *the Yidishe Shikse*
Sherman Gan ♦ **Bill Berle**
And also
on the screen:
all-star Warsaw cast

"Tkiyes Kaf"
[*Handshake Agreement*]
All places 50 cents and tax

This is the first mention of Irma Hasso. The title "the *Yidishe Shikse*" was bestowed on many performers. It is usually associated with Lillian Lux, of the New York husband and wife act, Burstein and Lux. Lux was as Jewish as the day is long, but she got the name, according to the *Forverts*, "because of her luxuriant blonde tresses." In other words, the emphasis was on "*Yidishe*." Irma Hasso, on the other hand, was a genuine Hungarian gentile whom Max taught to

sing Yiddish, so the emphasis was on "*shikse.*"⁷⁹ You can hear Irma Hasso's sweet classical soprano on a couple of tracks on "Music from the Jewish Hour." On the first one, Max introduces her with, "Coming to the microphone, the *yidishe shikse* Irma Hasso, with a lullaby. . ." Sherman Gan was the famous blind accordionist and composer. He and Irma would also perform at the December concert in the Victory Theatre. Bill Berle was a young pianist, featured on some of the tracks on "Music from the Jewish Hour." *Tkiyes Kaf,* as we've seen, was a Yiddish movie made in Poland before the war.

Another time, the show hosted some of the cast of a Workmen's Circle, Peretz School *Pesakh* Concert that took place in the Victory

---

79 In his autobiography, Lux's husband Pesch'ke Burstein mentions two other *yidishe shikses,* Paula Katarzhinsky and Vera Rosanko, and never mentions this term in connection with his wife, as opposed to the "Yiddish Jean Harlow." Pesach Burstein, *What a life! The autobiography of Pesach'ke Burstein, Yiddish matinee idol* (Syracuse, N.Y.: Syracuse University Press, 2003), pp. 72, 163, 231.

Theatre. The concert involved a children's choir and a mandolin orchestra, but the feature attraction was "VICTOR PACKER showman of great talent, recognized master of rhythm, word and sound, in a rich program of scene, song, rhythm and comedy." Also on the program was "LEO BARKIN artist-pianist — in some out of this world solo numbers." Packer was an unbelievably versatile phenomenon of New York Radio (the low-budget station WLTH from Brooklyn), a Yiddish avant-garde "beat" poet.

One of the sponsors of the CHUM hour was the Crown Bread Company run by Sam Gryfe and Max Hartstone. Gryfe's son went on to found Gryfe's Bagels. Hartstone finished out his years as the gregarious proprietor of the popular variety store "Steven's Milk" on Bathurst Street in Toronto. My son Max often spent hours in what Hartstone's son Marvin called "the library" there, i.e. reading comic books for free. The first bakery ads to mention the radio show appeared in the *Yidishe Zhurnal* in November, 1947: "Listen in to our radio hour CHUM 1050 on your dial, Sunday morning." A really delightful Crown Bread ad dates from 1949, when the show had moved to an afternoon slot on CHUM, with a happy mother and her two children laden with baked goods in front of the bakery:

There it is!
Another "Crown" product
"SOME TAM" FARFEL [80]

Get it in all the stores. Ask in the store for the farfel with the real taste

"SOME TAM" FARFEL

Is packed in sealed sanitary packages. Use as much as you want, seal it up again—no waste.

"SOME TAM" FARFEL

It can be used with soup, meat, dairy or greens to give a tasty and healthy twist to your meals

"SOME TAM" FARFEL

Is another example of how true it is: what Crown Bakery has is the "best in town" . . . buy a half pint of "Some Tam" farfel today.

It is kosher, it is *pareve*. [81]

> Don't forget to listen to your beloved Jewish Radio Program—The Crown Bread Hour—every Sunday 2.15 p.m.—CHUM 1050 on your dial.

CROWN BREAD COMPANY
319 Augusta Ave., Toronto   MI 9766 [82]

---

80 Means "Some Taste" Farfel
81 *Pareve* means food that is neither meat nor dairy and can, therefore, according to the Jewish dietary laws be eaten together with either milk or meat.
82 *Yidishe Zhurnal*, September 18, 1949, page 6.

The show had another bakery as a sponsor—not, one supposes, at the same time—which was Cohen's Bake Shop at 800 St. Clair Avenue West, the proprietor being Max's uncle, Harry Cohen. There is a commercial written on CHUM stationery in Max's hand for the bakery, a real artifact from the era:

Housewives know where to buy their baked goods
They know that they can get the best baked goods
in the new Cohen's Baker Shop at 800 St. Clair Ave.
near the St. Clair *shul*[83]
Their *shabbes khales* are really delicious
Telephone the Cohen Bake Shop
at 800 St. Clair whether it is a birthday cake, or a wedding.
Bar Mitzvah cakes.
Homemade farfel. Telephone Melrose 5823
And it can also be delivered.

The Last Years

"the tendency of the time which is to consolidate and make smaller"

On May 19, 1950 the *Kanader Nayes* switched to a new format in the shape of a tabloid with more pages but smaller ones, with heavier print "in order to please our advertisers who want their ads to stand out like headlines" and "in conformity with the tendency of the time which is to consolidate and make smaller. . . . We assure our readers and friends that the policy or our paper will remain unchanged."[84] In fact, the advertisers and the ads became far fewer, and the paper lost a lot of the vibrancy of the pre-1950s. Still, there were many elements of continuity. For instance, many of the old stalwarts stayed with the paper. Cantor Stolnitz continued writing on *khazunes*, as in the article "Jewish Melody in Lithuania," graced by a photo of Nathan and son Sam taken with *khazan* Moshe Koussevitsky, on the occasion of Koussevitsky's benefit concert of March, 1950 in Massey Hall (proceeds to build housing for new immigrants to Israel).[85] Koussevitsky, a Vilna-born Warsaw *khazan* who had escaped to

---

83 This was the Shaarei Shomayim Synagogue at 840 St. Clair Avenue West, newly completed in 1947.
84 Since February 28, 1947, the paper had switched from Sunday to Friday publication.
85 *KN*, November 24, 1950, p.9.

the Soviet Union during the Holocaust, had been billed, with some justice, as "the greatest *khazan* of the generation." With perhaps less justice, the picture was captioned "A Vilner *Khazanish* Trio." Koussevitsky, who had by then made his home in Brooklyn, was a frequent visitor-davener to Toronto, as was David, one of Moshe's younger cantor brothers, no slouch as a cantor himself.

Of course, *Khazan* Stolnitz also kept us informed of his own *Khazunish* engagements.[86] Professor Golecki continued to chime in with learned pieces on socialist politics and Max Federman was still battling his communist foes, as in the following:

> **An answer to my communist 'friend'**
> The Toronto *Vokhenblatt*, which is put out by and for the Communist Party has come to worry about the party '*Linke Poale Tsion*'[87] whose reputation is, poor thing, sullied by its member, Max Federman. This Federman has got so deep under the communists' skin that they can't forget him. Twelve years ago he tore their mask off and they appeared in their true light as traitors to the workers and the unions....[88]

Cold War

In fact, the paper had moved into full Cold War mode, with Federman its chief cold warrior. In his 1952 article on Labour Day "the *yontif*[89] of the worker," with Canadian troops fully engaged in the raging Korean War, Federman wrote:

> Without one hundred percent mobilization, we and the democratic world in general would be wiped out by aggressive, imperialist communism, with Comrade Stalin at its head.... The workers here know that their standard of living is now the highest in the world. There are two major reasons for our situation: first, our unions and second, our democratic way of life. The Stalinists in all countries have as their main goal to dominate and enslave the American and Canadian trade union movement.

---

86 *KN*, August 22, 1952 p.3: "Khazan Stolnitz engaged to daven *yomim norim* in Boston"; July 23, 1954 p. 4: "Khazan's and Musician's Meeting."
87 "Left Labour Zionists"
88 *KN*, August 4, 1950, p.7, responding to an article in the *Vokhenblatt*.
89 "Holy day."

This article provoked the usual attack from the *Vokhenblatt*, and Federman's usual full-page reply, "An Answer to 'Comrade' Gershman," which dismissed Joshua Gershman as a Stalin stooge and pointed out that Federman's Federation of Furriers Union won better contracts than the communist unions in Montreal and Winnipeg, finally invoking as a trump what Gershman had written about the Hitler-Stalin pact of a decade earlier:

> [T]he same Mr. Gershman and his little friends once wrote that Stalin's pact with Hitler—which brought war on the world, and the death of 65 million people, among them six million Jews—was the greatest good fortune for humanity; Mr. Gershman and his little friends once wrote, before Hitler went after Stalin, that Roosevelt and Churchill and the other great patriots were war mongers. So, I ask, was there a smidgen of truth in their scribbling? I could recount a lot more about Mr. Gershman's 'patriotism' to the worker, but it's not necessary. It is well-remembered. Mr. Gershman, if he will forgive me, did not then write the truth about the Hitler–Stalin pact; he did not then write the truth about Roosevelt and Churchill and the other great men; and he does not write the truth now about me and about our union.

But it wasn't only the communists that the paper opposed. The *Kanader Nayes* also opposed the CCF for its pacifism:

> **The CCF has overshot the mark**
> The opponents of the CCF party could not have hoped for a worse position for the party than that which the CCF party itself chose. That party is now agitating against the policy of NATO as it was formulated at the Lisbon meeting and which has the approval of the Canadian government. The CCF claims that a bigger portion of the funds which the meeting voted for arms and munitions should have gone to economic aid for poor and underdeveloped peoples of Europe and Asia.
>   This position cannot bring the CCF party any political value. On the contrary, it is full of grave dangers.... Every

Canadian citizen can understand the logic of uniting with other peoples to oppose, in a common opposition the communist giant that is ready to devour everything and everybody. In the time of our short lives we have twice had the tremendous success of cooperating with other people in defending against a common enemy. . . . [90]

Domestically, the paper stayed faithful to its liberal principles. It highlighted the work of the Jewish Labour Committee, of which Mrs. Dworkin was general secretary, in rooting out racial and religious discrimination in the workplace. In a famous debate between Reform Rabbi Abraham Feinberg of the Holy Blossom Temple and the Orthodox rabbis of Toronto over the American-born Feinberg's criticism of the Ontario government for requiring public school children to sing Christmas carols irrespective of their religion—the Orthodox rabbis thought the Christian orientation of the public schools was just fine and Feinberg should not "cause trouble"—the paper naturally took Feinberg's side in an article, "Rabbis and Priests United against Rabbi Feinberg," that was signed by "A. Democrat." [91]

Israel, of course, remained a major concern of the paper, increasingly so, even though it was enjoying a period of relative security. Besides a regular section on "Israel News," the paper supported the United Jewish Appeal each year. Its *Pesakh* edition of 1951 had this ad, a poignant variation on the traditional "four questions" that the youngest child asks at a Seder:

---

90 *KN*, April 18, 1952 p.2.
91 *KN*, December 8, 1950, p. 1. I remember well having to sing the carols at my overwhelmingly Christian public school and delighting in the fact that the phrase "the King of Israel" appeared in "The First Noel"! To this day I love singing Christmas carols on Christmas if I happen to find myself at a Christmas party.

> This child of immigrants in Israel asks the following four questions:
> If all Jews of the world are children of the same people, why am I, this Jewish child who has come back to our land—why am I worse off than other children?
> Why must I open up a land for you but no home for me?
> Why are all children fed and clothed but I have to live in want?
> Why do you burden me with your hopes of building this Jewish land and you do not even give me the means to do so? [92]

The paper supported campaigns for the Histadrut and the Jewish National Fund, welcomed Israeli dignitaries, mourned the death of the great Zionist leader Chaim Weizmann, and weighed in on the debate about whether Israel should have a written constitution. It was searing in its critique of the "Jewish fascists" who attacked the Knesset during the deliberations on war reparations. This provided the paper with an argument *in favour* of accepting reparations, because it proved there was little difference between "races" and thus, you could not blame all Germans for Hitler, just like you could not blame all Jews for the Jewish fascists:

> The shocking occurrences in Israel last week once again prove that, by and large, there is little difference between the members of the various races. . . . The infuriated mob which participated in the unholy march on the Knesset furnishes the strongest argument against the idea of collective guilt so frequently paraded before us by those who would condemn all the Germans, for all time, for the crimes of Hitlerist Germany.[93]

---

92 *KN*, April 4, 1951, p.7.
93 "An object lesson from Israel" *KN*, January 18, 1952, p. 8, an article in English by "M.G." The Knesset attackers were in fact led by future Prime Minister Menachem Begin. See, for a full account, Martin Gilbert, *Israel: A History* (London: Doubleday, 1998), p. 280ff.

The paper's anti-communism was at least in part a reaction to the Soviet Union's anti-Zionism and its increasing anti-Semitism. An editorial from December 19, 1952 entitled "With what will it end?" was provoked by the trial and execution in Prague of eleven former communist leaders and high Party officials of Czechoslovakia, eight of whom were Jews. The president of Czechoslovakia, Klement Gottewald, explicitly linked the conspirators to Zionism and indeed claimed a "doctor's plot" to take his life. This presaged, and, indeed, was part of Stalin's denunciation to the same effect of Russian Jewish "bourgeois nationalist" doctors in Russia, followed by mass arrests, the cutting off of diplomatic relations with Israel and the unleashing of an anti-Jewish campaign. The persecution was cut short by Stalin's death in March 1953 and the repudiation of the plot as a total fabrication by the regime that replaced him. The editorial on the Prague trials is worth quoting at length:

> **With what will it end?**
> Apart from the unholy psychopathic Stalinists, nobody doubts any more that Stalinist communism has taken up the whole anti-Semitic paraphernalia. Even such a dedicated friend of the Stalinists as Mr. B. Ts. Goldberg writes very often about this. The difference between him and the other writers on this theme consists only in that he calls it, not Stalinist anti-Semitism, but a "crusade against Zionism," as if it were a matter of Zionists being ten or fifty percent of the Jewish people. . . . The Jewish people consists today of at least ninety-five percent Zionists. With the exclusion of the swarm of Stalinists, who hold to the archaic principle that "the king can do no wrong," and the clump of 'Council for Judaism'niks' there are hardly any Jewish anti-Zionists. From this it is clear that no psychologically healthy and intelligent person can any longer be an anti-Zionist without at the same time being an anti-Semite.
> The sensation of the Prague trials has now made this matter public, and all the newspapers are dedicating a

large space to Stalin's anti-Semitism. In truth, however, the Soviet Union has practiced anti-Semitism for a considerable time already. Trials to eliminate Jews from leadership positions in the social, political and economic life of the Soviet Union have been going on now for some years. This has nothing to do with Zionism, which has been strongly forbidden in Russia for more than thirty years already. The prohibition of Yiddish, a language with which a struggle against Zionism and Hebraism has been conducted, is certainly no evidence that the Yiddish of Pfeffer and his colleagues is going arm in arm with Zionism, to the extent that to suppress Zionism one has also to suppress the Yiddish language. No, the decree excluding Jews from high positions and the ban on Yiddish were, in themselves, anti-Semitic acts, stone and bone, even without the Prague trials, notwithstanding the denials of our local professional communists.

Various explanations are being given for this sad phenomenon, as for example, that Stalinism has need of a scapegoat for the bad state of the Russian or the Communist economy, after more than thirty years of undisturbed Stalinist government; that the Kremlin wants to win the Arab world to its side for the struggle that it foresees with the free world; that the Jews, as an individualistic world-people will never remain a blind communist idol-worshipper; that an atavistic process of inborn anti-Semitism has come to a head among the Stalinists, and they cannot get it out of their skin; and yet other reasons. . . .

Only the Eternal knows how this will end. The lives of about two and a half million Jews are at play. If the government can 'legally' exclude Jews from their economic positions and from their culture, if the government can 'legally' murder eight communist Jews, on the basis of lying confessions, which they had extracted from the arrested through torture, why should not that people, and indeed all pious Stalinists, go a step further and embark on the path of Khmelnytsky[94] and the Tsarist pogrom makers? . . .

---

94 H. B. Khmelnytsky led a Ukrainian revolt against Polish rule in the 1650s that included the massacre of tens of thousands of Jews.

The Decline of Yiddish

The last years of the *Kanader Nayes* saw an anguished lament by the editors for what they regarded as an unnecessary decline in the use of Yiddish and had them deploying all their rhetorical skills in a vain effort to save it. Perhaps it would have been impossible for the language to survive the destruction of Eastern European Jewry. This choked off the source of Yiddish culture and native Yiddish speakers. Imagine Italian surviving the murder of two-thirds of the inhabitants of Italy. And Yiddish culture continued to suffer body blows even after the war. In Russia, the wave of anti-Semitism and anti-Zionism that engulfed Soviet Jews, a potentially huge wellspring of Yiddish speakers, had a distinct cultural side. The "Doctors' Plot" was preceded by an attack on Yiddish cultural figures and institutions that reversed the encouragement they had received in the early years of the Soviet Union, and that dashed the optimism engendered during the war when the prominent Jewish artists working in Yiddish, Mikhoels and Pfeffer, were sent as emissaries abroad. The onset of the Cold War led to renewed persecution. Mikhoels, as we've noted, was assassinated in 1948, while other Yiddish writers and actors were put on trial. The Yiddish Theatre GOSET (for which the painter Marc Chagall had designed some exceedingly beautiful sets) was closed, and those tried in 1948–49 were executed on August 12, 1952, the "night of the murdered poets." This could be said to have marked the definitive end of Yiddish culture in Eastern Europe. In Israel, Yiddish was also suppressed in favour of Hebrew, both officially and unofficially—sometimes violently.[95] So it was only the generation of immigrants like those who wrote the *Kanader Nayes*

---

95 D. Katz, *Words on Fire: The Unfinished Story of Yiddish* (New York: Basic Books, 2004), pp. 315-323.

who were the remaining bearers of it—the last of the Mohicans. Their lament became increasingly bitter, as in this editorial from May 18, 1951:

> **Why Not in Yiddish?**
> If a stranger would have entered Massey Hall on Sunday evening, May 6, at the Israel independence celebration and stayed there the whole evening not hearing one word of Yiddish, apart from the few with which the guest speaker, Dr. Nachum Goldman used to better express what he wanted to bring out—this stranger would have felt certain that, in Toronto, Yiddish is now a dead language, just like Latin, with the only difference that a number of Latin words and phrases are still used sometimes by the highly educated, and also by the ignorant who wish to be taken for educated, while with Yiddish, even a complete ignoramus would never do such a thing under any circumstances.
>
> This celebratory meeting looked otherwise, however, to a lot of the public in attendance and also to all those who heard the conversation that the public conducted among itself before the meeting opened. It's not an exaggeration to say that at least ninety percent of the people who had come to this meeting understood the mother tongue better than English and that they would have had much more enjoyment if the excellent program had been produced entirely in Yiddish.
>
> The organizers of such meetings are usually divided into two groups. One group, poor things, suffer from an inferiority complex and are simply ashamed of our Yiddish language, and the second group believes that, by carrying out this meeting in English, you will attract the younger generation, which understands little Yiddish. As regards the first group, we are dealing with people who are ill of spirit and who can be helped only by either the Supreme Being or by taking them in hand and scolding them for foolish inferiority feelings which have no basis in the light of logic.
>
> As for the second group of organizers, they must have learned from experience, which has already shown many times that the younger element, the born here, don't let themselves be attracted to mass-meetings just because

they are conducted in flawless English. The organizers of this meeting must have understood by now that, since those present at the meeting are Yiddish speakers, it probably stands to reason that the people who appear on stage will also be Yiddish speakers, so at least one of the speakers should speak in Yiddish.

Of course, there is no fear that if somebody should, God forbid, speak in Yiddish, the public would get up and leave the hall. And in the event one would truly find an "allrightnik" who wouldn't come to a meeting because somebody might speak Yiddish there, in his place ten others would come precisely because they would have the opportunity to hear a Yiddish word. Common people, normal people, are not ashamed of their mother tongue and, on the contrary, they get great pleasure from it.

Unfortunately, it is not only the unknowing born-here or the little knowing elements who suffer from feelings of inferiority in relation to Yiddish, but also, and perhaps even more, our *parvenus*, our *nouveau riche*, whose English you could place on a pinch of salt and even a grain wouldn't be displaced—these little people who whisper with their wives in Yiddish only in private so the Christians won't, God forbid, hear them, would rather break their hands and feet than speak Yiddish in the open and in their "society meetings." If one of them becomes an organizer of a meeting like Sunday's, he will be convinced that, if ever anyone spoke Yiddish at such a meeting, no one would come. That this assumption is false was confirmed by Mr. Shamrihu Levine with the splendid Yiddish talks he used to give to packed halls. Equally, Dr. Chaim Zhitlovsky was never the victim of a lack of listeners; and for long years people strove to hear Dr. Chaim Greenberg when he gave a Yiddish lecture. From the other side, one can often encounter yawning at well-advertised English meetings. And why shouldn't this be so, since it is not at all an infrequent occurrence that, at such a meeting, where the speaker uses the English language exclusively, one finds among the 'interested' who come there some who are fully asleep.

It is, without doubt, a tactical error to try and avoid the Yiddish language at public Jewish meetings here in Canada where the average Jew comes from Eastern Europe and his mother tongue is Yiddish. To what practical merchant would it ever occur to persuade a potential customer to be attracted to the merits of his goods in the language that the merchant speaks and not the language of the customer? To get the public into such a merchant's store, he would have to sell bargains, or what the customer thinks are bargains.

All of these meetings are aimed at attracting the listener to the ideals of the people who prepare these meetings or to popularize these ideals. If so, what is the wisdom in recounting the virtues of these ideals in a language that is partially strange to most listeners?

The editors returned to the subject when an American author, lamenting the same phenomenon of the absence of Yiddish at Jewish conferences in the United States, blamed the Jewish newspapers and argued for a boycott of Jewish organizations that neglected Yiddish.

About our Yiddish language
Mr. Louis Segal, the gifted general secretary of the Jewish National Worker Association has published a long article on the bad state of Yiddish in America. . . .

Mr. Segal wonders how the Jewish press and the Jewish culture institutions have been able to tolerate this state of affairs. He cites the various American Jewish social causes which the Jewish press helped develop, like Zionism, the relief actions in favour of our sisters and brothers on the other side of the sea, the boycott movement against Germany and the establishment of other Jewish institutions. Mr. Segal shows with a few examples that this is not a matter of bringing back to life a dead language which the people of today have either forgotten or have never understood. . . .

Mr. Segal also writes about the happier side of Yiddish in America. In Columbia University there now functions a complete Yiddish department. Other academies and institutions of higher learning now have sections where they study Yiddish. Yiddish courses are given in many high schools. And he comes to the conclusion that the Jewish newspapers bear a great deal of blame for the situation of Yiddish in the daily life of American Jews, and he writes further:

Those who must therefore be blamed for the unfavourable situation are the Jewish newspapers, the publishers and the editors. If a Jewish newspaper had the courage to not give any coverage to conferences, conventions and events (not to report them, not to write any news or articles) that ignore the Yiddish word; if the newspapers dealt that way with the leaders of certain organizations that ignore the Yiddish language, there would surely be a better result.

Yiddish lovers can easily agree with Mr. Segal that the leaders of the various Jewish movements, organizations and undertakings deserve to be condemned for their inferiority complex, for ignoring Yiddish and so on and so forth. The trouble, however, is that the first to suffer [from not reporting on conferences ignoring Yiddish] will not be the leaders but the institutions, organizations and undertakings which they represent. Mr. Segal himself is one of the pillars of the institutions, organization and undertakings whose leaders have so wronged our mother tongue. Would he want that these institutions, organizations and undertakings particularly in the State of Israel to suffer because of the sins of their leaders? . . . If the Jewish newspapers had relied on Mr. Segal's current advice, very few Israel Bonds would have been purchased in America. Mr. Segal, as an uncompromising Zionist, certainly would not have wanted that.

Newspapers cannot hold back from reporting news, whatever the language in which and through which the news is made. Even the stories of the mute must be reported in the columns of the newspapers. If the Jewish newspapers are guilty of something in relation to the abject state of Yiddish in America, it is surely through failing incessantly to remind their readers that Yiddish is a language like all languages, and perhaps even a lot more beautiful than some languages, and education is no less necessary to speak Yiddish well and correctly than to speak another civilized language; that Bialik, the great expert on language, was just joking when he said that all the other languages one has to know how to speak, but Yiddish speaks all by itself; and, therefore, that, if Jews are ashamed to speak Yiddish at public assemblies, they are demonstrating an inferiority complex that gives them no honour whatsoever. This and even more, must the Jewish newspapers rightly tell their readers.

Through such an initiative we can do something substantial for our Yiddish language, especially here in Canada, where the Jews of European origin constitute the majority of the Jewish people. These European Jews, who speak the King's English with a Yiddish accent and with a lot of mistakes, should not be hard to win over, since those born here, who, poor things, break their teeth over Yiddish, hold Canadian Jews of European origin in higher esteem if, at their public assemblies, they choose to speak even in a bad Yiddish rather than in a bad English; they will admire them even more if they speak in a good grammatical Yiddish.

Anyone who has had the opportunity to be at a Jewish meeting or a banquet will agree that a very large number of the English speakers cry out '*Oy* pity, *oy* travesty!' while they suffer, poor things, unable to escape from this linguistic web which they themselves have spun. When one asks these speakers why they did not choose to speak in the mother tongue, their usual answer is that it is because there are a few people in the audience who understand no Yiddish. It never occurs to these speakers that, for their own honour, it would have been a lot better if the few who could not understand Yiddish did not understand what they, the speakers, said in Yiddish, than that they did not understand what they said, such as it was, in English.

Thus, through such a reaction to this sorry situation can the Jewish newspapers best serve the cause of Yiddish, and bring it the importance that it deserves. Only ignoramuses and self-haters can speak badly of our Yiddish language. Educated people and people of normal spirit marvel at the beauty and richness of Yiddish. You just have to turn a page of Stutchkoff's *Thesaurus of the Yiddish Language* which the YIVO has published, to convince yourself that our Yiddish is a first-rank culture language; that it is very rich in diverse words, shrewd idioms and in clever expressions; and that one can bring out through it the finest nuances of human feelings and the deepest thoughts of the human mind.[96]

---

96 *KN*, October 10, 1952 p. 2.

Like Segal, the paper grasped at any reason for optimism. It declared a "victory for Yiddish" when the Encyclopedia Britannica recognized Yiddish as one of seven modern European languages: "It will be interesting to see if our 'all-rightniks' and unlearneds continue to ridicule our—yes and their—Yiddish language.... How this will affect our Jewish learning institutions who have tossed Yiddish out of their programs, also due to an inferiority complex, we don't need prophets to tell."[97]

In the early post-war period there seemed to be reasons for optimism. A flood of Yiddish talent hit Toronto. Mostly, however, they were the familiar pre-war stars, some of them getting a little long in the tooth. For instance when the great Aaron Lebedeff came to perform in a benefit concert for Moyshe Shapiro at Massey Hall February 22, 1953 he was panned ("somebody should remind him that 70 is not 17"). In his role as impresario, Shapiro also brought back Sadie Sheingold and Sam Auerbach to the Victory Theatre in August, 1952. An actors' union troupe, including Florence Weiss, Sarah Gingold, Gilt Stein (advertised as "the black mama" for reasons unknown), Pinchas Leaned, Yitzhak Lewinsky, Leon Schechter and others came for a five week run starting with *Children of Today* in November. "Jewish unions, organizations are asked to support the Jewish theatre and engage them for benefits from which they can earn nicely and at the same time not let the Yiddish word and Yiddish art die."[98]

Shapiro was also responsible for bringing back the *Kanader Nayes* darling Benny Adler, who in combination with local talent, put on his usual barrage of pieces: "The Delegate" in May, 1951, "A Friend

---
97 *KN*, February 12, 1954, p. 2.
98 David Mendelssohn, "Will we have a Yiddish Theatre in Toronto?" *KN*, October 31, 1952, p. 4.

in Life" ("a piece not a concert") in May, "Back to His People" in December and the "The Great Lie" in 1952. Sadly, bringing back Benny Adler was the old theatre man Shapiro's last act. During Adler's 1954 run of a couple of plays by Jacob Gordin (*The Wild Man* and *King Lear*), Shapiro died the prompter's death, on stage.

> **Morris Shapiro falls dead on the stage**
> He was participating as a prompter in an Adler show at the Victory Theatre and while they were setting up the last act he came out to make a theatre announcement. Mr. Adler says he noticed from Mr. Shapiro's talk that something was wrong. Shapiro ended his talk and went backstage behind the curtain and fell dead. According to theatre tradition "di show must go on no meter volt happens," [99] so they finished the show without letting on to the audience what had happened. Shapiro left his wife and six children. He was about seventy and had been in bad health in recent years.[100]

Besides Adler, many New York stars graced Toronto stages in the early 1950s, for example Max and Rose Bozik in concert at the Victory Theatre in December, 1953; and a blockbuster in March 1954, with Herman Yablokov, Chaim Tuber, Max Bozik, and Bella Meisel in *Children Don't Forget*. The red carpet was rolled out for international Yiddish literary figures such as Joseph Opatoshu and Zelman Schnook. The local talent included several recent European arrivals, refugees and Holocaust survivors such as singer Jenny Eisenstein, pianist Leo Spellman, Khayele Luxemburg, Mordecai Rothstein, Morris Nixon, Morris Turk's orchestra, his wife Eva Fishman, Philip Gravity, David Caiman, David Dubinsky, Sara Barkin, Sisal Gorlitz, Yakov Reinglass and even Harry Harris.

---

99 The entire passage in quotes is a transliteration of the English into the Yiddish: "די שָאו מאַסט גאָ אָן נאָ מעטער וואָט העפּענס"
100 *KN*, January 15, 1954, p. 8.

Isaac Swerdlow was back in supporting roles, along with his wife Adele, with Isaac now billed as "the showman and *Histadrut* leader." One local group that was enjoying a heyday was the Toronto Jewish Folk Choir, formerly the Freedom Singing Society that appeared on the early Greenfield Jewish Hour. They had maintained their strong political credentials, but were now under the baton of Emil Gartner who had considerably raised the choir's level of musical sophistication. Now the Choir was performing at Massey Hall with the likes of Metropolitan artists Jan Peerce and Regina Resnick, as well as the great activist bass, Paul Robeson. A review of the Resnick concert had her singing *Koll Nitre* and the choir singing the Russian song *Klink* (which I had the pleasure of singing with the Choir many years later), the latter being so well received that the Choir had to repeat it. (For the record, I got a big applause for my rendition, but I was no Resnick, so we only did it once.)

Jewish renewal was everywhere. On the same page in two successive editions of the paper, two fixtures of modern Toronto Jewish life were pictured in artists' renderings as construction was about to begin on the Bloor Street Young Men's Hebrew Association—now the Jewish Community Centre, and the Baycrest

"*Moesha Zikeynim*" ("Old Folks Home"), now the Baycrest Centre for Geriatric Care.

Jews were doing great, but Yiddish not so much. The signs of its decline were unmistakeable. Increasingly the Yiddish acts would mix in Hebrew and even English into their repertoire: "Zhigan and Shumacher, a comic duo in Yiddish, Hebrew and English in Eaton Auditorium"; "Ben Bonus, Mina Boyrn from Tel Aviv . . . In the repertoire: Israeli folks songs, sketches and one-acters." The first post-war Yiddish movie *Long is the Road* had an Israeli theme in it—how could it not?—"From Warsaw 1939 to Israel 1949, a powerful film of the rescued Jews, their struggle and aspirations for a new life. Artistically depicted, their love, hope and longing for Israel." It was also double-billed with an Israeli movie, *The Song of Tel Aviv*. In April 1952, the great Maurice Schwartz did a theatre piece at the Royal Alexandra entirely in English!

The newspaper itself had English pages more often, though it never went as far as the regular English page of the *Yidishe Zhurnal*. One of the most telling changes concerned Mrs. Dworkin herself. Of course, she was now specializing in flights to Bermuda and Israel, rather than boats to the old country:

> You will sit down on the airplane in Toronto and not get up until you are already in Bermuda. What Bermuda is, one does not need to tell anymore. It's enough to realize that Bermuda is the preferred playground of the richest people on the American continent.

She took her first well-advertised trip to Israel in 1954:

> Dorothy Dworkin makes her first trip to Israel on El Al in order to see with her own eyes, a life-long Zionist activist, what has been done in this wonder land and to check out the hotels for arrangement of future tours.[101]

---

[101] *KN*, March 5, 1954, p. 3.

But the day the music died may well have been March 19, 1954, the day the name of the company was changed—not just translated—from *shifs kontor* to "travel bureau," that is, the name *spelled out in Yiddish letters* was *Dvorkin's travel byuro*: דװאָרקינ׳ס טרעװועל ביורא̄[102]

Radio

As for Yiddish radio, Harry Harris stayed on CHML, Sundays 10 to 11, advertising daily in the *Yidishe Zhurnal*. Max also advertised in the *Yidishe Zhurnal*, often on the same page as Harris, but now it was as president of the Apter Friendly Society, which had just renovated its *shul* and was advertising its "modern" banquet halls:

> The Apter Center 216 Beverley Street announces that its two modern banquet halls, which can accommodate up to 800 people and are equipped with two kitchens for milk and meat, supervised under the new management of the well-known Greenberg caterers, are available to rent for weddings, bar mitzvahs, showers and other *simkhas*. The finest meals, strictly kosher.
> Beautifully decorated and affordable prices
> For reservations and information telephone
> Max Mandel, Lloydbrook 0686
> Apter Center Midway 0714
> Greenberg Caterers Waverley 1967 [103]

---

102 "Dworkin's Travel Bureau" in English appeared for the first time in the *Kanader Nayes* on April 17, 1953, p. 8; as late as December 19, 1952, p. 6, she was still calling it *shifs kontor*.
103 *YZ*, June 11, 1952. p. 6.

Max had left CHUM in January 1950 and was totally immersed in Apter work. He had taken over as president in 1948 on the sudden death of the prior president, David Freiberg and got caught up in the re-building of the Apter Centre on Beverley Street that housed both the synagogue and the Society. The centre, in Max's words, was meant to provide a meeting place for townsfolk, especially those newly arrived from the war, in a "clean and homelike atmosphere" where "our Apter traditions are not forgotten." The Society raised money for various Jewish causes, including the Histadrut, the United Welfare Fund, the Youth Aliyah, the Jewish Hospital, the Old Folks Home, the Morris Winchevsky School, the Jewish Folk Choir, and orphans and fire victims. Memorials were held for "the shining martyrs" killed in Apt during the war, and, generally, Apter townsfolk joined "the great family of Jewish societies linked to the national community of our people." [104]

Now his artistic endeavours, too, seemed to revolve around the Apter, with a series of famous relief concerts, first involving local and then international talent. The program from January 23, 1949 (billed as the "Second Annual Concert") had Max as headliner and director, with mostly local talent, but also including Isaac Swerdlow. Swerdlow was now a "field director" for the Canadian Histadrut (a labour-oriented group that raised funds for Israel), so he appeared "with permission of the Histadrut." [105]

---

104 Max Mandel, Leybish Dumsky, Pintche Teitel, "On the Fourth Annual Concert." *Fourth Annual Concert of the Apter Friendly Society under the direction of Max Mandel* (1951).

105 The local talent for the concert included Khayele Luxemburg, Mordecai Rotstein, Esther Ghan (a talented young soprano, the niece of Sherman Ghan, who went on to a distinguished musical career), dancers "Maxine and Dennis", Hazel Richell ("acrobatic dance"), N. Teitel ("in recitation"), Saul Firestone, emcee, with music by Maurice Turk and his orchestra.

Each subsequent January, Max organized, directed, emcee'd and usually performed in the Apter Concert at the Victory Theatre, with "proceeds for the relief fund."

The international stars were mostly performers from New York, including "the beloved show-woman and prima donna" Rachel Novikov Rozenfeld, "two great artist comedians from New York," Max and Reyzl Bozik,[106] and "two young artists from New York" Lilian Liliana and Leon Liebgold.[107] There were also Holocaust survivors who had settled in Toronto after the war, for instance Zisele Gorlitza and Yakov Reinglass, two Lodzer actors who had fled to the Soviet Union from Poland, and Leo Spellman, cousin of "The Pianist," as well as familiar faces from the Toronto Jewish musical scene, like Khayele Luxemburg, Mordecai Rotstein, Cantor Abraham Wantroff and Maurice Turk. Some of the locals had great futures ahead of them. Louis Jacobi, master of ceremonies in the 1950 concert, was then on the brink of a late-blooming stage, television and movie career, that would see him play stock Jewish characters into his 80s. The "famous dancer Zena Cheevers"—"*Shvivers*" as it was transliterated—would become Zena Cherry, the erstwhile society columnist for the *Globe and Mail*. Some were never heard of again: "the talented" Nchama-Nechele Teitel, "the famous dancers: Maxine and Dennis," the Bernstein Sisters.

...ONE OF CANADA'S GIFTED BARITONE SINGERS
Toronto Star

• Concert
• Oratorio
• Radio

ADOLPH WANTROFF
Studio:
399A PALMERSTON BLVD., TORONTO
TELEPHONE MELROSE 5983

---

106 Max Bozik had some major film credits, including a principal role in the pre-war Molly Picon vehicle *Yidl mitn fidl*. Reyzl had a major role in later life in *Crossing Delancey* as the busybody grandmother.
107 Liebgold also had a big role in *Yidl mitn fidl*.

The Fifth Concert on January 27, 1952 was dedicated to I. L. Peretz, claiming him—questionably, as was pointed out earlier—as a *landsman*:

> Together with the whole Jewish world, we are participating in the celebration of the hundredth year of Yitzkhak Leybish Peretz. We are proud of our great townsman, the Apter son-in-law, the father of Yiddish literature, Yitzkhak Leybish Peretz.

At this point, Max was in ill-health, suffering from uncontrollably high blood pressure and trying to make a living in the second-hand clothing business, in direct competition with his estranged brother and father, working out of a little store on McCaul Street, with my mother re-deploying her old seamstress skills to do the hemming. The story in our house was that he was not allowed by doctors to sing anymore, like Antonia in the *Tales of Hoffman*. However, in early 1953, he allowed himself to be persuaded by Yuchtman to launch a show on CKFH, a station owned by the famous Canadian sports broadcaster Foster Hewitt ("Hello Canada and hockey fans in the United States!"), which was building up an ethnic roster that included Johnny Lombardi, an associate from the CHUM days. According to my mother, Yuchtman only wanted to use Max's name. Nevertheless, Max seems to have thrown himself into the new show, which began on February, 15, 1953, right after the sixth annual Apter January Concert:

THE NEW TORONTO
JEWISH RADIO HOUR
CKFH – DIAL 1400
Today, Sunday 6.30 Evening
Every Sunday there will be heard heartfelt Jewish music [and] important social news on the new Jewish Hour,

which will give you great enjoyment. . .

**LISTEN IN EVERY SUNDAY
6.30 IN THE EVENING**

Organizations!
For all your activities contact:
MAX MANDEL
SAM YUCHTMAN
182 Pendrith St. – LL. 0686
40 Cecil Ct – KI. 0093

The new show caused much consternation on the part of the Harris camp. There was even a reputed confrontation one morning at a restaurant on College Street, no doubt over some Jewish delicacies of bagels and herring and such, that saw Mrs. Harris loudly accuse Max of taking away the Harris's livelihood. Apparently the women almost came to blows. But I only heard one side of the story. Before that, Max and Harris had been on more or less friendly terms,[108] but people who worked with Harris at the end of his career told me he still held a grudge.

The show went on for three Sundays and then, on the afternoon of the fourth show, March 8, 1953, in my bewildered four-and-a-half year old presence, my father cried out, "Oy, Hilda, do I have a headache!" He lay on the couch, very still, but with his eyes open, with a wet facecloth on his forehead, then he was gone from the couch, then the phone call came and my uncle announced that he was dead, there was chaos, and I was whisked away. The next day was the funeral, described in full detail in the *Yidishe Zhurnal*:

---

[108] In 1950, Max's picture appeared in a program for a concert celebrating Harry Harris's fifteen years in the radio business, with a "heartfelt greeting to our friend Harry Harris."

Deep sorrow at the funeral of Max Mandel

A deep sorrow reigned at the funeral of the young, deceased Max Mandel, who was yesterday taken to his eternal rest.

The chapel of Benjamin's Funeral Parlour was overflowing and hundreds of people who could not get inside stood outside and took part that way in the last honour which was bestowed on the deceased.

In the chapel a eulogy was made by Rabbi Hurwich, who spoke about the fine personality of the man who was lying in the casket. After that a *"moleh"*[109] was made by a friend of the Mandel family of many years, Khazan Akiva Bernstein.

At 12 noon the mourning procession began from Benjamin's Parlour to the Apter Center, on Beverley Street. The deceased was one of the builders of the Apter Center and he was also for many years the President of the Apter Society.

At the Apter Center a second eulogy was made. The eulogy was made by Rabbi Rappaport, himself an Apter, and one who knew the deceased well, after which Khazan Akiva Bernstein again made a *"moleh."* From there they went to the cemetery where Max Mandel found his eternal rest.

The deceased leaves behind in sorrow his beloved wife and three children, two daughters and a young boy.

Max Mandel died from a blood-clot in the brain which suddenly struck him Sunday afternoon before he prepared to go into the studio to conduct his weekly radio program, which he had started not long before, together with Sam Yuchtman. For many years he was usually taken up the whole day Sunday with Apter and other community undertakings. In the afternoon he was going to take his family for a drive in the car, when he suddenly complained that he was suffering from a severe headache.

Doctors were quickly called and an ambulance took him to the hospital. There he passed away.

Thus ended the career of a gifted Jewish man—a career which began brilliantly but which ended with a premature death.

Max Mandel had two things that he loved—Yiddish theatre and the Apter Society, and he loved both equally.

---

109 "El moleh rachamim" – "God full of mercy," the Jewish prayer for the dead.

He had a great affection for the Yiddish word and respect for everything that was involved with the Yiddish stage or with a Yiddish newspaper or a Yiddish book.

In Toronto he was one of the best known persons and he was loved in all circles.

His premature death was therefore shocking and the pain was great when the news of his death quickly spread.

The huge public that came to his funeral was an indication of the respect that was had for him.

The wife, children and family are sitting *shiva* at 182 Pendrith Street.

The previous day, the *Yidishe Zhurnal* had given front-page coverage to the news of his death, complete with a recent publicity picture of Max, along with the announcement of the funeral details and many condolence notices.[110] The obituary in the *Kanader Nayes* came in its next weekly issue:

Max Mandel Dead

On Sunday Mr. Max Mandel died suddenly, at 44 years of age. . . . Mr. Max Mandel was a man with an artistic nature. The stage was part of his life. Since coming to Toronto from Apt, Poland, he did not miss any opportunity to involve himself with the stage. He was considered a fine showman. He used to take active part in show troupes that came to Toronto from New York to do theatre. Those in the know say that if the Jewish stage would have been in a better state, he would have been an internationally known actor. The art of the stage was in his blood, and his talents were colossal.

The deceased was also a community man, who dedicated himself to the good of the community. He was one of the outstanding personalities of his townsfolk and a leader in the Apter association. His premature death has called forth sorrow in all the circles in which he was known. The editors and the management of the *Kanader*

---

110 *YZ,* March 9, 1953, p. 1. This was also the day after the announcement of Josef Stalin's death, so the front page also had such headlines as, "Europe is fearful of war on account of Stalin's death" and "Moscow absolves Stalin's doctors."

Nayes send their deepest sympathy to his family in their mourning. [111]

The new Jewish Hour continued on, of course, without Max. The next show had a talk by "the esteemed beloved Rabbi Monson" on "the deceased Max Mandel and his strivings for the good of the Jewish community in Toronto." After that, the show's ads in the *Yidishe Zhurnal* were identical to the first ones, except for a big space where the name Max Mandel had been. Yuchtman carried on with the Jewish Hour at CKFH for a while, then followed Johnny Lombardi to his own new radio station CHIN, where the show stayed until he handed over the reins to his daughter Zelda, who runs it as *The Zelda Show* to this day.

The Kanader Nayes closes

The newspaper did not outlive Max by very much. On September 24, 1954, in the Rosh Hashana edition, Maurice Goldstick announced that he was leaving the paper, with a quasi-revelatory op-ed:

> **Be well, dear friends**
> With today's eve of Rosh Hashana issue, your servant, the editor until now of the *Kanader Nayes*, bids you farewell. He asks you to pardon him for the personal remarks that he will make in taking leave of you. During the years in which he has served you, he has refrained from throwing himself in your eyes either through photographs, personal declarations or even the mention of his name in the newspaper. He has covered himself with anonymity in meeting with you. Today, for the first time, he makes an exception and speaks out from the heart, even signing his name to this editorial.
> He wants to unveil a secret to you, and that is, that, it seems, without exception, that he has written all of the lead editorials which have been published in the *Kanader*

---

[111] *KN*, March 13, 1953, p.8.

Nayes since April 1935 until today. May he not be put on trial for it; it has not been a light enterprise. Writing lead editorials is just like picking mushrooms. You not only have to know what to put in your basket, you must also know what you must not touch, because it is poison.

One is mistaken to believe that we have a free press in the sense that you can write about everything and everyone just what you will. According to our law, it is forbidden not just to make a libel on someone in a newspaper, but it is forbidden even to write the truth about the most loathsome soul. That clarifies why some scoundrels can be vested with public offices and taken for ethical people. . . .

Have we achieved something with our twenty years of Jewish journalism? The reader will forgive us our immodesty in answering—yes, even though, perhaps, this is not obvious to everybody. In this respect, we have been in the category of those medicinal and hygienic scientists who, thanks to their efforts, society is now protected from many plagues. Cities in civilized countries today do not know of afflictions such as typhus, diphtheria and small pox. If the researchers had not worked on it, each one of us could be a premature candidate for the cemetery.

Your servant believes that with what he has produced, he has helped eliminate a good deal of pestilence that tended to spread through our social institutions. If the circumstances did not force him to give back the suit he has been wearing for almost twenty years, almost without reward, and with great neglect of his other personal undertakings, he would have stayed longer at his journalistic work. If the Eternal will grant him the years, he might possibly return to you, and then in even better clothes.

At this opportunity, the writer of these lines wants to thank all those who have, orally or in writing, expressed their appreciation of his contributions. At the moment he cannot announce the name of his successor. Whoever it may be, this writer wishes him a happy future.

The *Kanader Nayes*, under its editor until now, has faithfully served the Zionist Organization and all of its local branches, in all of their undertakings. It has, with all means, helped promote the Canadian Jewish Congress, one of the most beautiful accomplishments of Canadian

Jewry. The *Kanader Nayes*, under its editor until now, has elicited a meaningful share of contributions from among the Yiddish-speaking elements of our city in favour of the United Jewish Welfare Fund, while politicians and petty people have fought against this undertaking with tooth and nail. The Toronto Jewish school leaders will testify that, when they turned to us to make something known or to fight their opponents, the *Kanader Nayes* was always ready to do what they asked of us.

The *Kanader Nayes*, under its editor until now, has a right to take 'credit' for the wonderful Mount Sinai Hospital which our city possesses and with which we are all now blessed. But the Jewish hospital was not always as accepted and popular as it is now. There was a time in the not-distant history of our city when they frowned from the 'high windows' on the 'Jewish apartness' which expressed itself with a Jewish hospital on Yorkville Avenue. And, with no good reason, there was also no lack of politicians who worked quietly at undermining the hospital so it would not be allowed to be realized. And if we had not, twenty years ago, built the little Jewish hospital on Yorkville Avenue, there would today be no big Mount Sinai Hospital on University Avenue. That is how it goes in Jewish history, from Moses's time until the present day. The presidents and the rich ones declare themselves only when there is already an ark, a strong Zionist movement and a place of honour—above all a place of honour. The *Kanader Nayes* incessantly advocated for the Toronto Jewish Hospital and encouraged its idealistic leaders, who were mostly women.

The *Kanader Nayes* never turned down a request for a good cause, whether the request came from an individual or a group. It is possible that the editor until now lacked the appropriate ability and proficiency that the position called for. He did not, however, lack in responsibility and good will.

The editor until now of the *Kanader Nayes* wishes you and all Israel and all decent people over the whole world a healthy and happy year. —*M. Goldstick*

Goldstick was not very forthcoming about the reasons for his retirement. Was it money? Was it health? According to his nephew

Harry Arthurs, Goldstick died in 1960, only about five years later, at about seventy-five years of age, so health is plausible. Whatever the reason, the paper simply could not survive his absence. In fact, the last issue of the paper, though it was not announced as such, was the next one, October 6, 1954, with the headline "State of Israel Accuses Egypt, Ambassador Abba Eban goes to the Security Council," a story about an Israeli ship in the Suez Canal being dealt with aggressively by an Egyptian patrol boat. On page 2, in lieu of Goldstick's usual editorial (and under the usual claim to have more readers than any other Jewish newspaper), there was this note:

> **To the subscribers of the Kanader Nayes and others**
> As readers already know, our editor until now has resigned. We have not yet been able to engage another in his place. Because of this, the *Kanader Nayes* has been constrained to temporarily cease distribution.
> In the meantime, negotiations are proceeding to reorganize the paper in accordance with the new circumstances. As soon as this can be done, the newspaper will again be published.
> Subscribers to the *Kanader Nayes* who do not wish to wait are asked to let us know and they will be paid back for their unfinished terms.
> Respectfully,
> *D. Dworkin, President*

And with that, the *Kanader Nayes* ceased publication.

There were still a lot of Yiddish speakers in Canada according to the census data, but their numbers were dropping fast. While, in 1931, 96% of the 155,700 Canadian Jews claimed Yiddish as their mother tongue ("first language learned and still understood"), by 1951, only 51% of the 204,800 Jews made the same claim. The numbers would drop to 32% of 254,400 in 1961, 18% of 276,000 in 1971 and 11% of 296,400 in 1981. Data for 1971 and 1981 showed that even these figures greatly overestimated the actual use of Yiddish at home, which was only 9.5% of Jews in 1971 and 3.6% in 1981.[112] By 2006, Yiddish as a mother tongue had dwindled to perhaps .05%, in other words near extinction.[113] It isn't hard to understand why. The Holocaust had destroyed European Jewry, the ultimate source of Yiddish-speaking Jews. Israel had turned its back on Yiddish in favour of Hebrew, so here in Canada the language of the Jewish schools became Hebrew. Hardly any Jews even know what *"Yidn redn yidish"* means anymore. And, anyway, it's not even *true*, let alone funny, having completely lost both ends of its original double *entendre*. Certainly, there are pockets of Yiddish spoken, especially among ultra-orthodox sects in Israel and North America. Yiddish is also studied in university courses and sung—there was, indeed, a big comeback for Yiddish music ("klezmer music") in the 1980s. But this was not nearly enough to sustain Yiddish newspapers and Yiddish radio.

Harry Harris died in 1960. The *Yidishe Zhurnal* lasted until 1975, Montreal's *Keneder Adler* until 1988. Nowadays, there are only increasingly isolated pockets. The *Forverts* itself cut back to a weekly in 1983 and, alongside of the Yiddish paper, launched a fully English—but still *Jewish*, of course—newspaper in 1990. Canada abounds in Jewish newspapers. *Forverts* now has a Yiddish section on its website and even a Yiddish radio program, but who knows how many people listen to it? Dovid Katz is optimistic that Yiddish might make a return in a "secular outburst" from the religious communities, precisely the way it did in the late nineteenth century,

---

112 Leo Davids, "Yiddish in Canada: Picture and Prospects," *Canadian Ethnic Studies*, 16:2 (1984) 89 at 92 and 94.
113 Statistics Canada, *Ethnicity Series. A Demographic Portrait of Manitoba. Volume 2 Population by Mother Tongue.*

and he may be right.[114] This has not, however, been a story about the Yiddish language, but about the people who spoke it, and who brought it to Canada, along with *gefilte* fish and a distinctive musical idiom and all the rest of *yidishkayt*. It has been a story about the world they lived in and tried to shape according to their ideals. We can learn a lot from these people and savour their insights and their music and all the rest, but we can't otherwise bring back their Jewish Hour, which has passed into history along with them.

---

114 D. Katz, *Words on Fire: The Unfinished Story of Yiddish* (New York: Basic Books, 2004), pp. 379 ff.

Mr. & Mrs. Max Mandel and family

APPENDIX

Music from the Jewish Hour

Note: Musical selections from the various Jewish Hours have been made available online free of charge. To access these tracks, please visit the website **www.soundcloud.com** and enter the search phrase "Jewish Hour - Mandel." (Subject to changing conditions.)

The music consists of digitally remastered 78 RPM recordings made for performance on Max Mandel's various Jewish Radio Hours between 1936 and 1953. Many of the original records were badly damaged from play and poor storage, but those on the website are the ones that remain listenable after all of these years. Besides containing some wonderful music and performances, they are a good example of the kind of music that was performed on the show.

The lyrics to sixteen songs are provided here in the original Yiddish, in Yiddish transliteration, and in English translation.

Musical selections have been made available online free of charge. To access these tracks, please visit the website www.soundcloud.com and enter the search phrase "Jewish Hour - Mandel." (Subject to changing conditions.)

1 Sheyn vi di levone/Bluestein's furniture store commercial (2:21)
2 Az der rebbe vil (4:11)
3 Unter boymer (3:22)
4 Shloymele-Malkele (3:14)
5 Shrayt zhe yidn, gevalt (3:34)
6 Hashkiveynu (3:33) (evening prayer)
7 Dray tekhterlekh (3:10)
8 Oy mamme, bin ikh farlibt (1:45)
9 Varshe (3:25)
10 Vu nemt men a Moyshe rabeynu (2:33)
11 Neyn, neyn, keynmol nit geven (3:13)
12 Av harakhamim (3:07)
13 Yidish redt zikh azoy sheyn (3:08)
14 Mahzel (2:37)
15 Der yidisher nign/A tfile fun a ghetto yid (3:13)
16 Fiddle Solo (Shloymele/Malkele) (1:22) *(no lyrics)*

שעהן ווי די לבנה
SHEIN VI DI L'VONE

WILLIAM ROLLAND PRESENTS
Menasha Skulnik and **Menachem Rubin**
IN
JOSEPH RUMSHINSKY'S
OPERETTA
"THE WISE FOOL"
Libretto by LOUIS FREIMAN

MENASHA SKULNIK

AS SUNG BY
Menasha Skulnik
and
Gertie Bulman

JOSEPH RUMSHINSKY

PRODUCED AT THE
PUBLIC THEATRE
2nd Ave. at 4th St., New York

GERTIE BULMAN

Price 30 cents net

Metro Music
58 SECOND AVE.
NEW YORK

MADE IN USA

Lyrics by

CHAIM TAUBER

(1)

BLUSTEIN'S FURNITURE STORE COMMERCIAL/BEAUTI-FUL AS THE MOON	Blusteyns fornitsher stor anons/ Sheyn vi di levone	בלושטיינס פֿאַרניטשער סטאָר אַנאָנס/שיין ווי די לבנה
Listen to this sensation	Hert nor a sensatsye	הערט נאָר אַ סענסאַציע
The best ensembles	Di greste combinatsye	די גרעסטע קאָמבינאַציע
Available to you.	Vos ir shtelt zikh for	וואָס איר שטעלט זיך פֿאָר
At the absolute lowest prices	Di prayzn gor di klenste	די פּרײַזן גאָר די קלענסטע
The most beautiful furniture	Di fornitsher di shenste	די פֿאַרניטשער די שענסטע
You can get everything	Alts krigt ir	אַלץ קריגט איר
In Blustein's Furniture Store	In Blusteyn's fornitsher stor	אין בלושטיינס פֿאַרניטשער סטאָר
Chesterfields and beds,	Tshesterfilds un betn,	טשעסטערפֿילדס און בעטן,
Kitchen sets and laundry machines,	Kitshn sets un gretn,	קיטשען סעטס און גרעטן,
All that you need, you get	Alts vos ir darft krigt ir	אַלץ וואָס איר דאַרפֿט קריגט איר
In Blustein's Furniture Store	In Blusteyn's fornitsher stor	אין בלושטיינס פֿאַרניטשער סטאָר

Beautiful as the moon	Sheyn vi di levone	שיין ווי די לבנה
And bright as the stars,	Un lekhtik vi di shtern,	און לעכטיק ווי די שטערן,
From heaven as a gift	Fun himl a matune	פֿון הימל אַ מתנה
You were sent to me.	Bistu mir tsugeshikt.	ביסטו מיר צוגעשיקט.
I won my happiness	Mayn glik hob ikh gevunen	מײַן גליק האָב איך געוואונען
When I found you,	Ven ikh hob dikh gefunen,	ווען איך האָב דיך געפֿונען,
You shine like a thousand suns,	Du shaynst vi toyznt zunen,	דו שײַנסט ווי טויזנט זונען,
You have made my heart happy.	Du host mayn harts baglikt.	דו האָסט מײַן האַרץ באַגליקט.
Your teeth White pearls	Dayne tseyndelekh Vayse perelekh	דײַנע ציינדעלעך ווײַסע פּעראַלעך
With your beautiful eyes	Mit dayne sheyne oygn	מיט דײַנע שיינע אויגן
Your graces,	Dayne kheyndelekh,	דײַנע חנדעלעך,
Your hair,	Dayne herelekh,	דײַנע העראַלעך
Have attracted me,	Host mir tsugetsoygn	האָסט מיך צוגעצויגן,
Beautiful as the moon	Sheyn vi di levone,	שיין ווי די לבנה
Bright as the stars,	Un lekhtik vi di shtern,	און לעכטיק ווי די שטערן,
From heaven as a gift	Fun himel a matune	פֿון הימל אַ מתנה
You were sent to me.	Bistu mir tsugeshikt.	ביסטו מיר צוגעשיקט.

Sung English lyrics:
Like the moon above you
The stars remind me of you,
The angels knew I loved you
So heaven sent you to me.
The moon so softly gleaming,
The stars have set me dreaming,
And now my heart is scheming
How happy we both could be.
You are wonderful
You're so loveable
Without you I'm so lonely
You're so beautiful,
So adorable
Oh my one and only,
Like the moon above you
The stars remind me of you,
The angels knew I loved you
So heaven sent you to me.

Notes

Music: Joseph Rumshinksy
Words: Chaim Tauber
Publication Date: 1938

From the operetta, *The Wise Fool* – Der Kluger Nar – דער קלוגער נאַר

In the Toronto telephone book for 1939 to 1941, there is a listing for "Blustein Saml new and sec hd furn 155 August av and 721 Queen w h same WA 6376." The buildings appear to have been replaced.

IF THE RABBI WANTS / Az der rebbe vil / אַז דער רבי װיל

1

The rabbi can be
a father to animals
How?
If he wants, he can.
The rabbi can make
a chicken from a cat
How?
If he wants, he can.
Oh. the rabbi can get
milk from a bear
And *shlog kapores* *with a fly
He can even make an ox
lay eggs
And don't ask how.

Chorus:
Because if the rabbi wants,
it's a trifle
If he wants, oh, oh, oh
Everything is within the rabbi's power
He lays his hands on you
You'll be saved right away
Because if the rabbi wants,
even a broom can shoot**
(Oh, do I have a rabbi! If
the great Moses caught
sight of him, his eye would
pop out.)

(Chorus)

2

The rabbi can help out
old maids
How?
If he wants, he can help
The rabbi can get
a bad guy into heaven
How?
If he wants, he can
Oh, the rabbi can display
such wonders

1

Der rebbe ken zayn
Tsu khayes a futer,
Vi azoy
Az er vil ken er.
Der rebbe ken makhn
Fun a katchke a kuter
Vi azoy,
Az er vil, ken er.
Oy der rebbe ken tsapn
milkh fun a ber
Un shlogn kapures mit a floy
Er ken makhn az an oks
Zol gor leygn eyer,
Un freygt nit vi azoy.

Korus:
Vayl az der rebbe vil
Eyn klenekeyt
Az er vil, oy oy oy
Alts ting mit dem rebns koyakh
Er leygt di hent off aykh
Vert ir geholfn glaykh
Vayl az der rebbe vil
shist a beyzem oykh
(Oy hob ikh a rebn! Er
kukt off fun moyshe
rabeynu an oyg zol im feln)

(Korus)

2

Der rebbe ken helfn
Farzesene meydn
Vi azoy,
Az er vil helft er.
Der rebbe ken shtipn
A rushe in gan eden
Vi azoy,
Az er vil shtipt er.
Oy der rebbe ken vayzn
azelkhe vinder

1

דער רבי קאָן זײַן
צו חיות אַ פֿאָטער,
װי אַזױ,
אַז ער װיל קאָן ער.
דער רבי קאָן מאַכן
פֿון אַ קאַטשקע אַ קאָטער
װי אַזױ,
אַז ער װיל, קאָן ער.
אױ דער רבי קאָן צאַפּן
מילך פֿון אַ בער
און שלאָגען כּפּרות מיט אַ פֿלױ
ער קאָן מאַכען אַז אַן אָקס
זאָל גאָר לײגן אײער,
און פֿרעגט ניט װי אַזױ.

קאָרוס:
װײַל אַז דער רבי װיל
אײן קלענעקײט
אַז ער װיל, אױ אױ אױ
אַלץ טינג מיט דעם רעבנס כּוח
ער לייגט די הענט אױף אײך
װערט איר געהאָלפֿען גלײַך
װײַל אַז דער רבי װיל
שיסט אַ בעזים אױך.
(אױ האָב איך אַ רבן! ער קוקט
אױף פֿון משה רבינו אַן אױג זאָל
אים פֿעלן)

(קאָרוס)

2

דער רבי קאָן העלפֿן
פֿאַרזעסענע מײדן
װי אַזױ,
אַז ער װיל העלפֿט ער.
דער רבי קאָן שטיפּן
אַ רשע אין גן עדן
װי אַזױ,
אַז ער װיל שטיפֿט ער.
אױ דער רבי קאָן װײַזן
אַזעלכע װינדער

He helps childless women With an "oy" He can make it so that widows have children, And don't ask how. (Oh, do I have a rabbi! He plays baseball too, does my rabbi.)	Akures helft er mit eyn "oy" Er ken makhn az almones zoln hobn kinder Un freygt nit vi azoy. (Oy hob ikh a rebbenyu! Er shpilt op beysbal oykh shpilt er op mayn rebbe)	עקרות העלפֿט ער מיט אײן "אױ" ער קאָן מאַכן אַז אַלמנות זאָלן האָבן קינדער און פֿרעגט ניט װי אַזױ. (אױ האָב איך אַ רביניו: ער שפּילט ער אָפּ בײסבאַל אױך שפּילט ער אָפּ מײן רבי)
(Chorus)	(Korus)	(קאָרוס)
3. The rabbi can bake a strudel from needles How? If he wants, he bakes The rabbi can sew a pelt without a needle. How? If he wants, he sews. Oh, the rabbi can recite the Song of Songs for Kol Nidre, And he can do the etrog ritual with a straw. At the Seder he can be thinking of Purim And don't ask how.	3 Der rebbe ken bakn fun shpilkes a shtrudl Vi azoy, Az er vil bakt er. Der rebbe ken neyen Funem pelts on a nodl Vi azoy, Az er vil neyt er, Oy der rebbe ken dos kol- nidre zogn shir hashirim Un bentshn esrog mit a shtroy Er ken tsum seder, trakhtn fun purim, Un freygt nit vi azoy.	3 דער רבי קאָן באַקן פֿון שפּילקעס אַ שטרודל װי אַזױ, אַז ער װיל באַקט ער. דער רבי קאָן נייען פֿונעם פּעלץ אָן אַ נאָדל װי אַזױ, אַז ער װיל נייט ער. אױ דער רבי קאָן דאָס כל נדרי זאָגן שיר השירים און בענטשן אתרוג מיט אַ שטרױ ער קאָן צום סדר טראַכטן פֿון פּורים. און פֿרעגט ניט װי אַזױ.
(Chorus) (Lively, lively, lively, lively!)	(Korus) (Leybedik, leybedik, leybedik, leybedik!)	(קאָרוס) (לעבעדיק, לעבעדיק, לעבעדיק, לעבעדיק)

Notes

Music: Abraham Ellstein
Words: Nakhum Stutchkoff
Publication Date: 1929

From the Khasidic operetta "Az der rebbe vil" (If the Rabbi Wants). First performed by Ludwig Satz at his Folks Theatre in New York.

* "*shlogn kapores*," literally "beating atonement," the orthodox ritual of transferring one's sins to a chicken that is swung around one's head and then slaughtered.
** Old Yiddish expression: *Az got vil, shist a beyzem*, literally, "If God wants, even a broomstick can shoot," meant to signfiy that there is no miracle God cannot perform.

Notes
Music: Alexander Olshanetsky
Words: Moishe Oysher; Publication Date: 1940
From the film, The Little Vilna Master, *Der Vilner Balebasl* (English title, *Overture to Glory*)
דער ווילנער באַלעבעסעל

(3)

| UNDER THE TREES | Unter Boimer | אונטער בוימער |

(Coming to the microphone, the *yidishe shikse*, Irma Hasso, with a lullaby, *Unter Boymer*)

(S'kumt tsu maykrofon, di yidishe shikse, Irma Hasso, mit a shlof-lid, Unter Boimer)

ס'קומט צו מיקראָפֿאָן, די אידישע שיקסע, ירמא האַסאָ, מיט אַ שלאָפֿליד, אונטער בוימער)

Under the trees the grass grows
Ay-lyu-lyu-lyu-lyu,
And the bad winds blow,
Sleep my little son.

Unter boimer vaksn grozn
Ay-lyu-lu-lu-lu,
Un di beyze vintn bloyzn,
Shlof zhe zunenyu.

אונטער בוימער וואַקסען גראָזען
אי לו לו לו לו,
און די בייזע ווינטען בלאָזען,
שלאָף זשע זונעניו.

Sit not, my son, by the window,
Because you can feel the wind there;
And I don't want you, my most beautiful
to heaven forbid to catch cold.

Zits mayn kind nit bay dem fenster,
Vayl du kenst dem vint derfiln;
Un ikh vil nisht, du mayn shenster
Zolst kholile zikh farkiln.

זיץ מיין קינד ניט ביי דעם פֿענצטער,
ווייל דו קענסט דעם ווינט דערפֿיהלען;
און איך וויל נישט, דו מיין שעהנסטער
זאָלסט חלילה זיך פֿאַרקיהלען.

The sky is already dark with clouds,
Just as it is here in my heart.

Himl iz shoyn khmarne shvarts,
Punkt azoy vi du bay mir in harts.

הימעל איז שוין כמאַרנע שוואַרץ,
פונקט אַזוי ווי דאָ ביי מיר אין האַרץ.

Under the trees grows the grass
Ay-lyu-lyu-lyu-lyu,
And the bad winds blow,
Sleep my little son.

Unter boimer vaksn grozn
Ay-lu-lu-lu-lu,
Un di beyze vintn bloyzn,
Shlof zhe zunenyu

אונטער בוימער וואַקסען גראָזען
אי לו לו לו לו,
און די בייזע ווינטען בלאָזען,
שלאָף זשע זונעניו.

Ay-lyu-lyu, ay-lyu-lyu,
Sleep my child,
Oh my heart,
Ay-lyu-lyu, ay-lyu-lyu,
Stay healthy for me.

Ay-lu-lu, ay-lu-lu,
Shlof zhe mayn kind,
Oy mayn hartz,
Ay-lu-lu, ay-lu-lu,
Blayb mir gezunt.

אי לו לו, אי לו לו,
שלאָף זשע מיין קינד,
אוי מיין האַרץ,
אי לו לו, אי לו לו,
בלייב מיר געזונד.

MENASHE SKULNIK

שלמהלע - מלכהלע

SHLOIMELE = MALKELE

From the
SENSATIONAL MUSICAL PRODUCTION
"THE GALICIAN RABBI"
Starring the Eminent Comedian
MENASHE SKULNIK

SONG FOR VOICE AND PIANO

WORDS BY
ISIDOR LILLIAN

MUSIC BY
JOSEPH RUMSHINSKY

Price 30 cents
NET NO DISCOUNT

JOSEPH RUMSHINSKY

SHLOYMELE-MALKELE

1
[M] A sister to you I'm a true one
Little brother, listen to me
[S] A picture you are a delight
Do I really have to be your brother?
[M] Brother I want to take care of you always and protect you at every step.
[S] Oh, kiss me and it won't seem as if I'm your brother.

Refrain:
Oh, Shloymele, oh, Shlyomele,
Brother, come closer to me,
Oh, Malkele, oh, Malkele,
I'm crazy about you.

2
[M] Little brother, you're a handsome one,
I am bold enough to say

[S] I see a roast goose

and I can't take a bite.

[M] Tell me, why are you acting so strangely? Little brother, don't you feel well?
[S] The evil impulse is boiling within me,
and it knows from no wisdom.

(Refrain)

Shloymele-Malkele

1
A Shvester bin ikh dir a traye
Briderl, her zikh nor ayn
A piktshe bistu a mekhaye
Darf ikh gor dayn bruder zayn
Brider, kh'vel dikh tomid akhten
Un hitn dir off shrit un trit.
Oy, kusht mir un zol zikh dir dakhtn
Az ikh bin dayn bruder nit.

Refreyn:
Oy, Shloymele, oy, Shloymele,
Bruder, kum neynter tsu mir,
Oy, Malkele, oy, Malkele
Ikh bin meshighe far dir.

2
Bruderl, bist a gerotns,

Ikh meg zikh groys haltn dermit,
A genzl zey ikh a gebrotns

Un aynbaysn ken ikh dos nit.
Zog, farvus git dir a tore?
Bruderl filstu nit git?

Es kokht in mir der yeytser hore
Un er veyst fun keyn khokhmes nit.

Refreyn...

שלמהלע מלכהלע

1
אַ שװעסטער בין איך דיר אַ טרייע
ברודערל, הער זיך נאָר איין,
אַ פּיקטשע ביזטו אַ מחיה
דאַרף איך גאָר דיין ברודער זיין
ברודער, כ'וועל דיך תמיד אַכטען
און היטען דיך אויף שריט און טריט.
אוי, קושט מיר און זאָל זיך דיר דאַכטען
אַז איך בין דיין ברודער ניט.

רעפרײן:
אוי, שלמהלע, אוי, שלמהלע,
ברודער, קום נעהנטער צו מיר,
אוי, מלכהלע, אוי, מלכהלע,
איך בין משוגע פאַר דיר.

2
ברודערל, ביזט אַ געראָטענס,

איך מעג זיך גרוים האַלטען דערמיט,
אַ גענזעל זעה איך אַ געבראָטענס

און אײנבײסען קען איך דאָס ניט.
זאָג, פאַרװאָס גיט דיר אַ טרה?
ברודערל, פילסטו ניט גוט?

עס קאָכט אין מיר דער יצר הרע,
און ער װײסט פון קיין חכמת ניט.

רעפרײן...

299

3	3	3

[M] I like to look in your face,
You're noble, you're good and you're fine;
[S] You're holding my happiness there
(Be a hero and restrain yourself!)
[M] You are your mother's son,
Your mother completely delights in you,
[S] I wish you were my little hen
and I was your rooster.

Ch'glaykh in dayn punim tsu kukn
Bist eydl, bist gut un bist fayn
Ot hostu dir mayne glikn

(Zay a held un gey halt zikh ayn)
Du bist doch der mamens a zindl
Di mame, zi kvelt dokh gor on,
Alevay geven volstu mayn hindl
Un ich volt gevezn dayn hon

כ'גלייך אין דיין פנים צו קוקען,
ביזט איידעל, ביזט גוט און ביזט פיין ;
אָט האָסטו דיר מיינע גליקען,

זיי א העלד און גיי האלט זיך איין
דו ביזט דאָך דער מאמענס א זונדעל,
די מאמע, זי קוועלט דאָך גאָר אָן,
הלוואי געווען וואָלסטו מיין הינדעל
און איך וואָלט געווזען דיין האָן.

Refrain...

Refreyn...

רעפריין...

4.

[M] Your little head is a sharp one,
I recognized your smartness right away,
[S] And you should know how I suffer,
I feel that I'm even going to burn up.
[M] I waited months, days and weeks,
And suddenly you've appeared,
[S] Alone, did I push myself in,
and now how they're pushing me out.

4

A kepl hostu fun di sharfe,
Dayn khokhme hob ikh bald derkent,
Un visn zolstu vi ikh sarfeh,
Ikh fil az ikh ver azh farbrent.
Khadoshim gevart, teg un vokhn,
Un plutsim gor ot vakstu oys,
Aleyn bin ikh arayn gekrokhn,
Un itzter vi krikht men aroys.

4

אַ קעפעל האָסטו פון די שאַרפע,
דיין חכמה האָב איך באלד דערקענט,
און וויסן זאָלסטו ווי איך סאַרפע,
איך פיהל, אַז איך ווער אזש פארברענט.
חדשים געווארט, טעג און וואָכען,
און פלוצים גאָר אָט וואקסטו אויס,
אַליין בין איך אריין געקראָכען,
און איצטער ווי קריכט מען ארויס.

Refrain...

Refreyn...

רעפריין:

Notes
Music: Joseph Rumshinsky
Words: Isidor Lillian
Publication Date: 1937
From the musical, *The Galician Rabbi - Dos galitsiyaner rebbe*

JEWS, RAISE A CRY!	(5) Shrayt zhe yidn gevalt!	שרייט זשע יידן גוואַלד
1 A time back, with beard and forelocks With all the virtues Answering difficult questions Learned in Gemara, learned in Yoreh De'ah He didn't even know about such afflictions as a tavern. Today, what does he do? What more does he need? So, what does he need Gemara for? What does he need Yoreh De'ah for? Because all he has on his mind are the lamentable taverns. Refrain: So, Jews, raise a cry Yes, right now Cry, Jews, that it's burning Our one and only Jewish world.	**1** A moll arop, mit bord un peyes Mit alle mayles Gepastn shvere shayles Gelernt Gemora gelernt Yureh Deya Hot afile nit geviss' Fun keyn tzure masbeya Haynt arop vos tit er? Vos darf er mer? "Zo" vos "nids" dem Gemora vos darft er Yureh Deya Az er hot gor in zin yamerkane masbeya Refreyn: Shrayt zhe yidn, gevalt Takeh, takeh bald Shrayt zhe yidn es brent, Di ayntsike yidishe velt	**1** אַמאָל אַראָפּ מיט באָרד און פּאהות מיט אַלע מעלות געפּאַסטן שווערע שאלהות געלערנט גמרא געלערנט יורה דעה האָט אַפֿילו ניט געוויזן פֿון קיין צרה מסבעה הײַנט אַראָפּ וואָס טוט ער וואָס דאַרף ער מער "זאָ" וואָס "נידס" דעם גמרא וואָס דאַרף ער יורה דעה אַז ער האָט גאָר אין זין יאָמערקאַנע מסבעה רעפֿריין: זאַ שרײַט זשע יידן גוואַלד טאַקע, טאַקע באַלד שרײַט זשע יידן עס ברענט, אוי די איינציקע אידישע וועלט
2 Once a cantor used to play a Jewish role He spoke Hebrew slowly and carefully He had learnt the various Torah portions in school Everybody got a pleasure from him Today's cantor comes with a big "borekh-habo" But he doesn't know a drop of Hebrew He's not even a bit observant And he looks just like a Russian butcher (Refrain)	**2** A mol a khazn hot geshpilt a yidishe roleh Ivri gezogt langsam un parvole Parsha milis gelernt in kheder Hanua gehat fun im, hot a yeder Haynt a khazn kumt mit a groysn borekh habo, Ober keyn tropn ivri iz bay er nito Frum iz er afile nit a kap Un er kikt gor oys vi a rusisher katsav (Refreyn)	**2** אַמאָל אַ חזן האָט געשפּילט אַ אידישע ראָלע עברי געזאָגט לאַנגזאַם און פּאַוואָליע פּרשה מיליאס געלערנט אין חדר הנאה געהאַט פֿון אים, האָט אַ יעדער הײַנט אַ חזן קומט מיט אַ גרויסן ברוך הבא, אָבער קיין טראָפּן עברי איז בײַ ער ניטאָ פֿרום איז ער אַפֿילו ניט אַ קאַפּ און ער קוקט גאָר אויס ווי אַ רוסישער קצב (רעפֿריין)

3
Once gentlemen used to have Jewish disputes.

For half the night they would devote themselves to them
They ran to shul with complete pleasure
And prayed and studied a chapter of the Mishnas
Today's gentlemen Involve theselves with business.
They crawl and act stupid in the speakeasies.
They play poker and pinochle and have such a good time.
And to go to shul, the poor things have no strength.

(Refrain)

3
A molikeh balebatim
Hobn gehat yidishe plikhtn.
Nokh halbe nakht fleygn zikh atzol tzu barikhtn

Gelofn in di shil mitn gantsen mekhaye
Gedavnt gelernt a perek mishnayes
Hayntikeh balebatim farnemen in biznes

Krikhtn un pratsof in di spikizis.
Me shpilt poker un pinokl
Az geyt aza royeh

Un in shil tsu geyn, hobn zey nebukh nisht kin koyekh

(Refreyn)

3
אַמאָליקע בעלי בתים
האָבן געהאַט אידישע פֿלוגתּן

נאָך האַלבע נאַכט פֿלעגן זיך אַ צאָל צו באַריכטן

געלאָפֿן אין די שול מיטן גאַנצן מחיה
געדאַוונט געלערנט אַ פּרק משניות
הײַנטיקע בעלי בתים פֿאַרנעמען אין ביזנעס

קריכטן און פּרצוף אין די ספּיק איזיס
מע שפּילט פּאָקער און פּינאָקל
עס גייט אַזאַ ראָיע

און אין שול צו גיין האָבן זיי נעבעך נישט קיין כּוח

(רעפֿריין)

Notes
Words by: unknown
Music by: unknown
Publication Date: unknown

(6)

| Lay us down to sleep | Hashkiveynu | הַשְׁכִּיבֵנוּ |

Lay us down to sleep, our Lord our God, in peace,
And raise us up, our king, to life,
Spread over us the cover of your peace
Set us right with good counsel from before your presence.
Save us for you name's sake.
And shield us,
And remove from us, foe, plague, sword, famine and woe;
And remove Satan from in front of us and behind us,

And shelter us under your wings.
Because you are the God who protects and rescues us,
Because you are the gracious and compassionate King:
And safeguard our coming and going
For life and for peace
From now to eternity.

Hashkiveynu adoshem elokeynu l'shaloym,
V'hamideynu malkeynu l'khayim.
Ufroys aleynu, sukas shloymekha.
V'sakneynu b'eytza toyva milfonekha.
V'hoshiyeynu l'ma'an sh'mekha.
V'hageyn badeynu.
V'hoseyr meyaleynu
Oyev dever, v'kherev v'rav v'yagon.

V'hoseyr Satan milfoneynu umeyakhareynu.
Uv'tseyl k'nofekha tastireynu.
Ki eyl shoymreynu matzileynu atah.

Ki eyl melekh chanun v'rakhum atah:

U'shmor tseseynu, u'vo'eynu
L'khayim ul'sholoym
Mey atah v'ad oylam

הַשְׁכִּיבֵנוּ ה' אֱלֹהֵינוּ לְשָׁלוֹם,
וְהַעֲמִידֵנוּ מַלְכֵּנוּ לְחַיִּים.
וּפְרוֹשׂ עָלֵינוּ סֻכַּת שְׁלוֹמֶךָ.
וְתַקְּנֵנוּ בְּעֵצָה טוֹבָה מִלְּפָנֶיךָ.
וְהוֹשִׁיעֵנוּ לְמַעַן שְׁמֶךָ.
וְהָגֵן בַּעֲדֵנוּ:
וְהָסֵר מֵעָלֵינוּ אוֹיֵב דֶּבֶר וְחֶרֶב וְרָעָב וְיָגוֹן.

וְהָסֵר שָׂטָן מִלְּפָנֵינוּ וּמֵאַחֲרֵינוּ.
וּבְצֵל כְּנָפֶיךָ תַּסְתִּירֵנוּ.
כִּי אֵל שׁוֹמְרֵנוּ וּמַצִּילֵנוּ אָתָּה.

כִּי אֵל מֶלֶךְ חַנּוּן וְרַחוּם אָתָּה:

וּשְׁמוֹר צֵאתֵנוּ וּבוֹאֵנוּ לְחַיִּים וּלְשָׁלוֹם
מֵעַתָּה וְעַד עוֹלָם:

---

*Evening Prayer. The musical setting cannot be attributed with certainty. However, the style is very close to that in the performance of *Av Harakhamim* on this disc, so there seems a strong probability that this *Hashkivenu* should be attributed to Pierre Pinchik as well.

דרײַ טעכטערלעך
DREI TECHTERLACH
(THREE DAUGHTERS)

Words and Melody by
Mordechai Gebirtig

Arranged for VOICE and PIANO by
Sholom Secunda

64 SECOND AVE.
NEW YORK

PRICE 40c net

Notes:
Words and Music by Mordekhai Gebirtig
Publication date: unknown.
The YIVO in New York has Gebirtig's original notebooks (#RG 740) with his hand-written lyrics to Dray Tekhterlekh in them. These were given away by him for safe-keeping before his murder in the Cracow Ghetto in 1942.

(7)

| THREE DAUGHTERS | Dray tekhterlech | דרײַ טעכטערלעך |

1.
When with luck, health and life, I marry off my eldest daughter.
Oh, will I dance, hop, hop, hop
A burden will be off my head,
Oh, will I dance, oh, will I dance
A burden will be off my head.

Play musicians! Play lively -
I'm marrying off my eldest girl today.
Only two girls remain to us.
And this will soon happen to them.
Play musicians! Take up your instruments!
So the whole world can be happy with us,
Only God knows our happiness, and whoever has girls.

2.
And when I see my second little girl
All done up in her little white wedding dress
Oh, will I drink and be happy --
A stone will be off my heart
Oh, will I drink, oh, will I drink,
A stone will be off my heart.

1.
Ven ikh vel mit mazl, gezint un lebn
Dos eltste tekhterel veln mir oysgebn
Vel ikh tantsn mir, hop, hop, hop
Oy arop an ol fun kop,
Oy, vel ikh tantsn, oy vel ikh tantsn --
Arop an ol fun kop.

Shpilt, klezmorim! Shpilt mit lebn –
dos eltste tekhterel mir haynt oysgegebn,
Undz geblibn nokh meydlekh tsvey,
Oy vi halt men shoyn bay zey
Shpilt, klezmorim
Nemt di kley-zayin!
Zol di gantse velt mit undz zikh freyen,
Undzer simkhe veys nor eyn got
Un der vos tekhter hot.

2.
Un ven ikh vel zeyn shoyn dos tsveyte meydl
Ongeton in vayse khipe-kleydel,
Oy vel ikh trinkn un freylekh zayn --
Arop fun harts a shteyn
Oy vel ikh trinkn, oy, vel ikh trinkn,
Arop fun harts a shteyn,

1.
װען איך װעל מיט מזל, געזונט
און לעבן
דאָס עלצטע טעכטערל װעלן מיר
אױסגעבן
װעל איך טאַנצן האָפּ, האָפּ, האָפּ
אױ אַראָפּ אַן עול פֿון קאָפּ,
אױ װעל איך טאַנצן, װעל איך
טאַנצן
אַראָפּ אַן עול פֿון קאָפּ.

שפּילט, קלעזמאָרים! שפּילט
מיט לעבן
דאָס עלצטע מײדלע מיר הײַנט
אױסגעגעבן,
אונדז געבליבן נאָך מײדלעך
צװײ,
אױ װי האַלט מען שױן בײַ זײ

שפּילט, קלעזמאָרים, נעמט די
כּלי-זײן!
זאָל די גאַנצע װעלט מיט אונדז
זיך פֿרײען,
אונדזער שׂמחה װײס נאָר אײן
גאָט
און דער װאָס מײדלעך האָט.

2.
און װען איך װעל זען דאָס
צװײטע מײדל
אָנגעטאָן אין װײַסן
חופּה-קלײדל,
אױ װעל איך טרינקען און
פֿרײלעך זײן
אַראָפּ פֿון האַרץ אַ שטײן,
אױ װעל איך טרינקען, אױ, װעל
איך טרינקען,
אַראָפּ פֿון האַרץ אַ שטײן,

Play, musicians, let's begin! I'm giving away my second daughter in joy. Only the littlest one remains to us, Oh, it will soon happen with her.	Shpilt, klezmorim, zol men toh opshnaydn! Dos tsveyte meydl gibn mir oys in freydn, Ot dos mizinikl nokh hobn mir, Oy vi halt men shoyn bay ir.	שפילט, קלעזמאָרים, זאָל מען טאָ אָפּשנײַדן! דאָס צווייטע מיידל גיבן מיר אויס אין פריידן, אָט דאָס מיזיניקל נאָך האָבן מיר, אוי ווי האַלט מען שוין בײַ איר.
Play musicians for us in-laws, For once poor people should also enjoy themselves, A child given away, oh my God, And a girl, too.	Shpilt, klezmorim, far undz mekhetonim, Zoln a leb ton oykh a mol kabtsonim, A kind oysgegebn, oy gotenyu, Un a meydl nokh dertsu.	שפילט, קלעזמאָרים, פֿאַר אונדז מחותּנים, זאָלן אַ לעב טאָן אויך אַ מאָל קבצנים, אַ קינד אויסגעגעבן, גאָטעניו, און אַ מיידל נאָך דערצו.
3. When with the last one I hear the music playing, Then I'll stand and think of something sad -- Oh, the last little daughter already gone away, What now is the purpose here? The last one, the littlest one, the youngest one, What now is the purpose here?	3. Ven baym letstn ikh vel shpiln hern, Vel ikh epes treyerik shteyn un klern -- Oy dos letste tekhterl shoyn oykh avek, Vos nokh iz do der tsvek? Dos letste, dos kleynste, dos yingste Vos nokh iz do der tsvek?	3. ווען בײַם לעצטן כ'וועל שפילן הערן, וועל איך עפּעס טרייעריק שטיין און קלערן אוי דאָס לעצטע טעכטערל שוין אויך אַוועק, וואָס נאָך איז דאָ דער צוועק? דאָס לעצטע, דאָס קלײנטשיקע, דאָס ייִנגסטע וואָס נאָך איז דאָ דער צוועק?
Play musicians! Enthrone the bride, They've taken away all our children, It was hard with three daughters, Oh but it's harder without them. Play musicians, chase away our tears, The last littel bed will today be empty, The whole room, her closet – Oh woe is me, how empty and sad.	Shpilt, klezmorim! Bazetst di kale, Tsugenumen bay undz di kinder ale, Shver geveyn undz di tekhter dray, oy shverer noch on zey. Shpilt, klezmorin, aroys undz di treren, Dos letste betl vet haynt leydik vern, Dos gantse shtibl ir kleyder-shank -- Oy vey iz mir, vi pust un bang,	שפילט, קלעזמאָרים! באַזעצט די כּלה, צוגענעמען בײַ אונדז די קינדער אַלע, שווער געוועןן אונדז טעכטער דרײַ, אוי שווערער נאָך אָן זיי. שפילט, קלעזמאָרים, אַרויס אונדז די טרערן, דאָס לעצטע בעטל וועט הײַנט ליידיק ווערן, דאָס גאַנצע שטיבל איר קליידער־שאַנק אוי ווי איז מיר, ווי פּוסט און באַנג.

Kammen Publication No. 449

"OH MOTHER! AM I IN LOVE!!"

OI MAMME!
BIN ICH FARLIEBT!!
.... MIT A KLESMER YINGEL ....

אוי מאמע, בין איך פארליבט!

Originally Introduced by MOLLY PICON

Words and Music by
ABE ELLSTEIN

VICTOR RECORD VOICE and PIANO
No. V-9073 35c

J. & J. KAMMEN MUSIC CO.
· MUSIC PUBLISHERS · 1619 BROADWAY
NEW YORK, N. Y.

Notes:
Words and music: Abraham Ellstein
Publication Date: 1941
Performers: The Harmony Girls – Di Harmoni meydlen – (identities unknown)

(8)

OH MOTHER! AM I IN LOVE!!	Oy mamme, bin ikh farlibt	אוי מאַמע בין איך פֿאַרליבט
Oh mother, am I in love
Oh mother, am I in love
A musician-boy, mother dear, is on my mind.
I laugh and cry and I don't know, mother, what world I'm in.
Oh mother, am I in love
Oh mother, am I in love
I want to embrace the whole world and hold it close to me
Oh! Oh mother, am I in love	Oy mamme, bin ikh farlibt
Oy mamme, bin ikh farlibt
A klezmer yingl mamme getrayeh ligt mir nor in zin
Ikh veyn un lakh un veyst nit mamme off velkhe velt ikh bin
Oy mamme, bin ikh farlibt
Oy mamme, bin ikh farlibt
Ikh volt di ganze velt arumgenumen un tsugedrikt tsu zikh
Oy! Oy mamme, bin ikh farlibt.	אוי מאַמע בין איך פֿאַרליבט
אוי מאַמע בין איך פֿאַרליבט
אַ קלעזמער ייִנגל מאַמע געטרייַע ליגט מיר נאָר אין זין
איך וויין און לאַך און ווייס ניט מאַמע אויף וועלכע וועלט איך בין
אוי מאַמע בין איך פֿאַרליבט
אוי מאַמע בין איך פֿאַרליבט
איך וואָלט די גאַנצע וועלט אַרומגענומען און צוגעדריקט צו זיך
אוי! אוי מאַמע בין איך פֿאַרליבט
When he plays a beautiful heartfelt Jewish song on his fiddle,
Oh mother, it's good and nice for me.
With his beautiful black eyes, he has attracted me so.
Oh, mother it's nice and good for me.
And when he says "Hi there girl, you are obviously sweet and refined"
And his playing creeps into my heart
It's like jumping, it's like dancing,
Oh, wow, I'm going to explode here.
Oh mother, I can't go on like this.	Ven er tsushpilt zikh off zayn fidl a sheyn hartsik yidish lidl
Oy, mamme vert mir gut un voyl
Mit zayne sheyne shvartse oygn hot er mir dan tsugetsoygn
Oy, mamme vert mir voyl un gut
Un ven er zogt mir "Hey, du meydl du bist dokh azoy lib un eydl"
Un zayn shpiln krikht in harts arayn
Tsuglikht off shpringen tsuglikht off tantsn,
Oy gevald ikh vel du platzn
Oy mamme ken ikh mer nit zayn	ווען ער צושפּילט זיך אויף זײַן פֿידל אַ שיין האַרציק אידיש לידל
אוי מאַמע ווערט מיר גוט און וווילֿ
מיט זײַנע שיינע שוואַרצע אויגן האָט ער מיר דאַן צוגעצויגן
אוי מאַמע ווערט מיר וווילֿ און גוט
און ווען ער זאָגט מיר "היי דאָ מיידל דו ביסט דאָך אַזוי ליב און איידל"
און זײַן שפּילן קריכט אין האַרץ אַרײַן
צוגליכט אויף שפּרינגען צוגליכט אויף טאַנצן
אוי, גוואַלד, איך וועל דאָ פּלאַצן
אוי מאַמע, קען איך מער ניט זײַן
Oh mother, am I in love…
Oh mother, oh mother of mine!... | Oy mamme, bin ikh farlibt….
Oy mamme…oy mammenyu… | אוי מאַמע בין איך פֿאַרליבט...

אוי מאַמע, אוי מאַמעניו!... |

THE EMINENT ARTIST

AARON LEBEDEFF

גאליציע

GALITZIE

Words by
Morris Rund

Music by
Aaron Lebedeff

ARRANGED FOR VOICE AND PIANO BY
Philip Laskowsky

As Sung With Great Success
By The Inimitable Comedian
Aaron Lebedeff

Price 30 Cents

WARSAW / Varshe / וואַרשע

(9)

1.

English	Yiddish (transliteration)	Yiddish
There's a band of wild animals over there,	A bande vilde khayes dortn existirn,	אַ באַנדע ווילדע חיות דאָרטן עקזיסטירן,
They're actually bathing in Jewish blood.	Zey bodn mamesh zikh In yidish mentshlekh blit,	זיי באָדן ממש זיך אין אידיש מענשליך בלוט,
Hitler the murderer* is ruling	Hitler der merder* Er tut regirn	היטלער דער מערדער* ער טהוט רעגירען
And ghosts and devils are dancing together with him.	Un sheydem un rikhes tantsn mit im mit	און שדים און רוחות טאַנצען מיט איהם מיט.
You don't see a happy face there any more	Ir zeyt dort nit mer ken freylekhn ponim	איהר זעהט דאָרט ניט מעהר קיין פֿריילעכן פנים,
Their life is bitter, dark and ugly.	Dos leben iz bitter, finster un mis.	דאָס לעבען איז ביטער, פֿינסטער און מיאוס,
With rifles and swords, soldiers are going around.	Mit biksn, shverdn, geyn um dort yevonim,	מיט ביקסען, שווערדען געהען אום דאָרט יונים,
They rob and slaughter and stomp on them with their feet.	Zey roybn, shekhtn un tretn mit di fis.	זיי רויבען, שעכטען און טרעטען מיט די פֿיס.

Refrain: / Refreyn: / רעפֿריין:

English	Yiddish (transliteration)	Yiddish
Oh, what has happened to Warsaw?	Oy, vos iz gevorn vi in Varshe,	אוי, וואָס עס איז געוואָרן ווי אין וואַרשע,
Everything is broken and burned.	Alles iz tsushtert dort un farbrent.	אלעס איז צושטערט דאָרט און פֿערברענט.
Oh, what has happened to Warsaw?	Oy, vos iz gevorn vi in Varshe,	אוי, וואָס עס איז געוואָרן ווי אין וואַרשע,
You wouldn't recognize it anymore, my friends.	Ir volt dos fraynde mer shoyn nit derkent.	איהר וואָלט דאָס פֿריינדע מעהר שוין ניט דערקענט.
Every little tree is broken,	Tsubrokhn yedes beymele,	צובראָכן יעדעס ביימאַלע,
Every little home is thrown over,	Tsuvorfn yedes heymele,	צאוואָרפֿן יעדעס היימאַלע,
Where people used to live comfortably,	Vi mentshen fleygn lebn zikh bakveym,	ווי מענטשען פֿלעגען לעבען זיך באַקוועם,
Where there was a little house,	Vi geveyn a shtibele,	ווי געווען אַ שטיבעלע,
you now see a hole.	Zeyt men yetst a gribele,	זעהט מען יעצט אַ גריבעלע,
Such a thing has happened to our old home.	A tel gevorn iz fun der alter heym.	אַ תּל געוואָרען איז פֿון דער אַלטער היים.

2._	2	.2
Who can forget Warsaw's beautiful times?	Ver ken di sheyne tsayt fun Varshe fargesn	ווער קען די שעהנע צײַט פֿון װאַרשע פֿערגעסען
When everything there was peaceful and quiet.	Ven ales iz geveyn dort ruig un shtil.	װען אַלעס איז געװען דאָרט רוהיג און שטיל.
Sabbath and holy days, every Jew went with pride and joy to the Eastern wall in the synagogue,	Shabbes un yontif iz yeder Yid gezesn mit shtoltz un mit freyd in mizrakh vand in shil,	שבת און יום טוב איז יעדער איד געזעסען מיט שטאָלץ און מיט פֿרייד אין מזרח װאַנד אין שול,
Today every holy place there is broken,	Haynt iz yeder mukom-koydesh dort tsubrokhn,	הײַנט איז יעדער מקום-קדוש דאָרט צובראָכען,
From weeping and wailing the ground has become wet.	Fun veynen, klogn iz di erd shoyn nas.	פֿון װײנען, קלאָגען איז די ערד שוין נאַס.
Sabbath and holy days and also on weekdays,	Shabbes un yontif un oykh in der vokhn,	שבת און יום טוב און אויך אין דער װאָכען,
It's terrifying and dangrerous to go out in the street!	A shrek, a moyre iz aroystsugeyn in gas!	אַ שרעק, אַ מורה איז אַרויסצוגיין אין גאַס!
(refrain)	(refreyn)	(רעפֿריין)

Notes
Words by Morris Rund
Music by Aaron Lebedeff
Publication date: 1938
The song was originally called *Galitsye* about the sad state of Jewish life in southern Poland just before the war. This version was recorded during the period of the Warsaw Ghetto, the title and some of the words changed accordingly, and a second verse added by an unknown author.
*in the published version "The ruler, a devil" - דער הערשער אַ טײַפֿיל

Words by Jacob Jacobs,
Music by Yasha Kreytsberg
Publciation date: 1944

WHERE CAN WE GET ANOTHER MOSES?

Where can we get another Moses?
A fighter the way he was long ago
Where can we get another Moses?
So he would free our people Israel.

He didn't lament
He just told Pharoah
You cannot enslave my people any longer
And as soon as he made his point,
The sea was quickly divided,
And Pharoah and his army were sunk.

Where can we get another Moses?
He would surely set things straight
Where can we get another Moses?
So he would free our Jewish people!

I often lie at night
Not sleeping but only thinking
How every villain has Trampled on the Jew
Enslaved by Pharoah,
He mistreated them
He made bricks and clay with them.
They were victims there for a bitter long time
Until Moses came and freed them.

So…

---

(10)

Vu nemt men a Moishe rabenu?

Vu nemt men a Moyshe rabenu?
a kempfer vi er iz geven amol
Vu nemt men a Moyshe rabenu?
er zol bafrayn undzer folk yisrol.

Er hot zikh nisht baklukt
Nor par'n glaykh gezugt
Du kenst mayn folk shoyn nisht farshklafn mer,
Un gevizn shoyn dem tam
Geshpoltn bald dem yam
Ayngezinken Par'n mit zayn militer

Vu nemt men a Moyshe rabenu?
Er volt zicher shoyn gemakht a tolk
Vu nemt men a Moyshe rabenu?
er zol bafrayn undzer Yidish folk!

Ikh leyg fil mol banakht,
ikh shlof nit nor ikh trakht,
Vi yeder rushe hot off dem yid getretn.
Geven by par'n knekht
Er hot zey bahandlt shlekht
Er hot mit zey tsigel un leym, gekneytn
Zey hobn dort gelitn a biter shtikl tzayt
Biz moyshe is gekomen un hot zey fun dort bafrayt

Az…

וואו נעמט מען אַ משה רבינו?

וואו נעמט מען אַ משה רבינו?
אַ קעמפער ווי ער איז געווען אַמאָל
וואו נעמט מען אַ משה רבינו?
ער זאָל באַפרייען אונזער פאָלק ישראל[אידיש פאָלק]

ער האָט זיך נישט באַקלאָגט
נאָר פרעה'ן גלייך געזאָגט
דו קאָנסט מיין פאָלק שוין נישט פארשקלאַפען מער,
און געוויזען אים דעם טעם
געשפּאַלטען באַלד דעם ים
איינגעזינקען פרעה'ן מיט זיין מיליטער.

וואו נעמט מען אַ משה רבינו?
ער וואָלט זיכער שוין געמאַכט אַ טאָלק
וואו נעמט מען אַ משה רבינו?
ער זאָל באַפרייען אונזער אידיש פאָלק!

איך ליג פיל מאָל ביינאַכט,
איך שלאָף ניט נאָר איך טראַכט
ווי יעדער רשע האָט דעם איד געטרעטן
געווען ביי פרעה'ן קנעכט
ער האָט זיי באַהאַנדעלט שלעכט
ער האָט מיט זיי ציגעל און ליים, געקנעטען
זיי האָבען דאָרט געליטען אַ ביטער שטיקעל צייט
ביז משה איז געקומען און האָט זיי פון דאָרט באַפרייט

אַז....

(11) NO, NO, NEVER / Neyn, Neyn, Keyn Mol Nit Geven

נײן, קיין מאָל ניט געווען

1.

Love is the happiness that makes life pleasant,
So I've been told and I have believed it.

To love a girl and even put up a wedding canopy
Now you're asking me about love and I'm going to tell you all about it.
It's not so, no, it never happened and it never will.

Not so, no, it never happened and it could not be otherwise.
They speak of sweet love, they keep affirming it and plead their case for it.
They write about true, pure love in novels.
It's not so, no, it never happened and it never will.

2.

King Solomon had a thousand little wives, you know,
And his opinion you all know, because he said it out loud,
He roared out that there is no good woman,
And all men have also given voice to this opinion.

1.

Libe iz dos glik vos makht dos lebn angeneym,
Azoy hot men gezogt mikh Un ikh hob gegloybt in dem.
Farlibt zikh in a meydl, geshtelt a khupe glaykh,
Itst fregst mikh fun libe vel ikh op dertseyln aykh.
S'iz nishtu, neyn, s'iz keyn mol nit geven, un s'vet keyn mol nit zayn,
Nishtu, neyn, s'iz keyn mol nit geven, un andersh ken dokh nit zayn.
Men redt fun zise libe, m'halt nor un eyntane,
Fun emes reyne libe shraybt men in di romanen.
S'iz nishtu, neyn, s'iz keyn mol nit geven, un s'vet keyn mol nit zayn.

2.

Shloyme hameylekh hot dokh toyznt vaybelekh farmugt,
Zayn meynung veyst ir ale vos er hot aroysgezugt.
Nishtu a froy a gitte hot er es tsugebrimt,
Un alle mener hobn oykh zayn meynung tsugeshtimt.

.1

ליבע איז דאָס גליק וואָס מאַכט דאָס לעבן אַנגענעם,
אַזוי האָט מען געזאָגט מיך און איך האָב געגלויבט אין דעם.

פֿאַרליבט זיך אין אַ מיידעל, געשטעלט אַ חופה גלײַך,
איצט פֿרעגסט מיך פֿון ליבע וועל איך אָפּ דערצײלן אײַך.
ס'איז נישטאָ, נײן, ס'איז קיין מאָל ניט געווען, און ס'וועט קיין מאָל ניט זײַן,
נישטאָ, נײן, ס'איז קיין מאָל ניט געווען, און אַנדערש קען דאָך ניט זײַן.
מען רעדט פֿון זיסע ליבע, מ'האַלט נאָר און אײַנטענה,
פֿון אמתע ריינע ליבע שרײַבט מען אין די ראָמאַנען.
ס'איז נישטאָ, נײן, ס'איז קיין מאָל ניט געווען, און ס'וועט קיין מאָל ניט זײַן.

.2

שלמה המלך האָט דאָך טויזנט ווײַבלעך פֿאַרמאָגט,
זײַן מיינונג ווייסט איר אַלע וואָס ער האָט אַרויסגעזאָגט.

נישטאָ אַ פֿרוי אַ גוטע האָט ער עס צוגעברומט,
און אַלע מענער האָבן אויך זײַן מיינונג צוגעשטימט.

NOTES: The composer and author of this song are not known. The first and second verse could have been written anytime, but the third verse refers specifically to the later stages of World War II after the Germans suffered their defeats at the hands of the Russians and had retreated, but, it seems before final victory. So the probable recording date is 1943-45. Most likely the 3rd verse was added to an earlier song.

It's not so, no, it never happened and it never will. Not so, no, it never happened and it could not be otherwise Not a good woman among a thousand of Eve's daughters And among a thousand men is there then one honest one? It's not so, no, it never happened, and it never will.	S'iz nishtu, neyn, s'iz keyn mol nit geven, un s'vet keyn mol nit zayn. Nishtu, neyn, s'iz keyn mol nit geven, un andersh ken es nit zayn. Nisthu a froy a gitte tsvishn toysend khaves tekhter, Un tsvishn toyznt mener iz den du eyner a rekhter? S'iz nishtu, neyn, s'iz keyn mol nisht geven, un s'vet keyn mol nit zayn.	ס'איז נישטא, ניין, ס'איז קיינמאל ניט געווען, און ס'וועט קיין מאל ניט זיין. נישטא, ניין, ס'איז קיין מאל ניט געווען און אנדערש קען דאך ניט זיין. נישטא א פרוי א גוטע צווישן טויזנט חוה'ס טעכטער און צווישן טויזנט מענער איז דען דא איינער א רעכטער? ס'איז נישטא, ניין, ס'איז קיין מאל ניט געווען, און ס'וועט קיין מאל ניט זיין.
3. The evil Hitler has spilled good people's blood, He wanted to annihilate and erase the Jew from the world. He got afraid of Russia, oh alas and alack, Because he was given a whiff of the powder of the Red Army. It's not so, no, it never happened and it never will, Not so, no, it never happened and it could not be otherwise Once Nazism has been annihilated and this has already been determined, America, Russia and England will build a new world. It's not so, no, it never happened and it never will.	3. Der rushe Hitler hot fargosn vertn mentshns blit, Gevolt farnikhtn un opmekn fun dem velt a yid. Far rusland hot er zikh dershrokn ven gevorn, vind un vey, Vayl er hot engegebn pilver shmekn fun der royter armey. S'iz nishtu, neyn, s'iz keyn mol nit geven, un s'vet keyn mol nit zayn, Nishtu, neyn, s'iz keyn mol nit geven, un andersh ken dos nit zayn. Farnikhtet dem natsism dos iz festgeshtelt, Amerike, Rusland, England vet shafn a naye velt. S'iz nishtu, neyn, s'iz keyn mol nisht geven, un andersh ken es nit zayn.	3. דער רשע היטלער האט פארגאסן ווערטן מענטשנס בלוט, געוואלט פארניכטן און אפמעקן פון דעם וועלט א איד. פאר רוסלאנד האט ער זיך דערשראקן ווען געווארן, ווינד און וויי, ווייל ער האט איינגעגעבן פולווער שמעקן פון דער רויטער ארמיי. ס'איז נישטא, ניין, ס'איז קיין מאל ניט געווען, און ס'וועט קיין מאל ניט זיין, נישטא, ניין, ס'איז קיין מאל ניט געווען, און אנדערש קען דאך ניט זיין. פארניכטעט דעם נאציזם דאס איז פעסטגעשטעלט, אמעריקע, רוסלאנד, ענגלאנד, וועט שאפן א נייע וועלט. ס'איז נישטא, ניין, ס'איז קיין מאל נישט געווען, און אנדערש קען עס ניט זיין.

(12)

| FATHER OF MERCY | Av Harakhamim | אַב הָרַחֲמִים. |

May the Father of mercy have mercy on the nation that is sustained by Him,	Av harakhamim, hu yerakheym am amusim,	אַב הָרַחֲמִים הוּא יְרַחֵם עַם עֲמוּסִים
And may He remember the covenant with the patriarchs,	V'yizkor bris eysanim,	וְיִזְכּוֹר בְּרִית אֵיתָנִים
And may he rescue our souls from evil times.	v'yatsil nafshoyseynu min hashuoys haruoys.	וְיַצִּיל נַפְשׁוֹתֵינוּ מִן הַשָּׁעוֹת הָרָעוֹת.
And may he check the evil inclination in those who have been sustained by him.	V'yigar b'yeytser hora min hanesowim.	וְיִגְעַר בְּיֵצֶר הָרָע מִן הַנְּשׂוּאִים.
And grace us with eternal deliverance,	V'yakhoyn oysanu lifleytas oylamim.	וְיָחוֹן אוֹתָנוּ לִפְלֵיטַת עוֹלָמִים.
and may he fulfill in good measure our petitions for salvation and mercy.	Vimaley mishaloysenu b'mida toyva yishua v'rakhamim.	וִימַלֵּא מִשְׁאֲלוֹתֵינוּ בְּמִדָּה טוֹבָה יְשׁוּעָה וְרַחֲמִים.

NOTES

Av Harakhamim is a synagogue prayer recited just before the reading of the Torah. There are many different musical settings of it. This particular one is the work of Pierre Pinchik (1893?-1971) (born Pinchas Segal), a Kiev-born khazan who emigrated to the United States in 1926 and recorded his version in 1928.

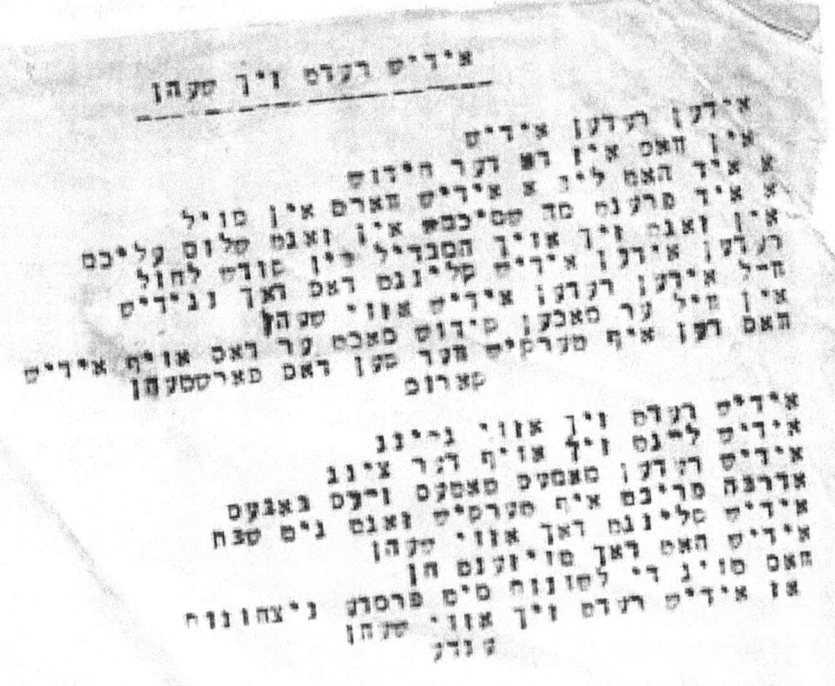

YIDDISH IS SO BEAUTIFUL TO SPEAK	(13) Yidish redt zikh azoy sheyn	ייִדיש רעדט זיך אַזוי שיין
1. Jews speak Yiddish And what's the big surprise? A Jew loves a Yiddish word in his mouth. A Jew asks "What's your name?" And says "Peace be with you" And says to himself "He who separates the sacred from the profane" Jews speak Yiddish It sounds rich, Because Jews speak Yiddish so beautifully And if he wants to make "Kiddush" He makes it in Yiddish What then, in gentile? Who could understand that?	1. Yidn redn yidish, Un vos is du der khidish, A yid hot lib a yidish vort in moyl. A yid freygt "Ma shemekhem?" Un zogt "Sholem aleykhem" Un zogt zikh "hamavdil ben koydesh l'khoyl" Redn yidn yidish, klingt es dokh negidish, Vayl yidn redn yidish azoy sheyn, Un vil er makhn kidish, Makht er dos off yidish Vos den off goyish? Ver ken dos farshteyn?	1. ייִדן רעדן ייִדיש, און וואָס איז דאָ דער חידוש, אַ ייִד האָט ליב אַ ייִדיש וואָרט אין מויל. אַ ייִד פֿרעגט ,,מה שמכם?" און זאָגט ,,שלום־עליכם" און זאָגט זיך ,,המבדיל בין קודש לחול" רעדן ייִדן ייִדיש, קלינגט עס דאָך נגידיש, ווײַל ייִדן רעדן ייִדיש אַזוי שיין; און וויל ער מאַכן קידוש, מאַכט ער דאָס אויף ייִדיש, וואָס דען אויף גויִיש? ווער קאָן דאָס פֿאַרשטיין?
Chorus: Yiddish is so easy to speak, Yiddish is just there on your tongue Mothers speak Yiddish, grandfathers, fathers, grandmothers, Otherwise, try saying "git shabes" (good Sabbath) in Gentile/Turkish* Yiddish is so beautiful to speak Yiddish has a thousand graces. What do you need of languages from strange places Since Yiddish is so beautiful to speak.	Kor: Yidish redt zikh azoy gring, Yidish leygt zikh off der tsing, Yidish redn mammes, zeydes, tattes, babbes Oderabe prift off goyish/terkish* zogt, "git shabbes" Yidish redt zikh azoy sheyn Yidish hot dokh toysnt kheyn, Vos toygn leshoynes fun fremde mikoymos? Az yidish redt zikh azoy sheyn.	כאָר: ייִדיש רעדט זיך אַזוי גרינג, ייִדיש לייגט זיך אויף דער צינג, ייִדיש רעדן מאַמעס, זיידעס, טאַטעס, באָבעס, אַדרבא פּרוּווט אויף גויִיש/טערקיש** זאָגט ,,גוט שבת" ייִדיש רעדט זיך אַזוי שיין ייִדיש האָט דאָך טויזנט חן, וואָס טויגן לשונות פֿון פֿרעמדע מקומות? אַז ייִדיש רעדט זיך אַזוי שיין.

317

2.
A Jewish rabbi is really a pleasure
When he gives such a caress to his text.
His two eyes squint
His brows are like two bows
When he wrenches out from his heart that "oy!"
Listen then Jewish children
To what I'm telling you now,
You also should speak Yiddish if you can.
Yiddish is easier to use when you're wiggling your thumb
Because Yiddish loves it when you speak it with your hands.

Chorus…

2.
A yidisher "rabaye" iz dokh a mekhayeh
Ven men git mit di vort a glet azoy.
Farshmuren tsvey di oygn
Di bremen vi tsvey boygn

Ven fun hartsn rayst zikh aroys der "oy"
Hert zhe yidishe kinder,

Vos ikh zog aykh atsinder,

Oykh ir darft redn yidish oyb ir kent.
Vayl yidish redt zikh gringer ven men dreyt mitn grobn finger
Vayl yidish hot lib ven men redt es mit di hent.

Kor…

2.
אַ ייִדישער ‏,,רביי‏`` איז דאָך אַ מחיה
ווען מען גיט מיט די וואָרט אַ גלעט אַזוי
פֿאַרזשמורען צוויי די אויגן
די ברעמען ווי צוויי בויגן

ווען פֿון האַרצן רײַסט זיך אַרױס דער ‏,,אױ``
הערט זשע ייִדישע קינדער,

וואָס איך זאָג אײַך אַצינדער,

אויך איר דאַרפֿט רעדן ייִדיש אויב איר קענט
ווײַל ייִדיש רעדט זיך גרינגער ווען מען דרייט מיטן גראָבן פֿינגער
ווײַל ייִדיש האָט ליב ווען מען רעדט עס מיט די הענט

כאָר...

Words by Isidor Lillian
Music by Maurice Rauch.
Publication date unknown

*first chorus "goyish" (gentile), second chorus "Turkish"

(14)
MAHZEL (MEANS GOOD LUCK)
(Sung in English)

There's a certain little word can mean a lot to you.
You gotta have and if you got it, there's nothing you can't do.
You've gotta have a little Mahzel.
'Cause Mahzel means 'Good luck'
And with a little Mahzel
You'll always have a buck.
And if you have no Mahzel and though you're on the ball.
You try and try and can't get by, you beat your head against the wall.
Don't ever try to figure why you seem to be the blame.
That some folks have a million and can't even write their name.
You've gotta have a little Mahzel and you never will get stuck.
'Cause with a little Mahzel, you'll always have good luck.

Notes:
Words and music by Artie Wayne and Jack Beekman
Publciation date: 1947
This was a big hit recorded by Benny Goodman, Louis Prima, and the Ravens, among others. Blue Barron (born Hershel Freidland) and His Orchestra, a big band of the era, pictured on the sheet music cover -- there is also an extant cover with Dennis Day -- "featured" it but it is not clear whether they recorded it.

The origins of the word Mahzel are ancient according to Dovid Katz:

> It goes back to the earlier Hebrew *mazzol* and Aramaic *mazzolo* which referred to a constellation, star, or planet. [*MM: in modern Hebrew, the signs of the Zodiac are all* מזל אריה *Leo* מזל דגים *Pisces etc.*] The modern sense of *mazel* on its own referring to "good luck" is a Yiddish development deriving from the Talmudic Hebrew and Aramaic sense of luck or fate, good or otherwise. That sense was derived from the pejorative biblical sense of idol worship ("those who burned incense to Baal, to the sun, to the moon, and to the *constellations*," 2 Kings 23:5). [*MM:* ולמזלות]. The biblical Hebrew term was borrowed from ancient Akkadian, a language that was widespread in Mesopotamia (largely covering the territory of today's Iraq from the third to the first millennium B.C.) In Akkadian, it was a neutral term for constellation or planet, but that neutrality implied belief in the godliness and power of these constellations vis-à-vis human affairs. By Old Testament times, the word referred to the cursed idol beliefs that seduced people away from belief in God. In Talmudic times it was softened, abstracted, and shifted to mean fate in general. That's how it eventually entered Yiddish and came to mean not just any luck but good luck. About five thousand years of history lie behind this one Yiddish word. Dovid Katz, *Words on Fire. The Unfinished Story of Yiddish* (New York: Basic Books, 2004), p. 12.

(15)

| THE JEWISH MELODY | Der Yidisher Nign | דער אידישער ניגו |

The Jewish melody / Der yidisher nign, off / דער אידישער ניגען אויף אייביג
Forever will it be, / eybig vet er zayn, / וועט ער זיין,
The Jewish melody / Der yidisher nign, / דער אידישער ניגען
It crawls right into your heart. / Es krikht in hartz arayn. / עס קריכט אין הארץ אריין
The Jew suffers in exile / In goles laydt der yid, / אין גלות ליידט דער איד,
Exhausted from wandering, / Fun vandern shoyn mid, / פון וואנדערען שוין מיד,
So his only consolation is this melody. / Zayn eyntsiger neckome iz dokh nor dos lid. / זיין איינציגער נחמה איז דאך נאר דאס ליד.
The Jew suffers many troubles, / Der yid laydt tsores fil, / דער איד ליידט צרות פיל,
so when he comes to the synagogue, / Dokh ven er kimt in shil, / דאך ווען ער קימט און שוהל,
He sings the beautiful old melody with feeling. / Dem altn sheynem nign zingt der yid mit a gefil. / דעם אלטען שיינעם ניגין זינגט דער איד מיט א גפיהל.

[The Prayer of a Ghetto Jew*] / [A Tfileh Fun A Ghetto-Yid*] / [א תפילה פון א געטאָ-ייִד*]
Great God, / Groyser Gott, / גרויסער גאָט,
Who was able from the void to create the world, / vos host gekont fun der lerkayt farshafn di velt, / וואס האָסט געקאָנט פון דער לערקייט באַשאַפן די וועלט,
From all creations to exalt me to the highness of a faith, / fun ale bashafenishn mikh derhoybn tsu der hoykhkayt fun a gloybn. / פון אלע באשעפענישן מיך דערהויבן צו דער הויכקייט פון א גלויבן,
Blessed with name of Man -- / Gebensht mit dem numen mentsh-- / געבענטשט מיט דעם נאָמען מענטש —
Hear my plea: / Her oys mayn gebeyt: / הער-אויס מיין געבעט:
I am a ghetto-Jew, dispossessed, alone and weary. / Ikh bin a ghetto-yid-- fartribn eynzam un mid. / איך בין א געטאָ-ייִד — פאַרטריבן, איינזאַם און מיד.
My heart is torn and empty, / Mayn hartz iz tserisn un ler, / מיין הארץ איז צעריסן און לער,
I have no more prayers. / Ikh hob kin tfiles mer. / איך האָב קיין תפילות מער.
Hear out my only plea and take from me the name of Man. / Her-oys mayn eyntsik gebet un nem fun mir tsu fun mensh dem numen / הער-אויס מיין איינציק געבעט און נעם פון מיר צו פון מענטש דעם נאָמען.

321

Take from me my suffering soul,	Nem fun mir tsu di farpaynikte neshume,	נעם פון מיר צו די פֿאַרפּייניקטע נשמה,
So sadness won't devour and gnaw at it.	es zol nit fresn, nit nogn der umet.	עס זאָל ניט פֿרעסן, נישט נאָגן דער אומעט.
Take from me the hearing of my ears,	Nem fun mir tsu dos banemen fun mayn oyer,	נעם פון מיר צו דאָס באַנעמען פון מיין אויער,
So I won't hear the sighs	Ikh zol nit hern dos geveyn	איך זאָל נישט הערן דאָס געוויין
from every ghetto-wall.	Fun yeder geto-moyer.	פֿון יעדער געטאָ-מויער.
Take from me my sight,	Nem fun mir tsu mayn blik,	נעם פון מיר צו מיין בליק,
So I won't see the wire, the brick –	ikh zol nit zen di drotn, di brik ---	איך זאָל נישט זען די דראָטן, די בריק –
Where my sisters and brothers are driven and pursued,	vi mayne shvester un brider vern getribn, geyogt,	ווי מיינע שוועסטער און ברידער ווערן געטריבן, געיאַגט,
Where we fall, and sink, day after day.	Vi mir faln, vi mir zinken fun tog tsu tog,	ווי מיר פֿאַלן, ווי מיר זינקען פֿון טאָג צו טאָג,
And transform me, God, Into an ox, into a horse, into a dog!	un farvandl mich, Got, in an oks, a ferd, in a hunt!	און פֿאַרוואַנדל מיך, גאָט, אין אַן אָקס, אין אַ פֿערד, אין אַ הונט!
I want to be an ox, or a horse, In harness, plowing the earth,	Ikh vil zayn an oks, oder a ferd, in shpan akern di erd,	איך וויל זיין אַן אָקס, אָדער אַ פֿערד, אין שפּאַן אַקערן די ערד,
And having a worth, a worth!	un hobn a vert, a vert!	און האָבן אַ ווערט, אַ ווערט!
I want to be a horse, or an ox,	Ikh vil zayn a ferd, oder an oks,	איך וויל זיין אַ פֿערד, אָדער אַן אָקס,
In rest, chewing the grass, not knowing that there is something better,	biminikhe kayn dos groz, nit visn, az epes besers iz du	במנוחה קיינ דאָס גראָז, נישט וויסן, אַז עפּעס בעסערס איז דאָ
And having peace, peace!	un hobn ru, ru!	און האָבן רו, רו!
I want to be a dog, To tear at and to bite your enemies with my teeth, Not leaving any limb, any bone.	Ikh vil zayn a hunt, dayne sonim tseraysn, tsebaysn mit di tseyn, Nit iberlozn kayn beyn.	איך וויל זיין אַ הונט, דיינע שונים צערייסן, צעבייסן מיט די ציין, נישט לאָזן קיין אבר, קיין ביין.

Great God,	Groyser Gott,	גרויסער גאָט,
make of me what you want:	makht fun mir vos du vilst:	מאַך פֿון מיר וואָס דו ווילסט:
nothing – or everything.	gornisht -- oder alts.	גאָרנישט – אַדער אַלץ.
Scatter me over the world as sand,	Tsevarft iber der velt in zamd,	צעשיט איבער דער וועלט אין זאַמד,
Bury me in the earth, as salt,	bagrob in der erd, in zalts,	באַגראָב אין דעק ערד, אין זאַלץ,
Transform me into a stone ---only a man,	farvundl mich in a shteyn - --nor a mentsh,	פֿאַרוואַנדל מיך אין אַ שטיין – נאָר אַ מענטש,
a man I can no longer be!	a mentsh ken ikh mer nit zayn!	אַ מענטש קאָן איך מער נישט זיין!
The Jewish melody	Der yiddisher nign,	דער אידישער ניגען
Forever will it be	off eybig vet er zayn,	אויף אייביג וועט ער זיין,
The Jewish melody	Der yiddisher nign,	דער אידישער ניגען,
It crawls right into your heart.	es krikht in hartz arayn.	עס קריכט אין הארץ אריין.

NOTES:
Words by Chaim Tauber
Music by Sholom Secunda
Publication date: 1940
The poem, "The Prayer of a Ghetto Jew" by Rivka Kwiatkowski.

The song is from the Joseph Seiden movie of the same name. The movie is a delightful, if sometimes embarassing, collage of recurring Jewish themes. An already-betrothed cantor's son, played by Chaim Tauber, studies music in Venice with a Yiddish speaking Italian music professor, whose few words of Italian are usually mispronounced: he addresses his daughter as "piccolo mio" – perhaps he always wanted a son -- and he calls his daughter Rosita, a nice Spanish name for an Italian girl! Tauber falls in love with Rosita, much to the horror of his cantor-father, who is already suffering from his son's rich future father-in-law's extortions. When father falls ill, the son has to return to New York and take over the *Kol Nidre* service. When asked at rehearsal if he remembers the old beautiful Jewish melody, Tauber sings the title song. There is a comic subplot, a surprise happy ending, and everything else, including the kitchen sink (shluging kapures with a fish). If people left the theatre humming this tune, as Peter Schickele once said, apropos of P.D.Q. Bach, it's because, they came in humming it. Sholom Secunda has taken this "old beautiful melody" almost note for note from the popular Ashkenazic tune for the prayer "*Avinu Malkeynu*," which, to be fair, actually fits into the plot, because the choir director wants to run through it before the service and asks Tauber if he remembers it, and then he sings these Yiddish words to it. According to Max's record label, he used this as his Jewish Hour theme song. In this recording, Max inserts his reading of a heart-rending poem by the Lodz Ghetto poet Rivka Kwiatkowski, *A tfileh fun a geto yid,* ("The prayer of a ghetto Jew") reprinted in Rivka Kwiatkowski-Pinchasik, *Di Letste – Di Ershte Vern* (Steven Spielberg Digital Yiddish Library No. 09840), p. 9. | 1980 ,חיפה, "אליין" פֿאַרלאַג ,ווערן ערשטע די -לעצטע די ,קוויאַטקאָווסקי־פּנכסיק רבקה]

ABOUT THE AUTHOR

Michael Mandel (1948–2013) was an author, teacher, activist and singer. Born in Toronto to Jewish immigrants, his love of music was first inspired by his father's Yiddish radio show.

Michael worked tirelessly to bring Jewish music to his community, by singing his father's repertoire and leading services at his synagogue.

As a professor at Osgoode Hall Law School for almost forty years, he taught Criminal and International Law, and Constitutional Politics. An outspoken anti-war activist, he wrote and spoke out against injustice throughout his life.

Previous publications include the books *The Charter of Rights and the Legalization of Politics in Canada* and *Illegal Wars: How America Gets Away with Murder* as well as numerous articles in both law journals and newspapers.

This was Michael's last work, and was completed in the final weeks of his life.

www.ingramcontent.com/pod-product-compliance
Lightning Source LLC
Chambersburg PA
CBHW060110170426
43198CB00010B/833